THE QURAN: IN EASY-TO-UNDERSTAND FORMAT
VOLUME 7

THE DESCRIPTION OF AFTERLIFE

DEATH AND BEYOND, THE LAST HOUR, RESURRECTION, JUDGMENT DAY, HELL, AND HEAVEN

FAROOQ MIRZA

The First-Ever Rendition of the Quran

According to Specific Topics and the Subject Matter

From

The Quran Foundation

Copyright © 2024 Farooq Mirza

All rights reserved.

No part of this book may be reproduced, stored in a retrieval system, or transmitted, in any form or by any means, electronic, mechanical, photocopying, recording, or otherwise, without prior written permission from the publisher, except for brief quotations embodied in critical reviews and certain other noncommercial uses permitted by copyright law.

Printed in the United States of America

DEDICATION

The seven-volume book series about the Quran is dedicated to the memory of Muhammad Asad, whose work, "The Message of the Qur'an," was the first-ever attempt at an idiomatic, explanatory rendition of the Quranic message in English. In my opinion, it is the best translation and commentary on the Holy Quran.

Muhammad Asad was born Leopold Weiss in July 1900 in Lviv, now Ukraine. He was the descendant of a long line of rabbis, a line broken by his father, who became a barrister. Asad himself received a thorough religious education that would qualify him to keep alive the family's religious tradition. He left Europe for the Middle East in 1922 for what was supposed to be a short visit to an uncle in Jerusalem. There, he came to know the Arabs and was struck by how Islam infused their everyday lives with existential meaning, spiritual strength, and inner peace. Weiss then became, at the remarkably young age of twenty-two, a correspondent for The Frankfurter Zeitung, one of the most prestigious newspapers in Germany and across Europe. As a journalist, he traveled extensively, mingled with ordinary people, held discussions with Muslim intellectuals, and met heads of state in Palestine, Egypt, Transjordan, Syria, Iraq, Iran, and Afghanistan.

Back in Berlin from the Middle East, a few years later, Weiss underwent an electrifying spiritual epiphany—reminiscent of the experiences of some of the earliest Muslims—that changed his mind and his life. "Out of the Quran spoke a voice greater than the voice of Muhammad," Weiss said. Thus, it was that Weiss became a Muslim. He converted in Berlin before the head of a small Muslim community in the city. He took the name Muhammad to honor the Prophet and Asad—meaning "lion"—a reminder of his given name, Leopold, which is derived from the Latin word for lion. Asad spent some six years in the holy cities of Mecca and Medina, where he studied Arabic, the Quran, and the "Hadith"—the traditions of the Prophet and Islamic history. He mastered the Arabic language not only through academic study but also by living with a tribe that spoke the Arabic dialect of the Holy Quran. At the age of eighty, after seventeen years of effort, he completed his life's dream, for which he felt all his life had been an apprenticeship: a translation and exegesis, or "tafsir," of the Quran in English: The Message of the Qur'an.

CONTENT

The Key To Understanding This Book 1

Part One Afterlife, Death And Resurrection

Chapter 1 Al-Ghayb 4

Chapter 2 Angels 8

Chapter 3 Jinn 12

Chapter 4 Satan 19

Chapter 5 Death 31

Chapter 6 Entering Afterlife 36

Cosmic Cataclysm And Resurrection Of The Dead

Chapter 7 The Last Hour 44

Chapter 8 The End Of The World 50

Chapter 9 Objections To The Resurrection Doctrine And The Quranic Rebuttal 55

Chapter 10 The Resurrection Of The Dead 65

Part Two Accounting Of Humanity

I. Accounting Of The Unrepentant Sinners 72

Chapter 11 Unrepentant Sinners' Excessive Love Of Life 73

Chapter 12 Sins Against God 82

Chapter 13 Sins Against Fellow Man 92

Torments Of Judgment Day For Unrepentant Sinners 108

Chapter 14 Welcome Of Unrepentant Sinners On Judgment Day 109

Chapter 15 The Day Of Regrets And Ransom Offer By Unrepentant Sinners 114

Chapter 16 Record Of Unrepentant Sinners 119

Chapter 17 Separation From Friends And Loved Ones And Witness Against Themselves 124

Chapter 18 Coming Face To Face With God For Final Judgment............. 129

Chapter 21 The Fire Of Hell 142

Chapter 20 Heavy Fetters 156

Chapter 21 Choking Food... 160

Chapter 22 Angels Guardians Of Hell... 165

Chapter 23 Dialogue Between The Righteous And The Unrepentant Sinners 168

Chapter 24 Begging For God's Clemency And Pardon Of All Sinners 173

(2) Accounting Of Sinners Who Repented And Attained Righteousness.. 177

Chapter 25 Sinners Ascending To Righteousness Through Repentance .. 178

Chapter 26 Forgiveness Of Sins Atonement Or Mitigation Of Sinful Deeds.. 183

Chapter 27 Easy Accounting Of Those Who Attained Righteousness 193

Chapter 28 Accounting Of The Righteous Of Other Monotheistic Faiths 196

Chapter 29 Paul/Augustine's Salvation Theology................................... 205

Chapter 30 What Did Jesus Say About Salvation?.................................. 208

Chapter 31 The Islamic Perspective Of Salvation................................... 214

Chapter 32 Accounting Of The Righteous Among Nonbelievers And Those In Limbo 221

(3) The Foremost Among The Righteous And Paradise 227

Chapter 33 The Foremost In Righteousness And Good Works 228

Chapter 35 Attributes Of The Blessed People Of Paradise 241

Chapter 36 The Prophet's Night Journey 247

Chapter 37 Pleasures Of Paradise And The Beautiful Vision Of God 251

Chapter 38 Infinite Gardens And Heavenly Drinks................................ 257

Chapter 39 Reuniting With Family And Spouses And Perfect Happiness 265

Bibliography... 274

THE KEY TO UNDERSTANDING THIS BOOK

PART ONE

Part one includes a general description of the afterlife. What happens after death and beyond? The Quran describes in detail the end of the world, the last hour, and the resurrection of all humanity.

PART TWO

HUMANITY DIVIDED IN THREE GROUP

After the resurrection, humanity will be gathered for the final judgment. Mankind will be divided roughly into three groups according to the burden of sins committed during their earthly life:

1. The **unrepentant sinners** abused their free will and defied God's commandments, attributable to their self-centeredness and false pride. They showed no regrets for their wrongdoings and did not alter their ways in the quest to better themselves. Their sinful life had negative effects in earthly life and therefore negative consequences in the afterlife. Lesser guilty among unrepentant sinners will face Judgment Day torments. They will avoid hellfire. Only the truly guilty and stubborn sinners shall suffer in hell.

2. **Sinners who have attained righteousness**. Those who commit sins and humble themselves through sincere repentance. They begged for God's mercy and forgiveness and thus attained excellence in conduct after stumbling. Their life on earth had net positive effects and happy endings in the afterlife as well. As they enter paradise, they will be spared the torments of Judgment Day.

Salvation in Islam is open to everyone who realizes God's oneness and surrenders himself to His will. By living righteously, they exemplified this spiritual attitude. Other monotheists will also be included in this group, such as righteous Jews, Christians, Sabians, and Zoroaster followers. Those who were helpless or never received proper religious guidance, and children who are considered innocent are likewise represented in this group. It will also include "the "indifferent ones" who in earthly life were neither inclined to right nor wrong. As a result of their lukewarm attitude, they were unable to do much good or harm.

3. The **foremost among the righteous** will enter paradise without accounting. All God's prophets and holy men will be in paradise described in glowing terms. Above all, man will finally have the glorious vision of God.

PART ONE
AFTERLIFE, DEATH AND RESURRECTION

CHAPTER 1
AL-GHAYB

This divine writ—let there be no doubt about it—is [meant to be] guidance for all the God-conscious who believe in [the existence of] that which is beyond human perception. (2:2-3)

Al-ghayb, commonly and erroneously translated as "the Unseen," is used in the Quran to denote all those sectors or hidden realities that lie beyond human perception and cannot, therefore, be proven or disproved by scientific observation or even adequately addressed within the accepted categories of speculative thought. The concept of a realm beyond human perception constitutes the fundamental premise for understanding the Quran's call. It is, indeed, a basic principle of almost every religion, for God Himself belongs to the realm of al-ghayb. All truly religious cognition arises from the fact that only a small segment of reality is open to man's perception and imagination. By far the largest part escapes his comprehension altogether. For instance, metaphysical subjects such as God's attributes, the ultimate meaning of time and eternity, the resurrection of the dead, the Day of Judgment, paradise and hell, the nature of beings or forces described as angels and Jinn, etc., all fall into the category of al-ghayb. Only a person who is convinced that the ultimate reality comprises far more than our observable environment can attain a belief in God and, thus, a belief that life has meaning and purpose. By pointing out that it is "guidance for those who believe in the existence of that beyond human perception," the Quran says, in effect, that it will remain a closed book to all whose minds cannot accept this fundamental premise. Belief in the last day or resurrection, judgment, and life after death is postulated as a logical corollary—almost a premise—of all beliefs in God.

HEREAFTER BEYOND HUMAN EXPERIENCE

Say: "None in the heavens or on earth knows the hidden reality [that exists, none knows it] except God. And neither can they [who are living] perceive when they shall be raised from the dead. Nay, their knowledge of life to come falls short of the truth. Nay, they are [often] in doubt about its reality. Nay, they are blind to it. (27:65-66)

They cannot truly visualize the hereafter, because its reality is beyond anything man experiences in this world. It cannot be overemphasized that it is an indirect explanation why all Quranic references to man's life after death are expressed in purely allegorical terms.

TWO TYPES OF VERSES

He has bestowed upon you from on high this divine writ. It contains messages that are clear, and these are the essence of the divine writ— as well as allegorical messages. Now those whose hearts are given to swerving from the truth seek after that part of the divine writ expressed in allegory. They seek out [what is bound to create] confusion and seek to arrive at its final meaning [in an arbitrary manner]. (3:7)

The "confusion" referred to is an attempt to interpret allegorical passages in an arbitrary manner and seek to arrive at their final meaning.

LOAN IMAGES

And it is not God's will to give you insight into what is beyond human perception. However, [to that end] God elects whomever He wills from among His apostles. Believe in God and His apostles; for if you believe and are conscious of Him, a magnificent reward awaits you. (3:179)

The glimpse of the afterlife was reserved exclusively for God's elected prophets. It is through these apostles that God grants man a partial glimpse of the reality of which He alone has full knowledge. The next question is how the events that will occur in the afterlife can be explained to common people without the benefit of experience of the afterlife or how religion's metaphysical ideas can be successfully conveyed to us. It is by borrowing images from our experiences, whether physical or mental. This is the innermost purpose of the term and concept of al-*mutashabihat* or allegory in the Quran.

Thus, the Quran tells us clearly that many of its passages and expressions must be understood allegorically. This is for the simple reason that they could not have been conveyed to us in any other way. How can you explain what a tree looks like to an unborn fetus who only knows the deep darkness of the womb? One can compare the placenta to the tree's root system, an umbilical cord to the tree's trunk, and various fetal arteries and veins to the branches of the tree. It will be an allegorical, highly imperfect, and vague description of a tree to a fetus.

If we took every Quranic passage, statement, or expression in its outward, literal sense, and disregarded the possibility of it being an allegory, a metaphor, or a parable, we would offend the very spirit of the divine writ. All Quranic references to hell, paradise, and men's conditions in the hereafter are, of necessity, highly allegorical. Therefore, they are liable to be grossly misunderstood if one takes them in their literal sense or, conversely, interprets them arbitrarily.

TIME-SPACE LIMITATION VERSUS INFINITY

They know only the superficial surface of this world's life, whereas of the ultimate things they are utterly unaware. Have they never learned to think for themselves? (30:7-8)

The possibility of an intellectual comparison between the two stages of human existence is to a large extent limited by the fact that all our thinking and imagining is connected with finite time and space. With the destruction of the cosmos, the canopy of space-time fabric rips apart, and the earthbound concept of time will disappear.

It is impossible for us to imagine infinity in time or space or a state of existence under such conditions. It would be improper to explain afterlife events literally. The Quran describes the hereafter as a concrete expression of an abstract concept. By analogy, the principle of comparison through allegory applies to all references to the afterlife.

The question arises whether "allegorical" means unreal. What is real or unreal from this life perspective cannot be applied to the afterlife. In the realm of infinity, there will emerge a more concrete reality that will be much more tangible than any reality in this life. Imagine that the people of paradise will stay young and live forever because of the everlasting quality of the hereafter. What is more real—the temporary life of this world or living forever?

There will always be genuine differences of opinion in understanding and interpreting the Quran. One should fully understand the Prophet's profound saying, "The differences of opinion among the learned men of my community are an outcome of divine grace." The human endeavor to understand God's words will never be complete.

Say: "If all the sea was ink for my Sustainer's words, the sea would indeed be exhausted before my Sustainer's words are exhausted! (18:109) "But none save God knows its final meaning." (3:7)

CHAPTER 2
ANGELS

There is no mention in the Quran about angel origins. According to the Prophet, "The Angels were created out of light, and the *Jinns* were born out of fire sparks, and Adam was born out of clay." Believing in angels is one of Islam's six articles of faith. Angels do not have free will and can only do God's will except fallen angels.

Who do not disobey God in whatever He has commanded them, and who [always] do what they are bidden to do. (66:6)

The more prominent angels are Gabriel, Michael, and Israfel. All angels appear in a graduated, individuated hierarchy. These ranks of angels offer God their praise, and they appear active throughout the universe as messengers from God and executors of divine will. They also function as guardians and recorders.

ANGELS SURROUNDING THE THRONE OF GOD

They extol His limitless glory by night and by day, never tiring of it. (21:20) They who bear [within themselves the knowledge of] the throne of [God's] almightiness, as well as all who are near it, extol their Sustainer's limitless glory and praise. They have faith in Him and ask forgiveness for all who have attained faith. (40:7)

God is encircled by a boundless realm of angels, who express their love and devotion to Him. Angels' "bearing" of God's throne of almightiness (*al-arsh*) must be understood metaphorically. Their carrying and surrounding the throne, or being near it, can be seen as a metaphor for their being mindful of it and acting in accordance therewith, or as a metonym for their closeness to the Lord of the Throne, their dignity in His sight, and their being instrumental in the realization of His will.

RESPECT FOR ANGEL GABRIEL AND MICHAEL

Say [O Prophet]: "Whosoever is an enemy of Gabriel"—who, verily, by God's leave, has brought down upon your heart this [divine writ] which confirms the truth of whatever there still remains [of earlier revelations], and is a guidance and a glad tiding for believers- "Whosoever is an enemy of God and His angels and His message-bearers, including Gabriel and Michael, [should know that,] verily, God is the enemy of all who deny the truth." (2:97-98)

According to several traditions of the Prophet, some learned men from among the Jews of Medina described Gabriel as "the enemy of the Jews," for three reasons. First, all the prophecies of misfortune for the Jews throughout their early history were said to have been transmitted to them by Gabriel, who thus became in their eyes a "harbinger of evil." In contrast to the angel Michael, whom they regarded as a bearer of happy predictions and, therefore, as their "friend." Second, the Quran repeatedly states that Gabriel conveyed his message to Muhammad. However, the Jews believed that a legitimate claim of divine revelation could only come from Israel's descendants. Third, the Quran—revealed through Gabriel—abounds in criticism of certain Jewish beliefs and attitudes and describes them as contrary to Moses' genuine message.

ANGELS AND DIVINE REVELATIONS

All praise is due to God, Originator of the heavens and the earth. He causes the angels to be [His] message-bearers, endowed with wings, two, or three, or four. (35:1) And [the angels say]: "We do not descend [with revelation], again and again, other than by thy Sustainer's command: unto Him belongs all that lies open before us and all that is hidden—from us and all that is in-between." And never does thy Sustainer forget [anything]—the Sustainer of the heavens and the earth and all that is between them! Therefore, worship Him alone, and remain steadfast in His worship! Do you know any whose name is worthy to be mentioned side by side with His?" (19:64-65)

Angels transmit God's message, communicating divine revelations to the prophets. Gabriel (Jibril) brought the Quran to Muhammad. The "wings" of the spiritual beings or forces comprised within the designation of angels are a metaphor for the speed and power with which God's revelations are conveyed to His prophets. Their multiplicity ("two, or three, or four") is perhaps meant to stress the countless ways in which He causes His commands to materialize within the universe created by Him. This assumption is supported by an authentic *hadith that Gabriel was "endowed* with six hundred wings."

ANGELS' PRAYER FOR FORGIVENESS

"O our Sustainer! Thou embrace all things with [Thy] grace and knowledge. Forgive, then, their sins unto those who repent and follow Thy path and preserve them from suffering through the blazing fire! "*And, O our Sustainer, bring them into the gardens of perpetual bliss which Thou hast promised them, together with the righteous from among their forebears, and their spouses, and their offspring—for, verily, Thou alone art almighty, truly wise—and shield them from [doing] evil deeds: for anyone whom on that Day [of Judgment] Thou wilt have preserved from [the taint of] evil deeds, him wilt Thou have graced with Thy mercy, and that will be the triumph supreme!" (40:7-9)*

WATCHFUL FORCES OVER HUMAN BEINGS

There are ever-watchful forces over you, noble, recording, aware of whatever you do! (82:10-12)

This is a reference to guardian angels who record, allegorically, all men's deeds. However, there may be another explanation; the "watchful force" (*hafiz*) set over every human being is his conscience, which "records" all his motives and actions in his subconscious mind. Since it is the most precious element in man's psyche, it is called "noble."

ANGELS DESCENDING ON DOERS OF GOOD

As for those who say, "Our Sustainer is God," and then steadfastly pursue the right way, upon them angels often descend, [saying]: "Fear not and grieve not but receive the glad tidings of that paradise promised to you! We are close to you in the life of this world and [will be so] in the life to come. In that [life to come] you shall have all that your souls may desire, and in it, you shall have all that you ever prayed for, as a ready welcome from Him who is much-forgiving, a dispenser of grace!" And who could be better of speech than he who calls [his fellowmen] unto God, and does what is just and right, and says, "I am of those who have surrendered themselves to God"? (41:30-33)

CHAPTER 3
Jinn

Somewhere between humans and angels are invisible, intelligent spirits called *jinn*. God is frequently spoken of as "the Sustainer of all the worlds" (*rabb al-alamin*), and the use of the plural clearly indicates that side-by-side with the world open to our observation, there are other worlds. The other forms of life are different from ours and presumably from one another. However, they subtly interact and perhaps even permeate beyond our comprehension.

In ancient pre-Islamic Arabian folklore, the term *jinn* denoted all manner of demons in the most popular sense of this word. This folkloristic image obscures the original connotation of the term and its self-explanatory verbal derivation. The root verb is *janna* (see 6:76 "he or it concealed" or "covered with darkness").

SPIRITUAL FORCES WITHOUT CORPOREAL EXISTENCE

The most commonly encountered is that of spiritual forces and because they have no corporeal existence are beyond the perception of our physical senses. Our inability to observe such phenomena doesn't justify denying their existence. Our physical senses can only communicate with them under exceptional circumstances. The very rare crossing of paths between their modes and ours may cause strange and unexplainable manifestations. These manifestations are interpreted as ghosts, demons, and other supernatural apparitions.

LEGENDS OF *JINN*

References to *jinn* are sometimes meant to recall certain legends deeply embedded in the consciousness of the people to whom the Quran was addressed in the first instance (e.g., in 34:12-14, 21:82, see under Solomon)—the purpose being, in every instance, not the legend as such but the illustration of a moral or spiritual truth.

CREATION OF *JINN*

The invisible beings We created [long] before that, from the fire of scorching winds. (15:27) He created invisible beings out of a confusing fire flame. (55:15)

Jinns can assume visible forms and, like humans, can be good and bad.

SURAH 114
MEN (AN-NAS)

In the Name of God, The Most Gracious, The Dispenser of Grace. Say: "I seek refuge with the Sustainer of men, the Sovereign of men, the God of men, from the evil of the whispering elusive tempter who whispers in the hearts of men-[Satan] from all [temptation to evil by] invisible forces as well as men." (114:1-6)

In Surah 114 (*An-Nas*), there is perhaps the oldest Quranic mention of the term and concept of *al-jinnah* (synonymous with *al-jinn*). The term probably denotes the intangible, mysterious forces of nature to which man's psyche is exposed. These forces sometimes make it difficult to discern between right and wrong. It is also possible to conclude that the "invisible forces" from which we are told to seek refuge with God are the temptations to evil emanating from the blindness of our own hearts, from our gross appetites, and from the erroneous notions and false values handed down to us by our predecessors.

CONFESSION OF FAITH

JINN ACCEPTING THE QURAN

And lo! We caused a group of unseen beings to incline towards thee, [O Muhammad], so that they might listen to the Quran. As soon as they became aware of it, they said [unto one another], "Listen in silence!" And when [the recitation] was over, they returned to their people as warners. (46:29)

JINN OF MOSAIC FAITH

They said: "O our people! We have been listening to a revelation bestowed from on high after [that of] Moses, confirming the truth of whatever remains [of the Torah]. It guides towards the truth, and to a straight way." O our people! Respond to God's call and have faith in Him. He will forgive your [past] sins and deliver you from grievous suffering [in the life to come]. But he who does not respond to God's call can never escape Him on earth, nor can he have any protector against Him [in the life to come]: all such are most obviously lost in error." (46:30-32)

It transpires that the *jinn* in question were the followers of the Mosaic faith. They refer to the Quran as "a revelation bestowed from on high after (that of) Moses," omitting the intervening prophet, Jesus. The occurrence mentioned in the passage above took place in the small oasis of Nakhlah, on the way from Mecca to Taif. Upon hearing the Quran recited by the Prophet, the "unseen beings" immediately recognized its truth. They returned to their fellow beings as preachers and warners of the Quranic creed.

The confession of faith of this group of *jinn* continues below in surah 72 *al-jinn* (verses 1-17).

SURAH 72
AL-JINN (THE UNSEEN BEINGS)

WONDERFUL DISCOURSE

Say: "It has been revealed to me that some of the unseen beings gave ear [to this divine writ] and said [unto their fellow beings]: 'Verily, we have heard a wondrous discourse, guiding towards consciousness of what is right, and so we have come to believe in it." (72:1-2)

GOD HAS NOT BEGOTTEN A SON

"And we shall never ascribe divinity to anyone beside our Sustainer, for [we know] that sublimely exalted is our Sustainer's majesty. No consort He has ever taken unto Himself, nor a son! And [now we know] that the foolish among us said outrageous things about God. [We were mistaken when] we thought that neither man nor [any of] the invisible forces would ever tell a lie about God." (72:2-5)

The invisible beings also rejected the Christian concept of the Trinity. Whatever the nature of these "unseen beings" matters little, for the context makes it abundantly clear that the speech of those beings is but a parable of the guidance that the Quran offers to a mind intent on attaining "consciousness of what is right."

The term *jinn* refers to what is described as "occult powers" or, rather, to a person's preoccupation with them. These forces apparently "tell a lie about God" as they induce their devotees to conceive all manner of fantastic, arbitrary notions about the nature of His Being and of His alleged relations with the created universe; notions exemplified in all mystery religions, in the various Gnostic and theosophical systems, in cabalistic Judaism, and in the many medieval offshoots of each of them.

GOD WILL NEVER SEND ANOTHER APOSTLE

"Yet [it has always happened] that certain kinds of humans would seek refuge with certain kinds of [such]invisible forces: but these only increased their confusion so much so that they came to think, as you [once] thought, that God would never [again] send forth anyone [as His apostle]." (72:6-7)

"Seeking refuge" is synonymous with seeking help or protection, which is an allusion to the hope of certain kinds of humans that the occult powers to which they have turned would successfully guide them through life and thus make it unnecessary for them to look forward to the coming of a new prophet. The overwhelming majority of Jews were convinced that no prophet would be raised after those explicitly mentioned in the Old Testament. This was why they rejected Jesus and Muhammad.

CONSCIOUSNESS OF RIGHT AND WRONG

"And we have come to know that we can never elude God [while we live] on earth, and that we can't elude Him by escaping [from life]. Hence, as soon as we heard this [call to His] guidance, we believed in it. He who believes in his Sustainer need not fear loss or injustice. Yet [it is true] that among us are such as have surrendered themselves to God—just as there are among us such as have abandoned themselves to wrongdoing. Now as for those who surrender themselves to Him, it is they who have attained consciousness of what is right. As for those who abandon themselves to wrongdoing, they are indeed fuel for [the fires of] hell! [Know] then, that if they [who have heard Our call] keep firmly to the [right] path, We shall certainly shower them with blessings abundant, to test them by this means. He who turns away from the remembrance of his Sustainer, him He will cause suffering most grievous.'" (72:12-17)

The above assertion ends the "confession of faith" of the beings described at the beginning of this passage as *jinn*. The phrase "water abundant" is rendered as a blessing abundant above, a metaphor for happiness. This echoes the allegorical reference so frequently occurring in the Quran to the running waters of paradise. God's bestowal of blessings is not just a reward of righteousness but, rather, a test of man's remaining conscious of, and grateful to, Him.

ASTROLOGY TO FORETELL THE FUTURE

"'And [so it happened] that we reached out towards heaven: but we found it filled with mighty guards and flames, notwithstanding that we were established in positions [which we had thought well-suited] to listening to [whatever secrets might be in] it: and anyone who now [or ever] tries to listen will [likewise] find a flame lying in wait for him! And [now we have become aware] that we [created beings] may not know whether evil fortune is intended for [any of] those who live on earth, or whether it is their Sustainer's will to endow them with consciousness of what is right: just as [we do not know how it happens] that some from among us are righteous, while some of us are [far] below that: we have always followed widely divergent paths.'" (72:8-11)

The above may refer to the old Jewish practice of astrology to foretell the future. Their "reaching out towards heaven" may be a metaphorical description of a state of mind that causes a man to regard himself as self-sufficient and delude himself into thinking that he is bound to master his fate. But we failed, despite our status, abilities, and learning. We do not know whether evil fortune awaits earthlings or if God will endow them with "consciousness of what is right," which is equated with the opposite of evil fortune—happiness. As the sequence shows (and as pointed out in 15:18), this relates to all attempts at predicting the future by astrology or esoteric calculations or at influencing the course of future events by the occult sciences.

FORETELLING FUTURE AND OCCULT ENDEAVORS

And, indeed, We have set up in the heaven's magnificent constellations, and endowed them with beauty for all to behold; and We have made them secure against every satanic force accursed—so that anyone who seeks to learn [the unknowable] by stealth is pursued by a flame clear to see. (15:16-18)

The phrase "every satanic force accursed" refers to endeavors strongly condemned in Islam, to divine the future through astrological speculations. God has made the heavens secure against Satanic forces. He has made it impossible for a person to obtain, through astrology or what is commonly referred to as the occult sciences, any real knowledge of "that which is beyond human perception" (al-Ghayb). Any attempt at fathoming the mysteries of the unknowable by such illicit means (by stealth) is inevitably followed by "a flame clear to see"—i.e., by burning, self-evident frustration.

Behold, We have adorned the skies nearest to the earth with the beauty of stars, and have made them secure against every rebellious, satanic force, [so that] they [who seek to learn the unknowable] should not be able to overhear the host on high, but shall be repelled from all sides, cast out [from all grace], with lasting suffering in store for them [in the life to come]; but if anyone does succeed in snatching a glimpse [of such knowledge], he is [henceforth] pursued by a piercing flame. (37:6-10)

A host on high is an angelic force whose "speech" represents God's decrees. The passage above points to the fact that human beings are precluded from really grasping the variety and depth of the universe created by Him. We have here an echo of 34:9: "Are they, then, not aware of how little of the sky and the earth lies open before them, and how much is hidden from them?"—and, thus, a new, oblique approach to the theme of resurrection, which is taken up in the sequence in the form of an indirect question.

CHAPTER 4
SATAN

THE FALLEN ANGEL

And Lo! Thy Sustainer said unto the angels: "Behold, I am about to establish upon earth one who shall inherit it." They said: "Wilt Thou place on it such as will spread corruption thereon and shed blood—whereas it is we who extol Thy limitless glory, and praise Thee, and hallow Thy name?" [God] answered: "I know that which you do not know." (2:30) When We told the angels, "Prostrate yourselves before Adam!" They all prostrated themselves, save Iblis, who refused and gloried in his arrogance, and thus, he became one of those who deny the truth. (2:34)

At the opposite end of the spectrum from God, the principle of good, is Satan (**Shaytan**), the principle of evil. Satan is the leader of other fallen angels, disobedient servants of God who tempt human beings in their earthly moral struggle.

And when they meet those who have attained faith, they assert, "We believe [as you believe]," but when they find themselves alone with their evil impulses, they say, "Verily, we are with you, we were only mocking!" (2:14)

Their evil impulses are literally, "their satans" (**shayatin**, plural of **shaytan**). In accordance with ancient Arabic usage, this term often denotes people "who, through their insolent persistence in evildoing, have become like Satan." (Zamakhshari) The term **shaytan**—derived from the verb **shatana** ("he was or became remote")—often denotes in the Quran a force or influence remote from and opposed to all that is true and good. Satan refers specifically to the chief fallen angel who does his bidding through evil impulses planted into men's hearts in the form of temptations and ungodly tendencies. The term is used in its broadest, most abstract sense to refer to an element of the "satanic force" or evil forces that are in opposition to every viable ethical principle. Evil forces are inherent in both the spiritual and physical worlds. According to several traditions, the Prophet was asked, Are there satans among men? He replied, "Yes, and they are more wicked than the Satans from among the Invisible beings *[al-jinn]* and Satan circulates in the human body as blood does."

SATAN IS NOT THE PRIMARY CAUSE OF SIN

Behold, he has no power over those who have attained to faith and in their Sustainer place their trust: he has the power only over those who are willing to follow him, and who [thus] ascribe to him a share in God's divinity. (16:99-100)

Satan will thus address the sinners on resurrection Day:

"I had no power at all over you: I but called you—and you responded to me. Hence, blame not me, but blame yourselves." (14:22)

Satan in the Quran is not an all-powerful monster lurking above human beings and forcing them to commit evil. Satan can only tempt men. There is no excuse as "Satan made me do it," as it contradicts free will. After committing a grave sin, many religious fundamentalists blame their actions on Satan, to avoid self-responsibility. Evil is not an independent, esoteric factor in life, but rather a result of men succumbing to Satan's evil temptations. In other words, the power of Satan's negative principle has no intrinsic reality. It becomes real only through men choosing willfully the wrong course of action.

SATAN'S GUILE IS WEAK

Those who have attained faith fight for God's cause, whereas those bent on denying the truth fight for evil powers. Fight, then, against those friends of Satan: Satan's guile is weak indeed! (4:76)

Fight against the power of evil; Satan's crafty or artful deception is weak indeed. In other words, Satan is not an invincible foe somewhere out there, and human beings are not helpless victims of evil.

SATAN TEMPTS MAN TO DISTINGUISH RIGHTEOUS FROM EVILDOERS

Indeed, Iblis proved his opinion was right. And yet, he had no power over them. [If We allow him to tempt man], it is only to the end that We might make a clear distinction between those who [truly] believe in the life to come and those who doubt it: for thy Sustainer watches over all things. (34:20-21)

MAN IS FREE TO ACCEPT OR REJECT EVIL

Are you not aware that We have let loose all [manner of] satanic forces upon those who deny the truth—[forces] that impel them [towards sin] with strong impulsion? Therefore, do not rush [to call down God's punishment] upon them: for We count the number of their days. (19:83-84)

The expression "We release all [manner of] satanic forces upon those who deny the truth" has here the meaning of "We have allowed them to be active among them," leaving it to man's free will to accept or reject those evil influences or impulses. Do not ask for hasty punishment because God has granted respite to all sinners.

STRATAGEMS OF SATAN

DECEPTIONS—WHEN EVIL DEEDS SEEM GOOD

By God, [O Prophet], even before thy time, We sent apostles unto [various] communities: but [those who were bent on denying the truth have always refused to listen to Our messages because] Satan has made all their doings seem good to them: and he is [as] close to them today [as he was to the sinners of the past]; hence, grievous suffering awaits them. (16:63)

SATAN INSTILLS FEARS OF HIS ALLIES

It is Satan who instills fear in you of his allies. So do not be afraid of them, but fear Me, if you are [truly] believers! And be not grieved by those who vie with one another in denying the truth. They can in no way harm God. It is God's will that they shall have no share in the [blessings of] life to come and tremendous suffering awaits them. (3:175-176)

WHISPERING HALF-TRUTHS

Thus, it is against every prophet that We set up as enemies the evil forces from among humans and from among invisible beings. These forces whisper glittering half-truth meant to delude the mind. But they could not do this unless thy Sustainer so willed: stand aloof from them and all their false imagery! (6:112)

The above verse refers to people who become allies with Satan by deliberately doing wrong. Evil forces whispering embellished speech or varnished falsehood by way of delusion or half-truths entice men with their deceptive attractiveness and cause them to overlook all moral values. Thus, the meaning of the above verse is that every prophet has had to contend with the spiritual—and sometimes physical—enmity of the evil ones who, for whatever reason, refuse to listen to the voice of truth and try to lead others astray.

SINFUL IMPULSES AS MASTERS

Some [of you] He will grace with His guidance, whereas, for some, straying from the right path will be unavoidable. For, behold, they will have taken [their own] evil impulses for their masters instead of God, thinking all the while that they have found the right path! (7:30)

It becomes inevitable for them to "stray from the right path" because of their own actions and attitudes. The term "satanic forces" is applied in the Quran to all kinds of wicked impulses or propensities that are near to the hearts of those who do not truly believe in God; hence, the term *shayatin* is rendered as "evil impulses."

SOWING DISCORD AMONG MEN

Satan is always ready to stir up discord between men—for, verily, Satan is man's open foe! (17:53) The evil impulses [within men's hearts] whisper unto those who have made them their own that they should involve you in the argument [as to what is and what is not a sin]; and if you pay heed unto them, lo! You will become [like] those who attribute divinity to other beings or forces beside God. (6:121)

Your evil impulses are trying to draw you into an argument about what constitutes a sin. This is to make you lose sight of God's clear ordinances in this respect. If you follow their arbitrary, deceptive reasoning, you will elevate them, as it were, to the position of moral lawgivers. This will ascribe to them a right belonging to God alone.

SATAN CASTING DOUBT IN PROPHETIC MESSAGES

For so it is that against every prophet We have set up enemies from among those lost in sin: yet none can guide and give succor as thy Sustainer does! (25:31) Yet whenever We sent forth any apostle or prophet before thee, and he hoped [that his warnings would be heeded], Satan would cast an aspersion on his innermost aims. But God renders null and void whatever aspersion Satan casts. God makes His messages clear in and by themselves—for God is all-knowing, wise. (22:52)

SINNERS ACCEPTANCE OF SATAN'S ASPERSIONS

[And He allows doubts to arise] so that He might cause whatever aspersion Satan may cast [against His prophets] to become a trial for all in whose hearts is disease and all whose hearts are hardened: for all who are [thus] sinning [against themselves] are most deeply in the wrong. (22:53)

SATAN THREATENS YOU WITH POVERTY

Satan threatens you with the prospect of poverty and bids you to be miserly. While God promises you His forgiveness and bounty. God is infinite, all-knowing, granting wisdom unto whom He wills and whoever is granted wisdom has indeed been rewarded with wealth abundant. But none remember this except those endowed with insight. (2:268-269)

THE RIGHTEOUS REJECT SATAN AND SUBMIT TO GOD

And [God renders Satan's aspersions null and void] so that they who are endowed with [innate] knowledge might know that this [divine writ] is the truth from thy Sustainer, and that they might believe in it, and that their hearts might humbly submit to Him. For, behold, God guides those who have attained faith. (22:54)

Every prophet had to contend with evil forces. Satan casts doubt upon the message-bearer's innermost aim by insinuating that the spiritual improvement of his community is not the real purpose of his message. It is rather the attainment of personal power and influence. Those who are prone to sinning readily accept such doubts, and it becomes a source of trial for them. Satan also tempts those who have attained faith. However, they reject the aspersions cast upon the prophetic message. This is because God's clear message speaks for itself, and any insinuation of prophets' hidden motives is automatically disproved.

FOLLOWERS OF SATAN

Nevertheless, among men there are many who argues about God without any knowledge [of Him]. They follow every rebellious satanic force. Those who entrust themselves to satanic forces will be led astray and guided towards the blazing flame of suffering! (22:3-4) Behold, Satan is a foe to you; therefore, treat him as a foe. He calls on his followers to the end they might find themselves among the destined for the blazing flame. (35:6)

SIN AND A MATERIALISTIC OUTLOOK

Tell them what happens to him to whom We vouchsafe Our messages and who discards them: Satan catches up with him, and he strays, like so many others, into grievous error. Now had We so willed, We could indeed have exalted him by means of those [messages]: but he always clung to the earth and followed his own desires. (7:175-176)

THE PARABLE OF AN EXCITED DOG

Thus, his parable is that of an [excited] dog: if you approach him threateningly, he will pant with his tongue lolling; and if thou leave him alone, he will pant with his tongue lolling. Such is the parable of those bent on giving the lie to Our messages. Tell [them], then, this story, so that they might take thought. (7:176)

SINNING AGAINST ONESELF

Evil is the example of people bent on giving the lie to Our messages. For it is against themselves that they are sinning! He whom God guides, he alone is truly guided; whereas those whom He lets go astray—it is they, they who are the losers! (7:177-178)

THEY ARE LIKE CATTLE

And most certainly have We destined for hell many of the invisible beings and men who have hearts with which they fail to grasp the truth, and eyes with which they fail to see, and ears with which they fail to hear. They are like cattle—nay, they are even less conscious of the right way: it is they, they who are the [truly] heedless! (7:179)

The kind of man spoken of here is one who has understood the divine message but refuses to admit its truth because, as pointed out in the next verse, his vain desires and a materialistic earthly outlook on life dominate him. His attitudes are influenced by what his earthbound desires represent to him as his immediate advantages or disadvantages, just as a dog follows only his instincts and natural needs and is not conscious of the possibility or necessity of a moral choice. The type of man alluded to in this passage is always, whatever the outward circumstances, prey to the conflict between his reason and his base urges. This leads to inner disquiet and imaginary fears. He cannot attain peace of mind, which a believer achieves through his faith.

DESTINED FOR THE BLAZING FLAME

Behold, Satan is a foe unto you; therefore, treat him as a foe. He but calls on his followers to the end that they might find themselves among such as are destined for the blazing flame—[seeing that] for those who are bent on denying the truth there is suffering severe in store, just as for those who have attained to faith and do righteous deeds there is forgiveness of sins, and a just reward. Is, then, he to whom the evil of his doings is [so] alluring that [in the end] he regards it as good [anything but a follower of Satan]? For, verily, God lets go astray him that wills [to go astray], just as He guides him that wills [to be guided]. Hence, [O believer], do not waste thyself in sorrowing over them. Verily, God has full knowledge of all that they do! (35:6-8)

ROLE OF EVIL IN GOD'S PLAN

But as for those who are bent on giving the lie to Our messages—we shall bring them low, step by step, without their perceiving how it came about. For, behold, though I may give them rein for a while, My subtle scheme is exceedingly firm! (7:182-183)

The term "subtle scheme" represents God's unfathomable plan of creation, of which man can glimpse only isolated fragments and never the totality; a plan in which everything and every event happening has a definite function and nothing is accidental. Indirectly, the above passage alludes to the question of why God allows so many evil persons to enjoy their lives to the fullest. In contrast, so many righteous people suffer. The answer is that during his life in this world, man cannot really understand where apparent happiness and unhappiness ultimately lead. He cannot also understand what role they play in God's "subtle scheme" of creation.

EVIL SOUL MATES

For [when they became oblivious of Us], We assigned to them [their own evil impulses as their] other selves. These made it seem good to them whatever lay open before them and beyond their ken. And so, the sentence [of doom] will fall upon them together with the [other sinful] communities of invisible beings [jinn] and humans that passed away before their time. Verily, they [all] will indeed be lost! (41:25)

The "other selves" refer to evil soul mates intimately associated or yoked together, one thing with another. Their evil impulses, which had become their "other selves," made them attracted to the unrestrained enjoyment, without moral discrimination. Their overindulgence in all the worldly attractions available to them caused them, at the same time, to dismiss as an illusion the idea of resurrection and God's judgment.

Giving them a false sense of security about something beyond their control.

SATAN COMPANION OF EVILDOERS

But as for anyone who chooses to remain blind to the remembrance of the Most Gracious, to him We assign an [enduring] evil impulse, to become his other self: whereupon, behold, these [evil impulses] bar all such from the path [of truth], making them think they are guided aright! But in the end, when he [who has thus sinned] appears before us [on Judgment Day], he will say [to his other self, "Would that between me and thee there was the distance of east and west!" For, evil indeed [has proven] that other self! On that Day, it will not profit you in the least [to know] that, since you have sinned [together], you are now to share your suffering [as well]. (43:36-39)

The above address is formulated in the plural and not in the dual; it relates to all sinners who were driven by their evil impulses—their "other selves," as it were—to "remain blind to the remembrance of the Most Gracious."

WORSHIP GOD AND SHUN EVIL

And indeed, within every community, We have raised up an apostle [entrusted with this message]: "Worship God and shun the powers of evil!" (16:36)

In Quranic terminology, "worship of God" implies man's sense of responsibility before Him. Hence, the above commandment comprises, in the most concise formulation imaginable, the sum total of all ethical injunctions and prohibitions. It is the basis and source of all morality as well as the one unchanging message inherent in every true religion.

SUFFERING IN HELL FOR IBLIS HOSTS

Thereupon they will be hurled into hell—they, as well as all [others] who were lost in grievous error, and the hosts of Iblis—all together. And there and then, blaming one another, they [who had grievously sinned in life] will exclaim: "By God, we were most obviously astray when we deemed you [false deities] equal to the Sustainer of all the worlds— yet they who have seduced us [into believing in you] are the truly guilty ones! And now we have none to intercede for us, nor any loving friend." (26:94-101)

The "hosts of Iblis" are the forces of evil, or Satan, frequently mentioned in the Quran in connection with man's sin.

WORSHIP OF SATAN

Did I not enjoin you, O you children of Adam, not to worship Satan—since, verily, he is your open foe—and you should worship Me [alone]? This would have been a straight way! And [as for Satan] he had already led astray a great many of you: could you not, then, use your reason? "This, then, is the hell of which you were warned again and again. Endure it today as an outcome of your persistent denial of the truth!" (36:59-64)

The phrase "this, then, is hell" points to sinners' realization of their mistakes despite repeated warnings from the prophets. It will be a source of intense suffering in the life to come.

SEEK REFUGE WITH GOD FROM SATAN

And but for God's bounty towards you, and His grace, all but a few of you would certainly have followed Satan. (4:83) And say: "O my Sustainer! I seek refuge with Thee from all the promptings of evil impulses, and I seek refuge with Thee, O my Sustainer, lest they come near unto me!" (23:97-98) Now whenever you happen to read this Quran, seek refuge with God from Satan, the accursed. (16:98)

Man is always, by virtue of his nature, prone to questioning the validity of the moral standards established through revelation. The believer is now called upon to seek, whenever he reads or meditates on this divine writ, God's spiritual aid against the whisperings of what the Quran describes as "Satan, the accursed."

SURAH 113
AL-FALAQ (THE RISING DAWN)

In The Name of God, The Most Gracious, The Dispenser of Grace, Say: "I seek refuge with the Sustainer of the rising dawn, "from the evil of aught that He has created, "and from the evil of the black darkness whenever it descends, "and from the evil of all human beings bent on occult endeavors, "and from the evil of the envious when he envies." (113:1-5)

The term *al-falaq* (or "the rising dawn") is often used to describe "the emergence of the truth after (a period of) uncertainty" (*Taj al-Arus*); hence, the "Sustainer of the rising dawn" implies that God is the source of all cognition of truth and that one's "seeking refuge" in Him is synonymous with striving after truth. The evil of black darkness refers to despair or approaching death. Occult endeavors, or literally "of those that blow upon knots" is an idiomatic phrase from pre-Islamic Arabia to designate all occult endeavors. It was probably derived from the practice of witches and sorcerers who tied a string into several knots while blowing upon them and murmuring magic incantations. In his explanation of the above verse, Zamakhshari categorically rejects all belief in the reality and effectiveness of such practices. He also rejects the concept of magic as such. The reason why the believer is enjoined to "seek refuge with God" from such practices despite their palpable irrationality is due to the inherent sinfulness of such endeavors, and from the mental danger in which they may involve their author, such as the moral and social effects that another person's envy may have on one's life, as well as from succumbing to the evil of envy.

CHAPTER 5
DEATH

FROM MORTALITY TO ETERNITY

REJECTION OF SOUL REINCARNATION

Islam rejects the suggestion that human souls will be reincarnated in different bodies for reparation and spiritual advancement. We have but one opportunity to earn the recompense that will determine our eternal existence. The Quran stresses, again and again, the principle of man's moral responsibility for all his conscious actions and behavior, and of the continuation of this responsibility, in the shape of inescapable consequences, good or bad, in a person's life in the hereafter. In other words, there is a direct continuity between this life and the next, linking our lives and actions on earth with the final dispensation of justice on Judgment Day.

LIFE: TWO STAGES OF ONE CONTINUOUS JOURNEY

Ours is [the dominion over] the life to come and [over] this earlier part [of your life]. (92:13)

This statement is meant to stress the fact that man's life in this world and the hereafter is two stages of one continuous entity. Life in this world is but the first stage—a very short stage—of life that continues beyond the hiatus called "death." God decides the life span of individuals and communities, and with the death of the body, the individual's soul enters the hereafter. Death is, therefore, a misnomer, as it is not an end. It is the beginning of a new journey for the soul, liberated from the limitations of the body, to travel into the realm of eternity.

STAGES OF HUMAN LIFE FROM BIRTH TO DEATH

He who created you out of clay, and then decreed a term [for you]—a term known [only] to Him. (6:2) And He it is who has brought you [all] into being out of one living entity, and [has appointed for each of you] a time-limit [on earth] and a resting-place [after death]. (6:98) There is no living creature on earth but depends for its sustenance on God, and He knows its time-limit [on earth] and its resting-place [after death]: all [this] is laid down in [His] clear decree. (11:6)

The above reference to man being created out of clay and dust points to his evolutionary origin. Only He knows a lifetime relating both to individual lives and to the world.

EVOLUTION FROM DUST AND FERTILIZED OVUM

It is He who creates you out of dust, and then out of a drop of sperm, and out of a germ-cell and brings you forth as children, and then [He ordains] that you reach maturity, and then you grow old—though some of you [He causes to] die earlier—and [all this He ordains] so that you might reach a term set [by Him], and you might [learn to] use your reason. (40:67)

FROM INFANCY TO OLD AGE

It is God who creates you [all in a state] of weakness, and then, after weakness, ordains strength [for you], and then, after [a period of] strength, ordains [old age] weakness and grey hair. He creates what He wills; and He alone is all-knowing, infinite in His power. (30:54) He will cause you to die, and in time resurrect you. God has created you, and in time will cause you to die. Many a one of you is reduced in old age to a most abject state, ceasing to know anything of what he once knew so well. Verily, God is all-knowing, infinite in His power! (16:70)

SLEEP AND WAKEFULNESS ARE AN ALLUSION TO LIFE AND DEATH

And He it is who causes you to be [like] dead at night and knows what you work during the daytime, and He brings you back to life each day in order that a term set [by Him] be fulfilled. In the end, unto Him you must return, and then He will make you understand all that you were doing [in life]. (6:60)

BARZAKH

We have [indeed] decreed that death shall be [ever-present] among you. (56:60) For behind those [who leave the world] there is a barrier [of death] until the Day when all will be raised from the dead! (23:100)

The entire Quran's message makes it clear that the person who has died will never return to earth again. The barrier of death (*barzakh*) represents the inability of departed souls to return to earth. There is very little explanation in the Quran as to what happens from the time between an individual's death and resurrection. All we know is that the soul lives on without a body.

EVERLASTING LIFE IS NEVER GRANTED

And [remind those who deny thee, O Prophet, that] never have We granted life everlasting to any mortal before thee: but do they, perchance, hope that although thou must die, they will live forever? Every human being is bound to taste death; and We test you [all] through the bad and the good [things of life] by way of trial: and unto Us; you all must return. (21:34-35)

Mecca's unbelievers questioned Muhammad's prophethood as he was a mortal like them. However, all of God's apostles were mortal men. And so, We shall not grant immortality to you, and you are bound to die. But when you die, will they live forever? This implies an assumption on their part that they would not be called to account after death and resurrection. However, in the end, you shall be returned for judgment.

TIMING AND PLACE OF DEATH

Wherever you are, death will overtake you—even though you are in towers raised high. (4:78) And none that is long-lived has his days lengthened—and neither is aught lessened of his days—unless it is thus laid down in [God's] decree: for all this is easy for God. (35:11) He (God) knows its time-limit [on earth] and its resting-place [after death]: all [this] is laid down in [His] clear decree. (11:6) Whereas no one knows what he will reap tomorrow, and no one knows in what land he will die. Verily, God [alone] is all-knowing, all-aware. (31:34)

VISIT FROM ANGELS OF DEATH

And He [God] alone holds sway over His servants. And He sends forth heavenly forces to watch over you [guardians over you] until, when death approaches any of you. Our messengers cause him to die, and they do not overlook [anyone]. (6:61) And [always] listen for the day when He who issues the call [of death] shall call [thee] from close-by. (50:41) Say: "[One day] the angel of death who has been given charge of you will gather you, and then unto your Sustainer, you will be brought back." [on the Judgment Day] *(32:11)*

HELPLESSNESS OF ONLOOKERS AND CERTAINTY OF DEATH

Why, then, when [the last breath] comes up to the throat [of a dying man], the while you are [helplessly] looking on—and while We are closer to him than you, although you see [Us] not. Why then, if [you think that] you are not truly dependent [on Us], can you not cause that [ebbing life] to return—if what you claim is true? (56:83-87)

The elliptic implication is: If then, as you claim, you are independent of any Supreme Power, why are you not able to prevent the death of your loved one?

CHAPTER 6
ENTERING AFTERLIFE

DEFINITION OF TERMS DUNYA AND AL-AKHIRAH

The term *dunya* means this world and its earthly concerns and possessions - unlike the ultimate reality of the spiritual realms of the hereafter or *al-akhirah*. God's creative abilities are not limited to creating the material world alone. The existence of this universe, although infinitely vast, is merely a small segment of reality open to man's perception and imagination.

VARIATIONS IN UNDERSTANDING AFTERLIFE

The question that preoccupies man above all others, whether there is life after death, has been answered in various ways throughout the ages. It is, of course, impossible to describe the innumerable variations of those answers; nevertheless, a few main lines of thought are clearly discernible, and their mention may be useful for a better understanding of the Quranic treatment of this concept.

Wishful Thinking: Some people, probably a minority, believe bodily death amounts to total and irreversible extinction. All talk about a hereafter is wishful thinking. Atheists and many pagans of pre-Islamic Arabia held this view.

Universal Soul: Others believe that after individual death, the human "life-essence" returns to the supposed source of its origin conceived as the "universal soul" and merges with it entirely.

Soul Incarnation: Hindus believe in the successive transmigration of the individual soul, at the moment of death, into another body, human or animal, but without a continuation of individual consciousness.

Existence Of Soul Only: Others, again, think that only the soul, and not the entire human "personality," lives after death in a purely spiritual, disembodied form.

Existence Of Soul and Individual Personality: And, lastly, some believe in the undiminished survival of individual personality and consciousness. They regard death and resurrection as the twin stages of a positive act of re-creation of the entire human personality, in whatever form this may necessarily involve. This is the Quranic view of life to come. Generally, it is also a Christian belief. Jews are vague on the topic.

MOVE ONWARD FROM THIS LIFE TO THE AFTERLIFE

I call to witness the sunset's [fading] afterglow and the night. It [step by step] unfolds, and the moon, as it grows to its fullness. [Even then, O men], you are bound to move from stage to stage. What, then, is amiss with them that they will not believe [in a life to come]? (84:16-20)

Thus God "calls us to witness" that nothing in His creation is ever at a standstill. Everything moves unceasingly from one state of being into another. A phenomenon of constant change, described by the Greek philosopher Heraclitus as panta rhei (everything is in a state of flux). There is an unceasing progression from conception, birth, growth, decline, death, and resurrection. The movement of all that exists from stage to stage corresponds to a fundamental law evident in all creation. It is unreasonable to assume that man alone should be an exception. His onward journey after death, is followed by a change into another state of being.

LIFE AFTER DEATH IS THE VERY TRUTH

Verily, what you are promised is truth [life after death], and judgment is bound to come! Consider the starry sky! Verily, [O men], you are deeply at odds with what to believe. He who deceives himself is perverted in his views! They destroy themselves and are prone to guessing at what they cannot ascertain. (51:5-10) And in heaven is [the source of] your sustenance and [of] all that you are promised [for your life after death]. By the Sustainer of heaven and earth, this [life after death] is the very truth—as true as you are endowed with speech! (51:22-23)

Think of the Creator of this magnificent universe and your responsibility to Him. You are at odds as to whether there is life after death, does God exists, whether there is any truth in divine revelation, etc. Belief in God and life after death is inherent in man's mind and feelings. Deviation from this belief is an intellectual perversion. "That which they cannot ascertain" is synonymous with *al-ghayb*, the reality beyond human perception. Heaven above is the source of sustenance, both physical (rain) in this life and spiritual (truth and guidance) in the afterlife. The reality of life after death is as true as man's ability to think conceptually and express himself as something he is absolutely, and unquestionably aware of.

WARN FOLLOWERS OF EARLIER SCRIPTURES

And warn hereby those [followers of earlier scriptures] *who fear lest they are gathered unto their Sustainer with none to protect them from Him or to intercede with Him. This is so that they might become [fully] conscious of Him. (6:51)*

"And warn hereby those" refers to followers of earlier scriptures—such as the Jews and the Christians—who share with the Quran followers the belief in life after death. It also refers to agnostics who, without definite beliefs on this point, admit the possibility of life after death.

THE ULTIMATE REALITY OF THE HEREAFTER

God has not created the heavens and the earth and all that is between them without [an inner] truth and a term set [by Him]. Yet, behold, there are those who stubbornly deny the truth that they are destined to meet their Sustainer! (30:8)

In contrast to God, who is eternal and unlimited, everything created is limited and subject to change and termination.

AFTERLIFE IS FAR BETTER THAN THIS LIFE

PASSING DELIGHT AND FLEETING PLEASURE

God grants abundant sustenance, or gives scant measure, to whomever He wills. They [who are given abundance] rejoice in the life of this world—even though, compared with the life to come, the life of this world is merely a fleeting pleasure. (13:26) The life of this world is nothing but a passing delight and play—whereas behold, the life in the hereafter is indeed the only [true] life if they knew this! (29:64) Say: "Brief is the enjoyment of this world, whereas the life to come is the best for all who are conscious of God—since none of you shall be wronged by a hair's breadth."(4:77) To happiness [in the life to follow] will indeed attain he who attains to purity [in this world] and remembers his Sustainer's name and prays [unto Him]. But nay, [O men], you prefer the life of this world, although the life to come is better and more enduring. (87:14-17)

LIFE TO COME IS EVERLASTING

And [remember] whatever you are given [now] is but for the [passing] enjoyment of life in this world, and for its embellishment—whereas that which is with God is [so much] better and more enduring. Will you not, then, use your reason? (28:60)

EARTHLY PLEASURES VERSUS ETERNAL HAPPINESS

Would you content yourselves with [the comforts of] this worldly life in preference to [the good of] the life to come? The enjoyment of life in this world is paltry compared to life to come! (9:38) Life in the hereafter is far better for God-conscious people. Will you not, then, use your reason? (6:32) Alluring to man is the enjoyment of worldly desires through women, children, horses of high rank, cattle, lands, heaped-up treasures of gold and silver. All this may be enjoyed in this world—but the most glorious goal is with God. Say: "Shall I tell you of better things than those [earthly joys]? For God-conscious there are, with their Sustainer, gardens through which running waters flow, there to abide, spouses pure, and God's goodly acceptance. (3:14-15)

THE LOGICAL NECESSITY OF THE AFTERLIFE

PERFECT JUSTICE IN THE AFTERLIFE

God designated man as His vicegerent and bestowed the gift of free will. Man's freedom and responsibility lead directly to Islam's doctrine of afterlife and resurrection. For Muslims, life on earth is the seedbed of an eternal future. Each soul will be held accountable for his actions on earth and how well he observed God's laws.

Would We treat those who have attained faith and do righteous deeds in the same manner as [We shall deal with] those who spread corruption on earth? Would We treat the God-conscious like the wicked? [All this We have expounded in this] blessed divine writ which We have revealed unto thee, [O Muhammad], so that men may ponder over its messages, and that those who are endowed with insight may take them to heart. (38:28-29)

Now as for those who indulge in sinful doings—do they think that We place them, both in their life and death, on an equal footing with those who have attained faith and do righteous deeds? Bad, indeed, is their judgment. For God has created the heavens and the earth in accordance with [an inner] truth, and [has therefore willed] that every human being shall be recompensed for what he has earned, and none shall be wronged. (45:21-22) One who is minded to ask might ask about the suffering that [in the hereafter] is bound to befall those who deny the truth. [Know that] nothing can ward it off. (70:1-2)

It is incomprehensible that lifelong suffering is often the lot of many righteous. In contrast, wrongdoers and deniers of the truth often remain unscathed and enjoy life. The Quran solves this apparent paradox by stating that the afterlife satisfies justice and morality. If good and evil have the same end, virtue and vice become meaningless. We must assume that God either does not exist or is unjust. Injustice is incompatible with the Godhead. Alternatively, there is a hereafter in which both the righteous and the unrighteous will harvest in full what they morally sowed during their lives on earth.

Without a differentiation between right and wrong—or true and false—there would be no "inner truth" in a divinely planned creation. A true believer faces worldly tribulations and death with inner peace and tranquility. Wrongdoers and deniers of the truth may have nagging anxiety. This is a feeling that often accompanies "fear of the unknown" at the time of dying.

REWARD AND PUNISHMENT

For, [in the life to come] all shall have their degrees in accordance with whatever [good or evil] they did. He will repay them in full for their doings, and none shall be wronged. (46:19) [Be conscious, then, of] the Day when every human being shall come to plead for himself [alone], and every human being shall be repaid in full for whatever he has done, and none shall be wronged. (16:111) To Him you all must return. This is, in truth, God's promise. He creates [man] first and then brings him forth anew to reward with equity all who attain faith and do righteous deeds. Those who are bent on denying the truth will suffer a draught of burning despair and grievous suffering because of their persistent refusal to acknowledge the truth. (10:4)

GOD WILL MAKE YOU UNDERSTAND WHAT YOU DID IN LIFE

They who are bent on denying the truth claim that they will never be raised from the dead! Say:

"Yea, by my Sustainer! Most surely you will be raised from the dead, and then, most surely, you will be made to understand what you did [in life]! For, easy is this for God!" Believe, then, [O men] in God and His Apostle, and in the light [of revelation], which We have bestowed [on you] from on high! And God is fully aware of all that you do. (64:7-8) And one Day, all [who have ever lived] will be brought back unto Him, and then He will make them [truly] understand all that they were doing [in life]: for God has full knowledge of everything. (24:64)

COSMIC CATACLYSM AND RESURRECTION OF THE DEAD

CHAPTER 7
THE LAST HOUR

The assertion of the godless that the universe is eternal—that is, without beginning and end and can never cease to exist—amounts to a denial of the fact that God alone is eternal and of resurrection and divine judgment as symbolized by the Last Hour. In other words, it is a denial of life after death and, hence, of all significance and purpose attached to human life.

As God appoints the life span of everyone, He determines the fixed limit of the earth and the duration of humanity upon it. At each instant, we are drawing near to the climax of time and history when all will be brought into the awesome presence of the Creator. In God's hands lies the fate of all He has created. One day, the world will end, followed by the resurrection and the Last Judgment.

DERISIVE QUERY OF ADVENT OF THE LAST DAY

The Prophet's contemporaries who refused to regard the Quran as a divine revelation made a sarcastic demand to be punished forthwith "if this be indeed the truth from God." Instead of willingly accepting the guidance offered by the Prophet, they mockingly challenged him to bring about the exemplary punishment with which, according to the Prophet, God threatened them.

Quranic references to the derisive question of the Last Hour and the Day of Judgment illustrate the attitude responsible for it. Such sarcasm is not restricted to an isolated historic incident but is symptomatic of most, if not all, people "who are bent on denying the truth."

Say: "There has been appointed for you a Day, which you cannot delay or advance by a single moment." (34:30) Behold, men look upon that [reckoning] as something far away—but We see it as near!

(70:6-7) Say thou: "It may well be that [in your ignorance] you so hastily demand has already drawn close to you." (27:71-72)

And thus, it is: if We defer their suffering until a time-limit set [by Us], [the Day of Judgment], they will ask, "What is preventing it [from coming now]?" Oh, verily, on the Day when it befalls them there will be nothing to avert it from them. They shall be overwhelmed by the very thing they deride. (11:7-8)

And for all thou knowest, the Last Hour may well be near. Those who do not believe in it [mockingly] ask for its speedy advent—whereas those who have attained faith stand in awe of it and know it to be the truth. Oh, verily, they who call the Last Hour in question have indeed gone far astray! (42:17-18)

Mentioning those who do not believe in the last hour and who ask to bring about their speedy chastisement in proof of his being God's message-bearer is not merely a reference to the sarcastic demand of Muhammad's opponents (mentioned several times in the Quran) but also an oblique allusion to unbelievers of all times who, without having any proof either way, categorically reject the idea of resurrection and judgment.

Say: [O Prophet] "I do not know whether that [judgment] you are promised [by God] is near or far [in time]. (21:109) But [for me], I do not know whether, perchance, this [delay in God's judgment] is but a trial for you, and a [merciful] respite for a while." Say: "O my Sustainer! Judge Thou in truth!" (21:111-112)

The Quranic allusions to the "nearness" of the Last Hour and the Day of Resurrection are not based on human time concepts. In other words, "drawn unto you" is the end of their own life, which must precede resurrection. The rejection by "those who are bent on denying the truth" of all revelation is motivated by their refusal to believe in the resurrection and God's judgment, and, hence, to admit the validity of absolute moral standards as postulated by every higher religion.

SUDDENNESS OF THE LAST HOUR

[The Last Hour] will weigh heavily on the heavens and the earth [and] fall upon you suddenly. (7:187) The advent of the Last Hour will manifest itself [in a single moment] like the twinkling of an eye, or closer still for God has the power to will anything. (16:77) [Answer this] if you are men of truth! Nothing awaits them beyond a single blast [of God's punishment], which will overtake them while they are still arguing [against the resurrection]. So [sudden will be their end that] no testament will they be able to make, nor to their own people will they return! (36:48-50) Nay, but [the Last Hour] will come upon them suddenly and stupefy them. They will be unable to avert it and will not receive respite. (21:40-41) Are they [whose hearts are sealed] waiting for the Last Hour that will come upon them suddenly? But it has already been foretold! And what will their remembrance [of their past sins] avail them of once it falls upon them? Know, then, [O man] that there is no deity save God, and [while there is yet time] ask forgiveness for your sins and for [the sins of] all other believing men and women: for God knows all your comings and goings as well as your abiding [at rest]. (47:18-19)

The Last Hour will manifest suddenly and unpredictably. This is an outcome of the absence of any time interval between God's decreeing it and its materialization. "Already been told," refers to the many Quranic predictions of its inevitability. It also refers to the evidence accessible to any unprejudiced mind of creation's temporal finality. When the Last Hour comes, what benefit will their belated repentance bring?

LAST HOUR AND GOOD DEEDS

[Although] I have willed to keep it hidden, the Last Hour is bound to come, so that every human being will be recompensed for what he strived for [in life]. (20:15)

The expression "what he strived for" implies a consciousness of endeavor, and thus excludes involuntary actions, and omissions irrespective of whether the relevant action or omission is morally acceptable or unethical. By enunciating the above principle, the Quran stresses the essential identity of ethical concepts underlying all true religions.

[People] who are filled with fear [at the thought] of the Day on which all hearts and eyes will be convulsed, [and who only hope] that God may reward them in accordance with the best that they ever did, and give them, out of His bounty, more [than they deserve]. God grants sustenance to whom He wills, beyond all reckoning. (24:37-38)

WORSHIP GOD ALONE AS THE LAST HOUR DRAWS NEAR

This is a warning like those warnings of old that the [Last Hour] is drawing ever nearer, [although] none but God can unveil it. Do you, perhaps, find this tiding strange? And do you laugh instead of weeping, and divert yourselves all the while? [Nay] but prostrate yourselves before God, and worship [only Him]! (53:56-62)

SIGNS OF THE HOUR: DESTRUCTION OF THE RAMPART

[The King] said, "This is a mercy from my Sustainer!" Yet when the time appointed by my Sustainer comes, He will make this [rampart] level with the ground and my Sustainer's promise always comes true!" (18:98) Hence, it has been unfailingly true of any community whom We have ever destroyed that they [were people who] would never turn back [from their sinful ways] until such a time as Gog and

Magog are let loose [upon the world] and swarm down from every corner [of the earth]. (21:95-96)

The breakthrough of the godless forces of "Gog and Magog" is one of the signs of the Last Hour approach. The terms Gog and Magog or *Yajuj* and *Majuj* in Arabic are also used in the Quran in allegorical terms. They refer to a series of social catastrophes, which will destroy man's civilization before the Last Hour.

"It has been unfailingly true" expresses the impossibility of conceiving anything to the contrary, that whenever God consigns a community to destruction, He does it not because of its people's occasional lapses but only because of their irremediable, conscious unwillingness to forsake their sinful ways. This will be until the Day of resurrection, heralded by the allegorical breakthrough of "Gog and Magog" (see 18:98 above) for it is on that Day that even the most hardened sinner will, at last, realize his guilt, and be filled with belated remorse. The expression "from all directions" or "from every corner [of the earth]" is used here idiomatically, signifying the irresistible nature of the social and cultural catastrophes that will overwhelm mankind before the Last Hour.

Lost indeed are they who consider it a lie that they will have to meet God—till the Last Hour suddenly comes upon them, [and] they cry, "Alas for us, that we disregarded it!" -- For they shall bear on their backs the burden of their sins: Oh, how evil the load with which they shall be burdened! (6:30-31) But nay, the Last Hour is the time when they truly meet their fate. That Last Hour will be calamitous, and bitter, for those who are lost in sin. [They will know that it is they who] were sunk in error and folly! On the Day when they shall be dragged into the fire on their faces, [they will be told]: "Taste now the touch of hellfire!" (54:46-48)

The signs by which to recognize the beginning of the end are the cataclysmic events upsetting the rhythm of the natural world, described in very vivid Quranic imagery (see next chapter). There is no specific mention in the Quran of moral decay before the signs of the hour. Much of this material is derived from the Prophet's traditions. However, it is alluded to in the invasion of Gog and Magog. One of Islam's most popular myths is Jesus' second coming before the end of the world. The Quran does not mention Jesus' second coming or the anti-Christ.

DENIAL OF THE LAST HOUR EVEN WHEN APPROACHING

But if they [who reject all thought of the Last Hour] saw a sign [of its approach], they would turn aside and say, "An ever-recurring delusion!" For they are bent on giving it the lie, [to the prediction of the Last Hour], *being always inclined to follow their own desires. Yet everything reveals its truth in the end. (54:2-3)*

Everything has an intrinsic reality of its own and is bound to reveal that reality either in this world or the next. Hence, everything must have a purpose or goal of its own. These two complementary interpretations reflect the repeated Quranic statement that everything that exists or happens has meaning and purpose.

CHAPTER 8
THE END OF THE WORLD

TRANSFORMATION (NOT ANNIHILATION) OF THE UNIVERSE

In the Quran's eschatology, the end of the world does not mean annihilation. It is not the reduction to the nothingness of the physical universe, but rather, its fundamental, cataclysmic transformation. Eventually, the earth and the universe will transform into something new. In other words, the disruption of the natural order can be seen as the reverse process of creation. Since that change will be beyond anything man has ever experienced or what the human mind can conceive, all the Quranic descriptions of what is to happen on that Last Day are expressed in allegorical terms.

THE APPROACH OF THE LAST HOUR

Wait, then, for the Day when the skies shall bring forth a pall of smoke which will make obvious [the approach of the Last Hour], enveloping all mankind. (44:10-11) [It will take place] on a Day when the sky will be like molten lead (70:8) and become red like [burning] oil. (55:37). [It will come to pass] on the Day the skies will be in a tumultuous convulsion. (52:9) And the sky is cleft asunder. (82:1) When the skies are opened [as wide flung] gates. (78:19) On that Day, We shall roll up the skies as written scrolls are rolled up. (21:104)

There will be a sudden change in sky color at the Last Hour. The sky or the heavens in the Quran often means "universe." Allegorically, the mysteries of the sky will be opened to man's understanding, thus further amplifying the concept of "the Day of Distinction between the true and the false."

THE FIRST BLAST OF THE TRUMPET

Hence, [bethink yourselves of the Last Hour], when the trumpet [of judgment] shall be sounded with a single blast. The earth and the mountains shall be lifted and crushed with a single stroke! And so, that which must come to pass will on that Day come to pass. (69:13-15)

With the first trumpet blast, the cosmos will be destroyed. The sun, moon, earth, and all the stars, galaxies, nebulae, and other heavenly bodies traversing vast cosmic spaces will be destroyed. The final catastrophe and death of every living thing underscore God's oneness (*tawhid*), His self-subsistence apart from and independent of any living creature. In this stark emptiness, God remains alone, as before creation.

DESTRUCTION OF THE SUN, MOON, AND STARS

On that Day all will be sundered. (30:43) Verily, it is God [alone] who upholds the celestial bodies and the earth, lest they deviate [from their orbits] for if they should deviate, there is none that could uphold them after He stops doing so. [But] verily, He is ever-forbearing, much-forgiving! (35:41)

God is forgiving and does not speed up the end of the world despite the sinfulness of most of its inhabitants. He does not punish without giving the sinner time to reflect and repent.

The last hour draws near, and the moon is split asunder! (54:1) And the moon is darkened, and the sun and the moon are brought together. (75:8-9) When the sun is shrouded in darkness, and when the stars lose their light. (81:1-2) Behold, all that you are told to expect will surely come to pass. Thus, [it will come to pass] when the stars are effaced. (77:7-8)

The Sun and the Moon will either lose their light or collide with each other.

DESTRUCTION OF EARTH

And they will ask thee about [what will happen to] the mountains [when this world ends]. Say, then: "My Sustainer will scatter them far and wide, and leave the earth level and bare, [so that] you will see no curve thereon, and no ruggedness. (20:105-107) You shall see the earth void and bare. (18:47) When the earth shakes violently, and the mountains are shattered like [countless] shards. (56:4-5) On the Day when the earth and the mountains will convulse, and the mountains will [crumble and] become like a sand dune on the move! Earth is shaken with a shaking [severe]. (73:14)

The mountains will move as if they were wool tufts or sand dunes on the move. (52:10) And when the mountains [crumble] and are shattered into countless shards, they become scattered dust and vanish as if a mirage. (78:20) And thou wilt see the mountains, which [now] you deem so firm, pass away as the clouds pass away: a work of God, who has ordered all things to perfection! (27:88)

God has ordered all things to perfection in accordance with the purpose for which He created them. Here, emphasis is placed on the transitory nature of the world, as we know it, compared to the lasting reality of an afterlife.

And when the seas boil over (81:6) and… burst beyond their bounds. (82:3) The earth will be a [mere] handful to Him on resurrection Day, and the heavens will be rolled up in His right hand. (39:67) And when the earth is leveled, and casts forth whatever is in it, and becomes utterly void, [and loses all its reality.] obeying its Sustainer, as in truth it must. (84:3-5)

The above is a metaphorical use of the term "hand" in reference to God's absolute power and dominion. All that has been hidden in the earth, including the bodies or remnants of the dead, will be revealed. On the Day of Judgment, the earth will bear witness, as it were, to all that has ever been done by man: an explanation given by the Prophet.

[His promise will be fulfilled] on the Day when the earth shall be changed into another earth, as shall be the heavens [universe]. (14:48) And the earth will shine brightly with her Sustainer's light. (39:69)

This describes the total, cataclysmic change, on the Last Day, of all-natural phenomena, and thus, of the universe as known to man. The Earth will shine brightly with a clear revelation of His will: an allusion to the universe's transformation or reverse creation.

REACTION OF MANKIND TO THE LAST HOUR

WOMEN WILL FORGET THEIR NURSLINGS

O men! Be conscious of your Sustainer: for, verily, the violent convulsion of the Last Hour will be awesome! On the Day when you behold it, every woman that feeds a child at her breast will utterly forget her infant, and every woman heavy with a child will bring forth her burden [before her time] (22:1-2)

NOW WE BELIEVE IN THEE

[The sinners will exclaim]: "Grievous is this suffering! O our Sustainer, relieve us of suffering, for, verily, we [now] believe [in Thee]!" (44:12) [But] how shall this remembrance avail them [at the Last Hour], seeing that an apostle had previously come unto them, clearly expounding the truth? They turned their backs on him and said, "Taught [by others], is he a madman?" (44:12-13) On the Day when We shall seize [all sinners] with a most mighty onslaught, We shall, verily, inflict Our retribution [on you as well]! (44:16)

"Taught by others," is a reference to the Prophet's opponents alleging that someone else imparted to him the ideas expressed in the Quran or at least helped him compose them.

MEN SWARMING LIKE MOTHS IN CONFUSION

Oh, the sudden calamity! How awesome the sudden calamity! And what could make you imagine that sudden calamity? [It will occur] on the Day when men will be like moths swarming in confusion, and the mountains will be like fluffy tufts of wool. (101:1-5) It will seem to thee that all mankind is drunk, although they will not be drunk—but vehement will be [their dread of] God's chastisement. (22:2) Yet in the end, when they see that [fulfillment] is close at hand, the faces of those who were bent on denying the truth will be stricken with grief; and they will be told, "This is what you were [sarcastically] calling for!" (67:27)

HEARTS THROBBING AND EYES DOWNCAST

So, think of the Day when a violent convulsion will convulse [the world], to be followed by further [convulsions]! On that Day [men's] hearts will throb, [and] their eyes will be downcast. [And yet] some say, "What? Are we indeed to be restored to our former state, even though we may have become [a heap of] crumbling bones?" [And] they add, "That, then, would be a return with loss!" [But] then, that [Last Hour] will be [upon them suddenly, as if it were] but a single accusing cry—and then, lo, they will be fully awakened [to the truth]! (79:6-14)

Men's hearts will throb and their eyes downcast upon realizing God's almightiness and, therefore, submitting to His ultimate judgment. Implying derisively that they would be proven wrong since they now believe that resurrection will never happen, and that would be a return with loss.

CHAPTER 9
OBJECTIONS TO THE RESURRECTION DOCTRINE AND THE QURANIC REBUTTAL

And yet they say: "There is nothing beyond our life in this world. We die as we come to life, [by accident, or as an outcome of blind forces of nature], *and nothing but time destroys us." But of this they have no knowledge whatsoever, they do nothing but guess. (45:24)*

Arabian belief in fatalism saw no meaning or accountability beyond this life – no resurrection, divine judgment, punishment, or reward in the afterlife. Islam introduced beliefs in the afterlife such as the Day of Judgment and the resurrection of the body. This added a dimension of human responsibility and accountability absent from the Arabian religion. The Meccans received with extreme skepticism and ridicule the Prophet Muhammad's message that all bodies would be resurrected.

Man's resurrection will be the result of what the Quran describes as "a new act of creation." It must be very different from anything man can experience in this world. The Quran appeals directly to man's intellect, using metaphors, allegories, and parables. Each emphasizes the absolute dissimilarity of all that man will experience after the resurrection from whatever he did or could experience in this world. The purpose of such an appeal is a visualization of the consequences in the hereafter of one's conscious acts and omissions here on earth.

BRING BACK OUR FOREFATHERS

And [so], whenever Our messages are conveyed to them in all their clarity, their only argument is this: "Bring forth our forefathers [as witnesses], if what you claim is true!" Say: "It is God who gives you life, and then causes you to die; and in the end, He will gather you together on resurrection Day, [the coming of] which is beyond all doubt—but most human beings understand it not." (45:25-26)

REJECTION BY THE YOUNGER GENERATIONS

But [there is many a one] who says to his parents [whenever they try to imbue him with faith in God]: "Fie upon both of you! Do you promise me that I shall be brought forth [from the dead], [resurrected] although [so many] generations have passed away before me?" And [while] they both pray for God's help [and say]: "Alas for you! For, behold, God's promise always comes true!" He answers: "All this is nothing but fables of ancient times!" (46:17-19)

The parabolic dialogue is not only meant to illustrate the ever-recurring and perhaps natural conflict between older and younger generations but also points to the transmission of religious ideas as the most important function of parenthood, and thus, in a wider sense, as the basic element of all social continuity.

DENYING RESURRECTION IS DENYING GOD'S UNLIMITED CREATIVE POWERS

Consider the sky full of magnificent constellations, and think about the Promised Day, [the Day of Resurrection], and [of] Him [God] who bears witness to all! (85:1-3) Are they, then, not aware that God, who created the heavens and the earth, has the power to create them anew in their own likeness, setting a term for their resurrection? (17:99)

A denial of resurrection implies doubt about God's unlimited power of creation and, thus, of His Godhead. By creating the universe, God bears witness to His Own almightiness and uniqueness. It is meant to illustrate God's creativeness as if to say, "Is not He who has created the universe equally able to resurrect and recreate man in whatever form He deems necessary?"

SUSTAINER OF THIS UNIVERSE

Say: "Unto whom belongs the earth and all that lives there? [Tell me this] if you happen to know [the answer]!" [And they will reply: "Unto God." Say: "Will you not, then, bethink yourselves [of Him]?" Say: "Who is it that sustains the seven heavens and He is enthroned in His awesome almightiness?" [Lit., "who is the Sustainer (rabb) of the seven heavens?"] *And they will reply: "[All this power belongs] to God." Say: "Will you not, then, remain conscious of Him?" Say: "In whose hand rests the mighty dominion over all things, and who is it that protects, while there is no protection against Him? [Tell me this] if you know [the answer]!" [And] they will reply: "[All this power belongs] to God." Say: 'How, then, can you be so deluded?"* ["as to deny the prospect of resurrection."] *Nay, We have conveyed the truth: and yet, behold, they are intent on lying [to themselves]! (23:81-90).*

They are indeed liars. They deceive themselves by asserting that they believe in God and, at the same time, rejecting the idea of a life after death. It is insolubly linked with the concept of divine justice that many wrongdoers prosper in this world while many righteous suffer. Apart from this, a denial of resurrection implies a doubt about God's unlimited power.

It is God who has raised the heavens without any supports that you could see and is established on the throne of His almightiness. He governs all that exists. Clearly, He spells out these messages, so that you might be certain in your innermost that you are destined to meet your Sustainer [on Judgment Day]. (13:2) Is, then, He who has created the heavens and the earth not able to create [a new] the like of those [who have died]? Yes, indeed—for He alone is the all-knowing Creator: His Being alone is such that when He wills a thing to be, He says unto it, "Be"— and it is. (36:81-82)

The "raising of the heavens without any supports" describes the cosmic space in which stars, solar systems (such as our own), and galaxies exist. You might realize that He who created the universe and governs all that exists can resurrect the dead. He can also judge you in the life to come in accordance with what you did when you were alive on earth.

THE RE-BIRTH OF MAN IS EASY FOR GOD

[For Him] the creation of you all and the resurrection is like [the creation and resurrection of] a single soul. (31:28) Are, then, they [who deny the truth] not aware of how God created [life] in the first instance, and then brings it forth anew? This is easy for God! Say: "Go all over the earth and behold how [wondrous] He created [man] in the first place. Thus, too, will God bring your second life— for God has the power to will anything! (29:19-20)

Because of His almightiness, there is no difference between the creation and resurrection of one or many. This is as if every soul is within His ken as is all humanity.

CREATION, SUBSISTENCE, DISSOLUTION, AND RECREATION

Out of this [earth] We have created you, and into it shall We return you, and out of it shall We restore you again. (20:55) As We brought the first creation, so We shall bring it forth anew— a promise We have willed upon Ourselves as We can do [all things]! (21:104) Nay - who is it that creates [all life] in the first instance, and then brings it forth anew? [This relates to man's life on earth and his resurrection after bodily death. It also relates to the this-worldly cycle of birth, death, and regeneration manifested in all organic nature.] *And who provides you with sustenance? Could there be any divine power besides God? Say: "[If you think so,] produce your evidence - if you truly believe in your claim!" (27:64)* [Lit., "if you are truthful" - the implication being that most people who profess a belief in a multiplicity of divine powers, or even in the possibility of the one God's "incarnation" in a created being, do so blindly, sometimes only under the influence of inherited cultural traditions and habits of thought, and not out of a reasoned conviction.] *Say: "None in the heavens or on earth knows the hidden reality [of anything that exists none knows it] save God." (27:65)* [In this context, the term Al-ghayb or "the hidden reality" - apparently relates to the "how" of God's Being, the ultimate reality underlying the observable aspects of the universe and the meaning and purpose inherent in its creation.]

GOD ALONE IS TRULY FORGIVING, ALL-EMBRACING IN HIS LOVE

VERILY, thy Sustainer's grip is exceedingly strong! Behold, it is He who creates [man] in the first instance, and He [it is who] will bring him forth anew. And He alone is truly forgiving, all-embracing in His love, in sublime almightiness enthroned, a sovereign doer of whatever He wills. (85:12-16) Say: "It is He who has multiplied you on earth, and it is unto Him that you shall be gathered [on resurrection]." (67:24)

Regarding the creation of man's body "out of the earth," and "return into it" signifies the dissolution of this body, after death, into the elementary organic and inorganic substances of which it was composed. All these facts—creation, subsistence, and dissolution—contain the message of God's almightiness and the ephemeral nature of man's life on earth, and of his future resurrection. "Bring forth anew" relates to man's life on earth and resurrection after bodily death.

REFLECT UPON YOUR OWN CREATION

O men! If you are in doubt as to the [truth of] the resurrection, [remember that] verily, We created [each of] you out of dust. (22:5) Let the man, then, observe out of what he has been created. He has been created out of seminal fluid issued from between the loins [of man] and the pelvic arch [of woman]. Now, verily, He [who thus created man in the first instance] is well able to bring him back [to life] on the Day when all secrets will be laid bare and [man] will have neither strength nor helper! (86:5-10)

As regards the expression "created out of dust," it is meant to indicate man's humble biological origin and his affinity for other earthy substances. The "pelvic arch," according to most authorities who specialize in rare Quranic expressions, relates specifically to female anatomy.

RAISING MEN FROM BONES AND DUST

If thou sayest [unto men], "Behold, you shall be raised again after death!" They who are bent on denying the truth are sure to answer, "This is clearly nothing but an enchanting delusion!" (11:7) "A strange thing is this! Why [how could we be resurrected] after we die and become dust? Such a return seems far-fetched indeed!" Well, do We know how the earth consumes their bodies, for with Us is a record unfailing? (50:2-4)) I call to witness the resurrection day! But no! I call to witness the man's accusing voice of conscience! Does the man think that We cannot [resurrect him and] bring his bones together again? Yea indeed, We are able to make the tips of his fingers whole! Nonetheless, man chooses to deny what lies ahead of him, asking [sarcastically], "When is that resurrection Day to be?" (75:1-6)

By "calling it to witness," and by speaking of the resurrection Day as if it had already occurred, the above phrase is meant to convey its certainty. The accusing voice of man's subconscious makes him aware of his own shortcomings and failings.

And [thus, too] they say, "After we become bones and dust, shall we, forsooth, be raised from the dead in a new act of creation?" Say: "[You will be raised from the dead even though] you be stones or iron or any [other] substance which, to your minds, appears yet farther removed [from life]!" And [if] thereupon they ask. "Who is it that will bring us back [to life]?" Say you: "He who has brought you into being in the first instance." And [if] thereupon they shake their heads at you [in disbelief] and ask, "When shall this be?" Say you: "It may well be soon." (17:49-51) [And so] he says, "Who could give life to bones that have crumbled to dust?" Say: "He who brought them into being in the first instance will give them life [once again], seeing that He has full knowledge of every act of creation." (36:78-79)

(3) THE PARABLE OF RAIN (LIFE–DEATH–LIFE)

Do they [who deny resurrection] never gaze at the clouds pregnant with water, [and observe] how they are created? (88:17) It is God who sends forth the winds, so that they raise a cloud, whereupon we drive it towards dead land and thereby give life to the earth after it has been lifeless: even thus shall resurrection be! (35:9) And He who sends down, again and again, waters from the sky in due measure and [as] We raise dead land to life, so will you be brought forth [from the dead]. (43:11)

Have they ever observed the miraculous, cyclic process of water evaporation, the skyward movement of vapor, its condensation, and, finally, its precipitation over the earth? The ever-recurring emergence, decay, and re-emergence of life, so vividly exemplified in all organic nature, is often cited in the Quran—not merely in support of the doctrine of resurrection but also as evidence of a consciously devised plan underlying creation as such and, thus, of the existence of the Creator. Denial of resurrection and life in the hereafter renders the concept of a conscious Creator meaningless.

MIRACULOUS TRANSFORMATION OF DEAD LAND TO LIFE

Do they not look at the sky above them - how We have built it and made it beautiful and free of all faults? And the earth - We have spread it wide, and set upon it mountains firm, and caused it to bring forth plants of all beauteous kinds, thus offering an insight and a reminder unto every human being who willingly turns unto God. And We send down from the skies water rich in blessings, and cause thereby gardens to grow, and fields of grain, and tall palm-trees with their thickly clustered dates, as sustenance apportioned to men; and by [all] this We bring dead land to life: [and] even so will be [man's] coming-forth from death. (50:6-11) Could We, then, be [thought of as being] worn out by the first creation? [I.e., by the creation of the universe or, more specifically, of man.] *Nay - but some people are [still] lost in doubt about [the possibility of] a new creation! (50:15)*

DECAY AND LIFE RE-EMERGENCE

Behold, then, [O man,] these signs of God's grace - how He gives life to the earth after it had been lifeless! Verily, this Selfsame [God] is indeed the One that can bring the dead back to life: for He has the power to will anything! (30:50) Remain, then, patient in adversity: verily, God's promise [of resurrection] is true indeed - so let not those who are devoid of all inner certainty disquiet thy mind! (30:60)

PARABLE OF FERTILE OR BARREN LAND

And [if, O man, you are still in doubt as to the resurrection, consider this]: you can see the earth dry and lifeless—and [suddenly,] when We send down water upon it, it stirs and swells and puts forth every kind of lovely plant! All this [happens] because God alone is the Ultimate Truth, and He alone brings the dead to life, and He has the power to will anything. (22:5-6)

By exercising the same life-giving power as God causes plants to grow, He will resurrect the dead at the end of time. The next sentence continues the parable by likening those whose hearts are open to truth to fertile earth, and those who are bent on denying it, to barren earth.

WHEN ANIMALS ARE GATHERED

And when pregnant camels with young, about to give birth, are left untended, and when all beasts are gathered. (81:4-5) Although there is no beast that walks on earth and no bird that flies on its two wings, which are not [God's] creatures like yourselves: no single thing have We neglected in Our decree. Lastly, unto their Sustainer shall they [all] be gathered. (6:38)

It is also said that animals loved by humans will live in the hereafter together with those who love them. Animals will crowd together in terror at the Last Hour or be indemnified by God for man's cruelty to them.

ALL THINGS GO BACK TO THEIR SOURCE

And God alone comprehends the hidden reality of the heavens and the earth, since all that exists comes back to Him [as its source]. (11:123) But if they [whose minds are perverted] give you the lie, [O Prophet, remember that] even so, before your time, have [other] apostles been given the lie: for [the unbelievers always refuse to admit that] all things go back to God [as their source]. O men! Verily, God's promise [of resurrection] is true indeed: let not, then, the life of this world delude you, and let not [your own] deceptive thoughts about God delude you! (35:4-5) He has dominion over the heavens and the earth, and all things go back unto God [as their source]. (57:5)

DO NOT ASK FOR SPEEDY DOOM

Remain, then, [O believer], patient in adversity, just as all of the apostles, endowed with a firmness of heart, bore themselves with patience. And do not ask for a speedy doom for those [who still deny the truth]: (46:35) And [know, O man] that the Last Hour is bound to come, beyond any doubt, and that God will [indeed] resurrect all who are in their graves. (22:7)

YOU CANNOT COMPEL THEM TO BELIEVE IN RESURRECTION

We are fully aware of what they [who deny resurrection] say, and you cannot force them [to believe in it]. Yet, remind them, through this Quran, that all those who may fear My warning. (50:45) Whoever looks forward [with hope and awe] to meeting God [on resurrection Day, let him be ready for it]: for, behold, the end set by God [for everyone's life] is bound to come—and He alone is all-hearing, all-knowing! (29:5)

PARABLE OF BRINGING A DEAD MAN TO LIFE

[Are you, O man, of the same mind] as he who passed by a town deserted by its people, with its roofs caved in, [and] said, "How could God bring all this back to life after its death?" God caused him to be dead for a hundred years. Whereafter He brought him back to life and asked: "How long have you remained thus?" He answered: "I have remained thus for a day, or part of a day." God said: "No, but you have remained this way for a hundred years! But look at your food and your drink-untouched by the passing of years—and look at your ass [donkey]! [And observe that it is alive]! And [We] did all this so that We might make you a symbol unto men. And when [all this] became clear to him, he said: "I know [now] that God has the power to will anything!" (2:259) How can you refuse to acknowledge God, seeing that you were lifeless, and He gave you life, and that He will cause you to die and then bring you back to life, after that you will be brought back. (2:28)

The story told above is a parable meant to illustrate God's power to bring the dead back to life. Thus, pointing out that God has the power to grant life indefinitely, as well as resurrect the dead.

CHAPTER 10
THE RESURRECTION OF THE DEAD

THE SECOND AND LAST BLAST OF THE TRUMPET

For what day has the term [of all this] been set? (77:12) Verily, the Day of Distinction [between the true and the false] has indeed its appointed time: the Day when the trumpet [of resurrection] is sounded, and you all come forward in multitudes. (78:17) And what could make you conceive what that Day of Distinction will be? Woe on that Day to those who give the lie to the truth! (77:12-14)

This is historically the earliest occurrence of the expression *Yawm al-fasl*, which refers to the Day of the Resurrection.

And then it will sound again [the judgment trumpet]-and lo! Standing [before the Seat of Judgment], they will begin to see [the truth]! (39:68) [And bethink thyself, too, of] the Day on which all [human beings] will hear the final blast—that Day of [their] coming forth [from death]. (50:42) The Day when they shall come forth in haste from their graves, as if racing towards a goal-post, with downcast eyes, with ignominy overwhelming them: that Day they were promised again and again. (70:43-44)

With the first blast of the trumpet, the cosmos will be destroyed and the universe will be transformed into something human minds cannot conceive. There will be the second and final trumpet blast. All the dead will be brought back to life in the second act of creation. For His justice and mercy to be demonstrated, there must be life again with God's living breath, by which humans will be brought forth whole, before the divine.

THE DAY OF DISTINCTION

For that [resurrection which they deride] will be [upon them suddenly, as if it were] but a single accusing cry—and then, lo! They will begin to see [the truth] and say: "Oh, woe unto us! This is the Day of Judgment!" [And they will be told]: "This is the Day of Distinction [between the true and the false—the Day] which you called a lie!" (37:19-21)

THE DAY WHEN CHILDREN'S HAIR WILL TURN GREY

How, then, if you refuse to acknowledge the truth, will you protect yourselves on that Day which shall turn children's hair grey, [the Day] on which the skies shall be rent asunder, [and] His promise [of resurrection] fulfilled? This, verily, is a reminder: let him who wills, set out on the way to his Sustainer! (73:17-19)

In ancient Arabian usage, a day full of terrifying events was described metaphorically as "a day on which children's locks turn grey," hence the use of this phrase in the Quran. Its purely metaphorical character is obvious since, according to the Quran, children are considered sinless- i.e., not accountable for what they do and remain untouched by the Day of Judgment.

THE SUMMONING VOICE

On the Day when the voice summons [man] to something that the mind cannot conceive. They will come forth from their graves, with their eyes downcast, [swarming about] like locusts scattered [by the wind], running in confusion towards the summoning voice. Those who [now] deny the truth will exclaim, "Calamitous is this Day!" (54:6-7)

RUSHING TOWARD THEIR SUSTAINER

They will all rush forth from their graves toward their Sustainer! They will say: "Oh, woe unto us! Who has roused us from our sleep [of death]?" [Whereupon they will be told]: "This is what the Most Gracious has promised! And His message-bearers spoke the truth!" (36:51-52)

GATHERING OF MANKIND AFTER RESURRECTION

On the Day when the earth is ripped asunder all around them as they hasten forth [towards God's judgment] that gathering will be easy for Us [to encompass]. (50:44) Herein, behold, lies a message indeed for all who fear the suffering [which may befall them] in the life to come, [and are conscious of the arrival of] that Day. When all humankind shall be gathered together—that Day [of Judgment] which shall be witnessed [by all that ever lived], and which We shall not delay beyond a term set [by Us]. (11:103-104) And We know well [the hearts and deeds of all human beings-both] those who lived before you and those who will come after you. Behold, it is thy Sustainer who will gather them all together [on Judgment Day]: verily, He is wise, all-knowing! (15:24-25) [Remember all this: for] in the end, when He will call you forth from the earth with a single call—lo! You will [all] emerge [for judgment]. For, unto Him belongs every being that is in the heavens and on earth; all things devoutly obey His will. It is He whom makes [all life] in the first instance, and then comes forth anew: and the easiest of things for Him, since He is the essence of all that is sublime in the heavens and on earth, and He is the only one Who is truly wise, the only one almighty. (30:25-27)

JUDGMENT DAY FOR THE JEWS AND CHRISTIANS ALSO

It may not accord with your wishful thinking—nor with the wishful thinking of the followers of earlier revelation—[that] he who does evil shall be requited for it, and shall find none to protect him from God, and none to bring him succor. (4:123)

Above is an allusion to the spiritual arrogance of the Jews that they are God's chosen people and, therefore, assured of His grace in the hereafter. It also alludes to the Christian dogma of vicarious atonement, which promises salvation to all who believe in Jesus as God's son.

THE END OF THE EARTHBOUND TIME CONCEPT

The resurrected sinners will realize the infinitesimal shortness of their lives on earth compared with the timeless realm in the hereafter. Sinners will guess how long they lived on earth, such as an hour, one night, a few days, ~~etc~~. In this parabolic manner, the Quran points to the illusory concept of "time" as experienced by the human mind—a concept that has no bearing on the ultimate reality to be unfolded in the hereafter. Sinners will offer self-deluding excuses that their lives on earth were too short to realize their errors and mend their ways. Man will become fully aware of his past life and be freed from self-deception.

And when the Last Hour dawns, those who had been lost in sin will swear that they had not tarried [on earth] longer than an hour. Thus, they were prone to delude themselves [all of their lives]! But those who [in their lifetime] were endowed with knowledge and faith will say: "Indeed, you have been tardy in [accepting as true] what God has revealed. [You waited] until the resurrection day. This, then, is the Day of resurrection but you were determined not to know it!" And so, on that Day their excuse will be of no avail to those who were bent on evildoing, nor will they be allowed to make amends. (30:55-57)

"What God has revealed" is that the dead shall be resurrected and judged by Him. Some have closed their minds to this promise of resurrection and judgment.

On the Day when they see [the fulfillment of] what they were promised, [it will seem to them] as though they had dwelt [on earth] no longer than one hour of [an earthly] day! (46:35) And on the Day when He gathers them [to Himself, it will seem to them] as if they had not tarried [on earth] longer than an hour of a day, knowing one another. Lost indeed will be those who [in their lifetime] considered it a lie that they were destined to meet God, and [thus] failed to find the right way. And whether We show thee [in this world] something of what We hold in store for those [deniers of the truth], or whether We cause thee to die [before that retribution takes place—know that, in the end], it is unto Us that they must return; and God witnesses all that they do. (10:45-46) On the Day when they behold it, [it will seem to them] as if they had tarried [in this world] no longer than one evening or [one night, ending with] its morn! (79:46)

All who turn away from it [God's guidance] *will bear an immense burden on the Day of resurrection. They will abide in this [state], and grievous for them will be the weight [of that burden] on the Day of resurrection – on the Day when the trumpet is blown. For on that Day, We will assemble all such as were lost in sin, their eyes dimmed [by terror], whispering unto one another, "You have spent but ten [days on earth]." [But] We know best* [We alone understand fully] *what they will say when the most perceptive of them shall say, "You have spent [there] but one day!" (20:100-104)*

The number "ten" is often used in Arabic to denote "a few."

BRIEF STAY ON EARTH VERSUS UNLIMITED HEREAFTER

On a Day when He will call you, and you will answer by praising Him, thinking that you have tarried [on earth] but for a short while. (17:52) And He [God] will ask [the doomed]: "What number of years have you spent on earth?" They will answer: "We have spent there a day, or part of a day, but ask those who [are able to] count [time]." [After that] He will say: "You have spent there but a short while: had you known [how short it was to be]! Did you, then, think that We created you in mere idle play, and that you would not have to return to Us?" (For judgment) *(23:112-115)*

"Answering God's call by praising Him" implies that as soon as they are resurrected, they will become fully aware of His existence and almightiness. This part of the "dialogue" between God and the doomed sinners touches upon the illusory, problematic character of "time," as conceived by man. It also touches upon the comparative shortness of this world's life within the context of the ultimate timeless reality known only to God. The disappearance, upon resurrection, of man's earthbound concept of time is indicated by the helpless answer, "Ask those who can count time." The Quran frequently points to the ever-recurring miracle of birth, preceded by the gradual evolution of the embryo in its mother's womb, as a visible sign of God's power to create—and therefore also to recreate life.

PART TWO
ACCOUNTING OF HUMANITY

I. ACCOUNTING OF THE UNREPENTANT SINNERS

CHAPTER 11
UNREPENTANT SINNERS' EXCESSIVE LOVE OF LIFE

IGNORING MORALITY

HUMANITY DIVIDED IN THREE GROUPS

Sin is usually equated with an individual's failure to live up to external standards of conduct or moral codes. Like Judaism, Islam teaches that sin is an act and not a state of being. Sin is disobedience or refusal to submit to the moral law. After the resurrection, all human beings will be gathered for the final judgment. Humanity will be divided into three groups according to the burden of sins committed during their earthly life:

1. The **unrepentant sinners** abuse their free will and defy God's commandments, attributable to their self-centeredness and false pride. They show no regrets for wrongdoings and did not mend their ways in the quest to being a better person.

2. Sinners who **attained righteousness.**

3. The **foremost among the righteousness**

1. ATTRIBUTES OF UNREPENTANT SINNERS

LACK OF BALANCED APPROACH TOWARD LIFE

Life is a positive gift from God and a source of blessings. The world is not to be rejected, because the earth is good. It provides sustenance and comfort for man, and it is the first and necessary arena for carrying out divine will. Our actions in earthly life form the foundation for quality of life in the hereafter. The reward of the Hereafter is for those who do not neglect their duties in this life. They focus on the afterlife. The

Quran does not suggest abandoning this world for the next. This is because in the light of one can the other attain its full meaning; this world must be seen in harmony with the hereafter.

DUNYA: ONLY CONCERN FOR THIS LIFE

There are people who simply pray, "O our Sustainer! Give us in this world and such shall not partake in the blessings of the life to come. (2:200) To him who desires [but] a harvest in this world, We [may] give something thereof—but he will have no share in [the blessings of] the life to come. (42:20)

The gift of life loses its positive quality if it is indulged in recklessly, blindly, and disregarding spiritual values and considerations. Those who strive exclusively after worldly (Dunya) rewards may or may not achieve all of their aims in this life, but they should not expect "a share of the blessings" that awaits the righteous in the hereafter.

DISREGARD OF ALL ETHICAL VALUES

Is it that they [who care for no more than this world] believe in forces supposed to have a share in God's divinity, which enjoins them as a moral law something that God has never allowed? Now were it not for [God's] decree on the final judgment, all would indeed have been decided between them [in this world]: but grievous suffering awaits the evildoers [in the life to come]. (42:21-22)

Usually, they believe that circumstantial phenomena like wealth, power, luck, etc., have something divine about them. The belief in such forces is usually at the root of men's exclusive pursuit of worldly ends. This causes them to abandon themselves with almost religious fervor to something God disapproves of—namely, the striving after purely materialistic goals and a corresponding disregard for all spiritual and ethical values.

TURN OTHERS AWAY FROM GOD

But woe unto those who deny the truth for severe suffering awaits those who choose the life of this world as the sole object of their love, preferring it to [all thought of] the life to come, and who turn others away from God's path and try to make it appear crooked. Such as these have indeed gone far astray! (14:2-3)

The above verses indicate that an all-absorbing, exclusive love of this world leads inevitably to moral denial.

DENIAL OF GOD

Behold, they [who are unmindful of God] love this fleeting life and leave behind them [all thought of] a grief-laden Day. [They will not admit to themselves that] it is We who have created them and strengthened their make—and [that] if it is Our will, We can replace them entirely with others of their kind. (76:27-28)

Those who love this fleeting life forget that it is God who has endowed their bodies and minds with the ability to enjoy it. If God so wills, He can replace them with other human beings who would have the same powers of body and mind but put them to better use.

GREED FOR MORE AND MORE

Know [O men] that this world is but a play and a passing delight, and a beautiful show. It is [the cause of] your boastful vying with one another, and [of your] greed for more and more riches and children. Its parable is that of [life-giving] rain: the herbage it grows delights the soil tillers; but then it withers, and you can see it turn yellow, and in the end, it crumbles into dust. (57:20)

This is the sole instance in the Quran where the participial noun *kafir* (in its plural form *kuffar*) has carried its original meaning of "tiller of the soil." For the etymology of this meaning, see 74:10, where the term *kafir* (in the sense of "denier of the truth") appears for the first time in the sequence of Quranic revelation.

SPIRITUAL AND SOCIAL CONFUSION

While you call them to a straight way, those who do not believe in the life to come are bound to deviate from that way. (23:72) Say: "Go all over the earth and behold what happened in the end to those [who were thus] lost in sin!" But do not grieve over them, and neither be distressed by the false arguments they devise [against God's messages]. (27:69-70) Nay, but they [who refuse to believe in the resurrection] have been wont to give the lie to this truth whenever it was proffered to them, and so they are in a state of confusion. (50:5)

They deny the reality of life after death and, hence, man's ultimate responsibility for his conscious actions. The unavoidable consequence of this denial is the loss of all sense of right and wrong. This leads to spiritual and social chaos, and to the downfall of communities and civilizations. Since they reject all thought of life after death, they are perplexed by the lack of any answer to the "why" and "what for" of man's life, by the evident inequality of human destinies, and by what appears to them as senseless, blind cruelty of nature. Problems that can be resolved only against the background of a belief in a continuation of life after bodily "death" and, hence, in the existence of a purpose and plan underlying all creation.

SUFFERING IN THIS WORLD

As against this, they who are bent on denying the truth say [unto all who are of like mind]: "Shall we point out to you a man who will tell you that [after your death] when you will have been scattered in countless fragments, you shall—lo and behold!-be [restored to life] in a new act of creation? Does he [knowingly] attribute his own lying inventions to God—or is he a madman?" No, [there is no madness in this Prophet] but they who will not believe in the life to come are [bound to lose themselves] in suffering and in a profound aberration. (34:7-8)

The concept of aberration is meaningless in the context of life to come, and the last phrase points to suffering in this world (in contrast with suffering in the hereafter). It has an obvious meaning of moral and social confusion—and, hence, of individual and social suffering—which is the unavoidable consequence of people's loss of belief in the existence of absolute moral values and, thus, in an ultimate divine judgment based on those values.

THOSE WHO DENIED THE AFTERLIFE

Verily, as for those who do not believe that they are destined to meet Us, but content themselves with the life of this world and do not look beyond it and are heedless of Our messages—their goal is fire in return for all [the evil] that they used to do. (10:7-8)

And some [of the unbelievers] say, "There is nothing beyond our life in this world, for We shall not be raised from the dead. If you could see [them] when they shall be made to stand before their Sustainer [and] He will ask, "Is not this the truth?" They will answer: "Yea, indeed, by our Sustainer!" [Whereupon] He will say: "Taste, then, the suffering that comes from your refusal to acknowledge the truth!" (6:29-3130)

The most pertinent question is why people should be mindful of the hereafter (akhirah) as well as, or even more than, their present life. In comparison with life to come, life in this world is a brief moment. It is only in the hereafter that man's destiny reveals itself in all its true aspects. The brief enjoyment of this world is self-delusion, if it is indulged in without thought of the hereafter.

SINNING AGAINST THEMSELVES

Are they [who deny the truth] waiting for angels to appear to them or for God's judgment to manifest? Even thus did behave those [stubborn sinners] who lived before their time. And [when they were destroyed], it was not God who wronged them, but they who wronged themselves. They were overwhelmed by the very thing they deride. For all the evil they had done fell [back] upon them. (16:33-34)

Similar phrases occur in many places in the Quran, always referring to the derision of divine messages. This is a particular case of predictions relating to God's chastisement of reprobate sinners. The Quran points out here that this "chastisement" or "suffering" is a natural, unavoidable consequence of deliberate wrongdoing. Hence, he who becomes guilty of it is "doing wrong to himself" or "sinning against himself" as he destroys his own spiritual integrity and must suffer for it.

THE PARABLE OF ICYWIND

The parable of what they spend on the life of this world is that of an icy wind which smites the tilth of people who have sinned against themselves and destroys it: for, it is not God who does them wrong, but it is they who wrong themselves. (3:117)

The above Quranic phrase is meant to stress the completeness of loss of all efforts in the case of those who knowingly deny the truth. In the end, tilth, or gainful achievement, is lost in its entirety. On the other hand, the tilth of a believer is never lost. In the future, he expects a reward for his patience in adversity.

THE FATE OF UNREPENTANT SINNERS

Those who lived before them did [too] give the lie to the truth - whereupon suffering befell them without knowing where it came, and thus, God let them taste ignominy [even]in the life of this world.

Yet, how much greater will be the suffering of [sinners] in the life to come - if they [who now deny the truth] knew it! (39:25-26) Hence, leave them alone until they face that [Judgment] Day of theirs, when they will be stricken with terror. The Day when none of their scheming will be of any use to them, and they will receive no succor. (52:45-46)

ARRAIGNED BEFORE GOD

Is, then, he to whom We have given that goodly promise [of better and enduring happiness in the hereafter] *which he shall see fulfilled [on his resurrection] comparable to one on whom We have bestowed [all] the enjoyments of this worldly life but who, on resurrection Day, will find himself among those to be arraigned [before Us]? (28:61)*

They will be arraigned for having misused God's gifts and attributed them to powers other than God.

DEATH OF AN UNREPENTANT SINNER

TWILIGHT OF DEATH BRINGS THE FULL TRUTH

And [then] the twilight of death brings with it the [full] truth [full insight into one's own self] *that [very thing, O man] from which you would always look away! (50:19)*

FUTILITY OF REPENTANCE CLOSE TO DEATH

When [the last breath] comes up to the throat [of a dying man], and people ask, "Is there any wizard [that could save him]?" The while he [himself] knows that this is the parting and is enwrapped in the pangs of death. At that time towards thy Sustainer does he feel impelled to turn! [Useless, though, will be his repentance]: for [as long as he was alive] he did not accept the truth, nor did he pray [for enlightenment]. On the contrary, he gave the lie to the truth and turned away [from it], and then went arrogantly back to what he had come from. [And yet, O man, your end comes hourly] nearer unto thee, and nearer and ever nearer unto thee, and nearer! Does man, then, thinks that he is to be left to himself, to go about at will? (75:26-36)

He returned to the arrogant belief, rooted in the materialism of his social environment, that man is self-sufficient and therefore not in need of any divine guidance. Does he think that he will not be held morally responsible for his actions?

THOSE WHO DENIED THE EXISTENCE OF THE HEREAFTER

[As for those who will not believe in the life to come, they go on lying to themselves] until, when death approaches any of them, he prays: "O my Sustainer! Let me return, let me return [to life], so that I might act righteously in whatever I have failed [aforetime]!" No, it is indeed but a [meaningless] word that he utters. (23:99-100)

FORSAKEN BY FALSE OBJECT OF WORSHIP

Whatever has been decreed to be their lot [in life] will be theirs—till there shall come unto them Our messengers [angels of death] to cause them to die, [and] shall say, "Where now, are those beings whom you used to invoke beside God?" And [those sinners] will reply, "They have forsaken us!" And [thus], they will bear witness against themselves that they had denied the truth. (7:37)

They will have in their lifetime, like all other people, all the good or bad fortune envisaged for them in God's eternal decree, till the "messengers" referred to be the angels of death pay a visit.

TORMENTS OF THE GRAVE

If thou could but see [how it will be] when these evildoers find themselves in the agonies of death, and the angels stretch forth their hands [and call]: "Give up your souls!" (6:93) And if thou could but see [how it will be] when He causes those who are bent on denying the truth to die. The angels will strike their faces and their backs, and [will say]: "Taste suffering through a fire in return for what your own hands have wrought—for, never does God do the least wrong to His creatures!" (8:50-51) Hence, how [will they fare] when the angels gather them in death, striking their faces and their backs? This, because they were wont to pursue what God condemns, and to hate [whatever would meet with] His goodly acceptance: and so, He has caused all their [good] deeds to come to nought. (47:27-28)

THE TORMENTS OF THE GRAVE

The accounting and punishment of the unrepentant sinner begins soon after death. The beating of the sinners' faces and backs is an allegory of their final suffering to come, in consequence of their having denied the truth while alive in this world. The torments of the grave both prefigure and predict the final outcomes. However, this is not the final judgment that will happen on Judgment Day after the resurrection. What happens to the human soul between death and resurrection is not clear. There are no Quranic verses that shed light on this period of hiatus.

CHAPTER 12
SINS AGAINST GOD

Since man is created weak, he is prone to sinning. No human being is exempt from making mistakes. Only God is sinless. Prophets like Moses, David, and Jonah all sinned. Moses was guilty of Egyptian manslaughter; David was an accessory to murder; and Jonah defied God's command and abandoned his mission. Jesus made racist remarks and called a Canaanite woman a dog when she brought her daughter suffering from epilepsy. She pleaded repeatedly with Jesus to save her daughter. Jesus was also baptized to be forgiven of his sins. The Prophet Muhammad was not exempt from sin, as the following verses indicate:

[O Muhammad], We have placed before thee a manifest victory so that God might show His forgiveness of all thy sins, past and future. And [thus], bestow upon you the full measure of His blessings, and guide you on a straight path. God will provide you with mighty help. (48:1-3)

Sins of omission: A sin of omission involves not doing what is right or failing to do as instructed. The duties we owe God are the five articles of faith and the five pillars of Islam. In Islam, sins of omission such as not performing rituals, dogmas, practices, and beliefs usually fall under God's rights (Huquq Ullah).

A sin of commission involves the willful act of doing something that violates God's commands such as man's rights (Huquq al abad).

RIGHTS OF GOD (HUQUQ ULLAH)

The following offenses may be considered sins against God.

DENYING GOD's EXISTENCE

As for those who will not believe, in their ears is deafness, and so (the Quran) remains obscure to them. They are [like people who are] called from too far away. (41:44) None does He cause thereby to go astray save the iniquitous, who break their bond with God after it has been established [in their nature] and cut asunder what God has bidden to be joined and spread corruption on earth. It is they who will be the losers. (2:26-27)

The fundamental sin, according to the Quran, is denying the existence of God. It is the arrogance and ingratitude of those who forget or turn away from their Creator and Sustainer. This will gradually stifle the voice of conscience until it becomes a distant call coming "from a far-off place" and they only hear the words but cannot understand their meaning. The primordial "bond with God" stands for something rooted in the human situation and that can be perceived instinctively and through conscious experience. It is man's moral obligation to use his inborn gifts—intellectual and physical—in the way intended for them by God. The establishment of this bond arises from the faculty of reason, which if properly used, must lead man to a realization of his weakness and dependence on a causative power and, thus, to a gradual cognition of God's will concerning his own behavior. In this passage, God's oneness and uniqueness are emphasized. Without belief in God and His ultimate judgment, there is no basis for acceptance of absolute moral values—i.e., values independent of time and social circumstances. For an explanation of the subsequent reference to "what God has bidden to be joined", see 13:25 under "Sins Against Fellow Man" in this chapter.

ATTRIBUTING RIVALS TO GOD

And yet there are people who believe in beings that allegedly rival God, loving them as [only] God should be revered. While those who have attained faith love God more than anything. If they who are bent on doing evil could but see as they will when they are made to suffer [on Resurrection Day] - that all might belongs to God alone, and that God is severe in [meting out] punishment! (2:165)

Say: "Verily, my Sustainer has forbidden only shameful deeds, be they open or secret, and [every kind of] sinning, and unjustified envy, and the ascribing of divinity to aught beside Him - since He has never bestowed any warrant therefor from on high and the attribution unto God of aught of which you have no knowledge." (7:33)

Do not set up any other deity side by side with God, lest thou find thyself disgraced and forsaken: for thy Sustainer has ordained that you shall worship none but Him. (17:22-23) Say: "My Sustainer has forbidden the ascribing of divinity to aught beside Him, since He has never bestowed any warrant therefor from on high for attributing unto God of aught of which you have no knowledge." Do not set up any other deity side by side with God, lest you find yourself disgraced and forsaken: for thy Sustainer has ordained that you shall worship none but Him; lest you be cast into hell, blamed [by thyself] and rejected [by Him]! (17:39)

FALSE ATTRIBUTION TO GOD

Whenever they commit a shameful deed, they say, "We found our forefathers doing it and God enjoined it upon us." Say: "Never does God enjoin abominations. Would you attribute to God something of which you have no knowledge?" (7:28) O mankind! Partake of what is lawful and good on earth and do not follow Satan's footsteps. He is your open foe, and bids you only to do evil, and commit abominations. He also bids you to assign to God something you have no knowledge. (2:168-169) And who could be more wicked than he who attributes his own lying inventions to God, or gives the lie to the truth when it comes [through revelation]? Is not hell the [proper] abode for all who [thus] deny the truth? (29:68)

This refers to assigning to God commandments or prohibitions beyond what has been clearly ordained. "Own lying inventions," by persuading himself that there is, side by side with God or even independently of Him, any power that could govern men's destinies.

DISTORTING GOD'S MESSAGE

They who distort the meaning of Our messages are not hidden from Us: hence, which [of the two] will be in a better state—he that is [destined to be] cast into the fire, or he that shall come secure [before Us] on Resurrection Day? Do what you will: He sees all that you do. (41:40)

TURNING OTHERS AWAY FROM GOD

Those bent on denying the truth, and turning others away from God's path, have certainly gone far astray. God will indeed not forgive them, nor will He guide them onto any road but the road that leads to hell, where they will abide beyond time: and this is indeed easy for God. (4:167-168)

DO NOT INCLINE TOWARD OR RELY ON EVILDOERS

And do not incline towards, nor rely upon, those who are bent on evildoing lest the fire [of the hereafter] touch you: for [then] you would have none to protect you from God, nor would you ever be succored [by Him]. (11:113)

God will not succor those who incline toward or rely on deliberate and persistent evildoers.

MISLEADING OTHERS INTO SIN

[He is aware, too, that] they who are bent on denying the truth speak to those who have attained faith: "Follow our way [of life], and we shall indeed take your sins upon ourselves!" But never could they take upon themselves the sins of those [whom they would thus mislead]: they are liars indeed! Yet most certainly they will have to bear their own burdens, and other burdens besides their own; and most certainly they will be called to account on Resurrection Day for all their false assertions! (29:12-13)

The above "saying" is a metaphor for the way deniers of truth view believers. People who deny the validity of any spiritual commitment arising out of faith are unwilling to tolerate such faith and commitment in others. They try to persuade believers to their way of thinking by a sarcastic, contemptuous reference to the alleged irrelevance of the concept of "sin" as such.

DENIAL OF AFTERLIFE

And on the Day when those who were bent on denying the truth will be brought within sight of the fire, [they will be told:] "You have exhausted your [share of] good things in your worldly life, enjoying them [without any thought of the hereafter]. Today you shall be repaid with the suffering of humiliation for having gloried on earth in your arrogance, offending against all that is right, and for all your iniquitous doings!" (46:20)

This refers to arrogantly asserting that there is no life after death.

FALSE PRIDE

Pursue, then, the right course, as you have been instructed by God, together with all who, with you, have turned unto Him. Let none of you behave arrogantly for He sees all that you do. (11:112) "Turn not your cheek away from people out of [false] pride and walk not haughtily on earth. God does not love anyone who, out of self-conceit, acts boastfully. "Hence, be modest in your bearing, and lower your voice: for the ugliest of all voices is a loud voice of asses." (31:18-19)

He (God) does not love those who are given to arrogance, and [who], whenever they are asked, "What is it that your Sustainer has bestowed from on high?" They answer, "Fables of ancient times!" [And not divine revelations]. Hence, on Resurrection Day they shall bear the full weight of their own burdens, as well as some of the burdens of those ignorant ones whom they have led astray. Oh, how evil the load they shall bear! (16:23-25)

This injunction, expressed in the second person plural, is addressed to all believers, and to their behavior towards everyone. Be humble before God and do not show false pride or overbearing behavior. Do not overstep God's bounds or exceed equity limits. Satan's arrogance and false pride were the first sin. They will also bear the burden of those ignorant ones whom they have led astray. The Prophet's saying: "Whoever calls others to the right way shall have a reward equal to the combined rewards of all who follow him until Resurrection Day. However, who calls to the way of error will have to bear a sin equal to the combined sins of all who follow him until Resurrection Day."

And walk not on earth with haughty self-conceit; for, verily, thou can never rend the earth asunder, nor grow as tall as the mountains! The evil of all this is odious in thy Sustainer's sight. This is part of that knowledge of right and wrong with which thy Sustainer inspires thee. (17:37-39)

"Which thy Sustainer inspire thee," the noun hikmah, usually signifying "wisdom", which prevents evil or ignorant behavior and leads to conscious insight into excellence. This term refers here to what is "odious in God's sight," which implies ethical discrimination or the knowledge of right and wrong, and this, in turn, presupposes the existence of an absolute, God-willed standard of moral values.

MAKING MOCKERY OF GOD'S MESSAGE

Woe unto every sinful self-deceiver who hears God's messages when they are conveyed to him, and yet, as though he did not hear them, persists in his haughty disdain! Hence, announce to him grievous suffering—for when he becomes aware of any of Our messages, he makes them a target of his mockery! For all such, shameful suffering awaits. Hell is ahead of them. All that they may have gained [in this world] shall be of no avail to them. Not one of those things which, instead of God, they regard as their protectors, for awesome suffering awaits them. [Paying heed to God's signs and messages] is guidance. On the other hand, for those bent on denying the truth of their Sustainer's messages, there is grievous suffering in store as an outcome of [their] vileness. (45:7-11)

A sinful self-deceiver lies to himself because he is perverted in his intellect and judgment. They regard their protectors as false deities to which they attribute a quasi-divine influence on their lives.

SCOFFING AT BELIEVERS

There were among My servants who prayed, 'O our Sustainer! We have come to believe [in Thee]; forgive, then, our sins and bestow Thy mercy on us, for Thou art the true bestower of mercy!' But you made them a target of your derision to the point where it made you forget all remembrance of Me. You laughed at them. [But] today (the day of judgment) I rewarded them for their patience in adversity. It is they who have triumphed!" (23:109-111)

HYPOCRISY

The verses below relate to a group of half-hearted Muslims in Medina. These hypocrites openly professed Islam, but they weren't convinced of its authenticity. They played a double game, adopting a wait-and-see strategy to pick the winner of the conflict between Muslims and pagans of Mecca. Their sympathies were with the pagans, a much more powerful group than Muslims.

God has promised the hypocrites, both men and women—as well as the [outright] deniers of the truth—the fire of hell, therein to abide; this shall be their allotted portion. God has rejected them, and long-lasting suffering awaits them. (9:68) The hypocrites shall be in the lowest depth of the fire, and you will find none who could save them. (4:145)

APOSTASY

As for those bent on rejecting the truth after attaining faith, and then grow [ever more stubborn] in their refusal to acknowledge the truth, their repentance [of other sins] shall not be accepted. It is they who have truly gone astray. On the Day [of Judgment] some faces will be dark [with grief]. And as for those with darkened faces, [they shall be told]: "Did you deny the truth after attaining faith? Taste then, this suffering for denying the truth!" These are God's messages: We convey them unto you, setting forth the truth, since God wills no wrong to His creation. And unto God belongs all that is in the heavens and all that is on earth, and all things go back to God [as their source]. (3:106-109)

But as for him who, after guidance has been vouchsafed to him, cuts himself off from the Apostle and follows a path other than that of the believers - him We shall leave unto that which he himself has chosen, [A stress on man's freedom of choice] and shall cause him to endure hell, and how evil a journey's end. (4:115) Such as these who have hell as their goal, and they shall find no way to escape. (4:121)

Apostasy will be punished in the afterlife. God has bestowed the freedom to choose or reject a religion in this life. It's a good riddance to those who want to leave Islam. Usually, such apostates become celebrities in the Islamophobic Western media. They should keep their opinions about modernizing Islam to themselves and let the bygone be bygone.

ASTROLOGY

The "evil ones" are the astrologers. They have made stars objects of their guesswork, claiming to know what will happen in the future from the position and aspects of stars. Since only God knows about the future and "that which is beyond the reach of a created being's perception" (al-ghayb), any attempt at such an understanding would be blasphemy (kufr).

SINFUL THOUGHTS VERSUS EVIL DEEDS

The Prophet said, "God has forgiven my followers for the evil thoughts that occur in their minds, as long as such thoughts are not put into action or uttered." Some Christians are taught that even thinking about sin is a sin. It's challenging to control what we think, but we can usually control what we do.

ENTERTAINMENT AND MUSIC

There is no reference to music or singing in the Quran; however, the Prophet encouraged others to do so. Salama narrated: We traveled with the Prophet to Khaybar. A companion said, O Amir! Let us hear some of your camel-driven songs. So, he sang some of them in harmony with the camel's walk. The Prophet asked, "Who is the driver of these camels?" They replied, "Amir." The Prophet said, "May God bestow

His mercy on him." Amir was martyred the next day in the battle of Khaybar.

Calling to prayer and recitation of the Quran is a form of singing. Horse racing was one of the Prophet's pastimes. When a group of Africans came to Medina and performed in the Mosque compound, the Prophet himself showed this performance to his wife Aishah.

CHAPTER 13
SINS AGAINST FELLOW MAN

VIOLATING THE HUMAN RIGHTS OF FELLOW MEN

Some modern-day Muslims believe that if they fasted, prayed, and pilgrimed to Hajj (Huquq ullah), it did not matter how they treated people (Huququl Ibad). Nothing could be further from the truth. Human beings depend upon the fulfillment of certain natural rights to live a dignified life, Huququl Ibad is more important to fulfill than God's rights. The rights of man are considered universal and should be stringently observed without exception. This and the next chapter describe various sins as mentioned in the Quran. Idol worship (shirk) is the only unforgivable sin, however, if the idol worshiper repents and returns to the worship of one God, the sin of shirk is also forgiven. The major or minor sins can be differentiated by the level of punishment. The major sins are those for which hellfire is explicitly mentioned as a punishment.

BREAKING BOND OF BLOOD TIES

But as for those who break their bond with God after it has been established [in their nature] and cut asunder what God has bidden to be joined and spread corruption on earth - their due is rejection [by God], and theirs is a most evil fate [in the life to come]. (13:25)

The phrase "what God has bidden to be joined" refers to all ties arising from human relationships—e.g., family bonds, and neighbors' mutual rights and duties. In short, man must treat all living beings with love and compassion. The Prophet said, "The person who breaks the bond of kinship will not enter paradise." Rejection whenever it is attributed in the Quran to God concerning a sinner signifies the latter's exclusion from God's grace. In the present context, this meaning is reinforced by reference to "a most evil fate" (lit., "abode") in the afterlife.

SIN OF DEVOURING ORPHANS' POSSESSIONS

Hence, render to the orphans their possessions, and do not substitute the bad things [of your own] for the good things [that belong to them], and do not consume their possessions together with your own: this, verily, is a great crime. (4:2) Behold, those who sinfully devour orphans' possessions fill their bellies with fire. For [in the life to come] they will have to endure a blazing flame! (4:10)

MISTREATING OLD PARENTS

And [do not offend but] do good unto your parents. (6:151) Should one of them, or both, attain to old age in your care, never say "Ugh" to them or scold them, but [always] speak unto them with reverent speech, and spread over them humbly the wings of your tenderness, and say: "O my Sustainer! Bestow Thy grace upon them, even as they cherished and reared me when I was a child!" (17:22-24)

God is the ultimate cause of man's coming to life, and his parents are its outward immediate cause: and so, the injunction to honor and cherish one's parents. The rest of the passage shows that kindness and just dealings between man and man are an integral part of the concept of "striving for the good of life to come." In Arabic, "ugh" is a word or sound indicative of contempt, dislike, or disgust. "The wings of your tenderness" is a metonymical expression evocative of a bird that lovingly spreads its wings over its offspring in the nest.

THE THREE CARDINAL SINS: IDOL WORSHIP, ADULTERY, AND MURDER

But whoever deliberately slays another believer, his punishment shall be hell, therein to abide; and God will condemn him, and reject him, and prepare for him awesome suffering. (4:93) Never invoke any [imaginary] deity side by side with God, and do not take any human being's life—[the life] which God has willed to be sacred—

otherwise than in [the pursuit of] justice, and do not commit adultery. And [know that] he who commits aught thereof will [not only] meet with a full requital [but] have his suffering doubled on Resurrection Day: for on that [Day] he shall abide in ignominy. (25:68-69)

Zina means both adultery and fornication, (24:2) which is sex outside the marriage, regardless of whether either party is married or not. Zina is generally translated as adultery since English has no equivalent word. There is no direct verse in the Quran about suicide. However, it is clear from the Prophet's tradition that suicide is a mortal sin just like murder.

ANTI-SOCIAL BEHAVIOR

Defer not to the contemptible swearer of oaths, [or to] the slanderer that spreads about with defaming tales, [or] the withholder of good, [or] the sinful aggressor, [or] one who is cruel, possessed by greed, and, in addition to all this, utterly useless [to his fellow men]. (68:10-13)

[Whereupon God will command]: "Cast into hell every [such] stubborn enemy of the truth, [every] withholder of good [and] sinful aggressor [and] fomenter of distrust [between man and man—everyone] who has set up another deity beside God. Cast him, then, cast him into severe suffering!"

Man's other self will say: "O our Sustainer! It was not I that led his conscious mind into evil— [no], but it had gone astray [independently]! [And], He will say: "Contend not before Me, [O you sinners], for I gave you a forewarning [of this Day of Reckoning]. The judgment passed by Me shall not be altered, but never do I do the least wrong unto My creatures!" (50:24-29)

Man's other self is its counterpart, namely, the complex of the sinner's instinctive urges and inordinate and unrestrained appetites. Man's evil impulses cannot gain ascendancy unless his conscious mind wanders astray from moral verities. This explains the purpose, in the present context, of the verses above.

ENVY

Say: "My Sustainer has forbidden shameful deeds, be they open or secret, and [every kind of] sinning, and unjustified envy. (7:33) He forbids all that is shameful and all that runs counter to reason, as well as envy: [and] He exhorts you [repeatedly] so that you might bear [all this] in mind. (16:90)

The phrase "that which is wrong" or shameful has the original meaning of anything reprehensible and runs counter to reason and good sense, which the mind or the moral sense rejects, or ought to reject. Thus, fully in tune with the Quran's rational approach to ethics questions as well as its insistence on reasonableness and moderation in man's behavior.

CONTENTION AS A SIN

Thus, indeed, We have given in this Quran many facets to every kind of lesson [designed] for [the benefit of] mankind. However, man is, above all else, always prone to contention. For, what is there to keep people from attaining faith now that guidance has come unto them, and from asking their Sustainer to forgive them their sins? Unless it be [their wish] that the fate of [sinful] people of ancient times should befall them, [as well], or that the [ultimate] suffering should befall them, in the hereafter? But We send [Our] message-bearers only as bearers of glad tidings and warners. While those who are bent on denying the truth contend [against them] with fallacious arguments to render void the truth thereby, and to make My messages and warnings a target of their mockery. And who could be even more wicked than he to whom his Sustainer's messages are conveyed and who turns away from them, forgetting all [the evil] that his hands may have wrought? (18:54-57)

The Prophet said, "The most hated person in God's sight is the most quarrelsome person."

BLAMING OTHERS FOR ONE'S OWN SIN

He who commits a fault or a sin and then throws the blame on an innocent person burdens himself with calumny and [yet another] flagrant sin. (4:112)

BREAKING AN OATH

And do not use your oaths as a means of deceiving one another—or else [your] foot will slip after being firm, and then you will have to taste the evil [consequences] of having turned away from the path of God, with tremendous suffering awaiting you [in the life to come]. (16:94)

By making a false pledge, you will offend God because every pledge given by man to man is synonymous with a pledge to God. The breaking of a promise inevitably leads to a gradual disappearance of all mutual trust and to the decomposition of the social fabric.

ANGER

Hence, if Satan prompts you [to blind anger], seek refuge in God: He alone is all-hearing, all-knowing! (41:36)

PERSECUTION OF BELIEVERS

As for those who persecute believing men and women, and do not repent, hell's suffering awaits them. Yes, suffering through fire awaits them! (85:10) Would any of you like to have a garden of date palms and vines, through which running waters flow, and have all manner of fruit therein—and then be overtaken by old age, with only weak children to [look after] him—and then [see] it smitten by a fiery whirlwind and utterly scorched? In this way God makes clear His message unto you, so that you might take thought. (2:266)

In the above parable, this man devotes his entire life to worldly pleasures represented by the earthly garden producing all kinds of fruit and his children. Earthly pleasures are temporarily represented by the burning of the garden and weak children. He ignored the afterlife in his younger days. Now in his old age, he desperately needed good deeds whose fruits will last forever.

CRUELTY TO ANIMALS

Although there is no direct Quranic reference to cruelty to animals, the Prophet's Traditions make it clear that those who inflict cruelty on animals risk damnation in eternal life. In this context, read the story of the Thamud tribe and the prophet Salih (volume 3). In this story, a camel was brutalized, resulting in the destruction of the Thamud tribe. Cruelty to animals is not only a grave sin but is symptomatic of a deep mental disturbance. Murderers often start out killing and torturing animals as kids. People who commit acts of cruelty to animals do not stop there and move on to their fellow humans.

SOCIAL SINS

SPREADING RUMORS

O you who have attained faith! If any iniquitous person comes to you with a [slanderous] tale, use your discernment, lest you hurt people unwittingly and be filled with remorse for what you have done. And know that God's apostle is among you. If he were to follow your inclinations in every case, you would be bound to suffer [as a community]. (49:6-7)

Man is prone to believe malicious rumors devoid of real evidence. The talebearer is characterized as "iniquitous" because the very act of spreading unsubstantiated rumors affecting other persons' reputations constitutes a spiritual offense. God's apostle ought to be an example for you as regards your behavior towards one another: i.e., he would not accept rashly a hearsay tale affecting the honor of third persons but would either refuse to listen to it altogether or, should a clarification become necessary in the interests of the community, would insist on ascertaining the truth objectively. There is a moral imperative to safeguard the honor and reputation of every community member, man and woman alike.

SLANDER

Never concern yourself with anything of which you have no knowledge. [Your] hearing, sight and heart—all of them—will be called to account for it [on Judgment Day]! (17:36) Those who like [to hear] foul slander spread against [any of] those who have attained to faith— grievous suffering awaits them in this world and in the life to come, for God knows [the full truth], whereas you know [it] not. (24:19)

This relates to groundless assertions about events or people, to statements based on guesswork unsupported by evidence. This Quranic warning against slander and against any attempt at seeking out other people's faults finds a clear echo in several well-authenticated sayings of the Prophet: "Beware of all guesswork [about one another], for, behold, all [such] guesswork is most deceptive." "Do not spy upon one another, and do not seek to expose other people's failings." "Do not hurt those who have surrendered themselves to God, and do not impute evil to them, and do not try to uncover their nakedness [i.e., their faults]: for behold, if anyone tries to uncover his brother's nakedness, God will uncover his own nakedness [on the Day of Judgment]." "Never does a believer draw a veil over the nakedness of another believer without God drawing a veil on his own nakedness on the Resurrection Day."

SELF-RIGHTEOUSNESS

O you who have attained faith! Follow not Satan's footsteps: for he who follows Satan's footsteps [will find that] he enjoins deeds of abomination and all that run counter to reason. And were it not for God's favor for you and His grace, not one of you could have remained pure. For [thus it is] God who causes whomever He wills to grow in purity: for God is all-hearing, all-knowing. (24:21) He is fully aware of you when He brings you into being out of dust, and when you are still hidden in your mother's wombs. Do not, then, consider yourselves pure-[for] He knows who is conscious of Him. (53:32)

No human being is immune to the temptation to do evil, which befalls both the righteous and those bent on denying the truth. The warning against self-righteousness implies that no matter how good a person may be, there is always a possibility of him or her doing a moral wrong and then conveniently forgetting this sin. Do not, then, consider yourself pure, and never boast about your purity. Instead, remain humble and remember that God causes whomever He wills to remain pure. No one will feel entirely secure of Sustainer's chastisement on Judgment Day (70:28).

What runs counter to reason is the unreasonable self-righteousness of so many people who "follow Satan's footsteps" by imputing moral failings on others and forgetting that it is only due to God's grace that man, in his inborn weakness, can ever remain pure.

DO NOT RIDICULE, DEFAME, INSULT, SPY AND BACKBITE

O you who have attained faith! No men shall deride [other] men. It may well be that those [whom they ridicule] are better than themselves. No women [shall deride other] women. It may well be that those [whom they mock] are better than themselves. And neither shall you defame one another, nor insult one another by [insulting] epithets. Evil is all imputation of iniquity after [one has attained to] faith. They who [become guilty thereof and] do not repent—it is they, they who are evildoers! O you who have attained faith! Avoid most guesswork [about one another]. For some of [such] guesswork is [in itself] a sin. Do not spy upon one another, and never allow yourselves to speak ill of one another behind your backs. Would you like to eat his dead brother's flesh? No, you would loathe it! And be conscious of God. God is an acceptor of repentance, a dispenser of grace! (49:11-12)

Backbiting is a loathsome sin and is like eating a dead human being.

INTRIGUE AND CONSPIRACY

Are you unaware that God knows all that is in the heavens and on earth? Never can there be a secret confabulation between three persons without His being the fourth of them, nor between five without His being the sixth of them; and neither between less than that, or more, without His being with them wherever they may be. But in the end, on Resurrection Day, He will make them truly understand what they did: for God has full knowledge of everything. Are you not aware of those who have been forbidden [to intrigue through] secret confabulations, and yet [always] revert to that which they have been forbidden? They conspire with one another to sinful doings, aggressive conduct, and disobedience to the Apostle.

[Hence] O you who have attained faith, when you hold secret confabulations, it should be in the cause of virtue and God-consciousness: and [always] remain conscious of God, unto whom you all shall be gathered. [All other kinds of] secret confabulations are Satan's doing, so that he might cause grief to those who have attained faith. Yet he cannot harm them in the least, unless it be by God's leave: in God, then, let the believers place their trust! (58:7-10) "No good comes, as a rule, out of secret confabulations—save those which are devoted to enjoining charity, or equitable dealings, or setting things to rights between people." (4:114)

Although the "secret confabulations" spoken of in this passage relate to intrigues aimed against the Prophet and his followers by some of their unbelieving contemporaries, the passage also has a general import, and is, therefore, valid for all times.

CORRUPT AND OPPRESSIVE LEADERS

Blame attaches to those who oppress [other] people and behave outrageously on earth, offending against all right, for them, there is grievous suffering in store! (42:42) And you will see them exposed to that [doom], humbling themselves in abasement looking [around] with a furtive glance. Oh, the evildoers will fall into long-lasting suffering. (42:45)

SECTARIANISM

Verily, as for those who have broken the unity of their faith and become sects, thou hast nothing to do with them. Behold, their case rests with God: and in time He will make them understand what they were doing. (6:159) And be not like those who have drawn apart from one another and have taken to conflicting views after all evidence of the truth has come unto them: so tremendous suffering is in store for them. (3:105)

The followers of the Bible became "Jews," and "Christians." The followers of the Quran, the Muslims split into various sects, although all three communities have a common belief source and are based on the same spiritual truths.

TRIBALISM, NATIONALISM AND JINGOISM

Say: "If your fathers and your sons and your brothers and your spouses and your clan, and the worldly goods which you have acquired, and the commerce whereof you fear a decline, and the dwellings in which you take pleasure—[if all these] are dearer to you than God and His Apostle and the struggle in His cause, then wait until God makes manifest His will. (9:24)

While recognizing differences in status, wealth, and tribal origin, the Quran teaches the ultimate unity and equality of all believers before God. It includes Jews, Christians, Muslims, and followers of other monotheist faiths. Common faith, not tribal or family ties, binds the community together. The passage above rejects the tendency to regard ties of kinship and national affiliation expressed in the term "your clan" as the decisive factors of social behavior. This may be an allusion to communities' inevitable degeneration and decline, which place narrow self-interest above ethical values.

WORSHIP OF WEALTH

To him who cares for [no more than the enjoyment of] this fleeting life, We readily grant thereof as much as We please, [giving] to whomever it is Our will [to give]; but in the end, We consign him to [the suffering of] hell, which he will have to endure disgraced and disowned! (17:18) Is it because he is possessed of worldly goods and children and whenever Our messages are conveyed to him, he says, "Fables of ancient times"? [For this], We shall brand him with an indelible disgrace! (68:14-16)

Visible signs of material success, including children or sons, are considered evidence of the righteousness of the person concerned. This is, therefore, evidence that he does not require further guidance. We shall stigmatize him with an indelible disgrace.

CONSUMING ORPHANS' WEALTH

Those who sinfully devour orphans' possessions but fill their bellies with fire: for [in the life to come] they will have to endure a blazing flame! (4:10)

DISCARDING INHERITANCE LAWS

These are God's bounds (referring to the laws of inheritance). And whoever rebels against God and His Apostle and transgresses His bounds, He will commit to fire; shameful suffering awaits him. (4:13-14)

This severe punishment has been promised for breaking inheritance laws, such as depriving women or weaker family members of their due inheritance.

AMASSING WEALTH AND GORGING ON USURY

All [that awaits him] is a raging flame, tearing his skin! It will claim all those who turn their backs [on what is right], and turn away [from the truth], and amass [wealth] and withhold [it from their fellowmen]. (70:15-18) As for those who return to it [the practice of usury], they are destined for fire, therein to abide. (2:275)

LUST FOR WEALTH BY RELIGIOUS LEADERS

O you who have attained faith! Many of the rabbis and monks do indeed wrongfully devour men's possessions and turn [others] away from the path of God. But as for all who lay up treasures of gold and silver and do not spend them for the sake of God—give them the tiding of grievous suffering [in the life to come]. On the Day when that [hoarded wealth] shall be heated in the fire of hell and their foreheads and their sides and their backs branded therewith, [those sinners shall be told:] "These are the treasures which you have laid up for yourselves! Taste then, [the evil of] your hoarded treasures!" (9:34-35)

And they should not think - they who are stingy and cling to all that God has granted them out of His bounty - that this is good for them: nay, it is bad for them. That to which they [so] miserly cling will, on the Day of Resurrection, be hung about their necks: for unto God [alone] belongs the heritage of the heavens and the earth; and God is aware of all that you do. (3:180)

Above is an allusion to the wealth of the Jewish, Christian, and Muslim communities and their misuse of this wealth. These communities hoard their wealth without spending it on righteous causes. See the parallel allegory, in 3:180, of the suffering that will befall the avaricious and the miser in the life to come.

MATERIAL OUTLOOK AND MORAL DECAY

Now there is a kind of man whose views on the life of this world may please you greatly, and [the more so as] he cites God as witness to what is in his heart and is, moreover, exceedingly skillful in argument. But whenever he prevails, he goes about the earth spreading corruption and destroying [man's] tilth and progeny: and God does not love corruption. And whenever he is told, "Be conscious of God," his false pride drives him into sin: hell will be his allotted portion—and how vile a resting place! (2:204-206)

This signifies a person who always defeats his opponent in a controversy using extremely adroit and often misleading arguments. This passage refers to people who hold admirable views regarding a possible improvement of human society and of man's lot on earth. At the same time, they refuse to be guided by what they regard as "esoteric" considerations—like belief in a life after death—and justify their exclusive preoccupation with the affairs of this world by seemingly sound arguments and stress on their own ethical objectives ("they cite God as the witness to what is in their hearts").

The expression "tilth" signifies gain or acquisition through labor, and it often signifies worldly goods, especially the crops obtained by tilling land, as well as the tilled land itself. It would apply, metaphorically, to human endeavors in general, and to social endeavors in particular. This expression may also stand here for wives ("your wives are your tilth," 2:223): in which case the "destruction of tilth and progeny" would be synonymous with an upsetting of family life and, consequently, of the entire communal fabric. The passage has the following meaning: As soon as the attitude described above is generally accepted and made the basis of social behavior, it unavoidably results in widespread moral decay and social disintegration.

GRANT OF RESPITE

Now if God were to hasten for human beings the ill [which they deserve by their sinning] in the same manner as people themselves would hasten [the coming to them of what they consider to be] good, their end would indeed come forthwith! But We leave them alone [for a while] - all those who do not believe they are destined to meet Us: [We leave them alone] in their overweening arrogance, blindly stumbling to and fro. (10:11)

Now if God were to take men [immediately] to task for all the evil they do [on earth], He would not leave a single living creature on its face. However, He grants them respite for a term set [by Him]. When the end of their term approaches, they can neither delay it by a single moment, nor can they hasten it. (16:61)

Repentance shall not be accepted from those who do evil deeds until their dying hour and then say, "I now repent" nor from those who die as deniers of the truth: it is these for whom We have readied grievous suffering. (4:17-18)

In Arabic usage, the term "hour" signifies not merely the astronomical hour - i.e., the twenty-fourth part of a mean solar day - but also "time" in an absolute sense, or any fraction of it, whether large or small. In the above context, it means "a least fraction of time" or "a single moment."

WHEN REPENTANCE IS TOO LATE?

When they [clearly] beheld Our punishment, they said: "We have come to believe in the One God, and we have renounced all beliefs in which we used to ascribe a share in His divinity!" But their attaining to faith after they had beheld Our punishment could not possibly benefit them - such being the way of God that has always obtained for His creatures -: and so, then and there, lost were they who had denied the truth. (40:84-85)

Their newly acquired faith will be of no benefit to them because, firstly, this belated faith could not unmake a reality that had already come into being, and, secondly, because it could not contribute to their spiritual growth as it was not an outcome of free choice but had been, rather, forced on them by the shock of an irreversible calamity. The "way of God" (Sunnat Allah) is the Quranic term for the totality of natural laws instituted by the Creator: in this case, the law is that faith has no spiritual value unless it arises out of genuine, inner enlightenment.

VAIN REPENTANCE OF PHARAOH AT HIS LAST HOUR

When he was about to drown, [Pharaoh] exclaimed: "I have come to believe there is no deity save Him in whom the children of Israel believe, and I am of those who surrender themselves unto Him!" *[Allah said]: "Whenever before this you have rebelled [against Us] and have been among those who spread corruption. But today, We shall save only your body so that you may be a [warning] sign to those who will come after you: for many people are heedless of Our messages!" (10:90-92)*

At his dying hour, it is too late for the Pharaoh to repent (see 4:18: "Repentance shall not be accepted from those who do evil deeds until their final hour, and then say, behold, now I repent"). "Today, We shall save only your body," an allusion to the ancient Egyptian custom of embalming kings and nobles and preserving them for posterity.

TORMENTS OF JUDGMENT DAY FOR UNREPENTANT SINNERS

CHAPTER 14
WELCOME OF UNREPENTANT SINNERS ON JUDGMENT DAY

Unrepentant sinners because of self-pride and arrogance will not humble themselves before God, and thus forgo the opportunity to reduce the burden of sins during their lifetime. Those lost in sins and failed to repent will suffer through the process of catharsis or cleansing of their soul through spiritual punishment on Judgment Day. The lesser guilty ones will endure the terror of Judgment Day. God will forgive them through His mercy, and they will be saved from Hell. Truly guilty and hardened sinners will suffer hellfire. Hell's suffering will be limited in time, and in the end, God through his mercy will pardon all sinners.

He governs all that exists, from the celestial space to the earth; and in the end, all shall ascend unto Him [for judgment] on a Day the length of will be [like] a thousand years of your reckoning. (32:5)

The Day of Judgment will seem endless, a thousand years to those who are judged. In the ancient Arabic idiom, a day that is trying or painful is described as "long," just as a happy day is spoken of as "short."

WELCOME ON JUDGMENT DAY FOR THE UNREPENTANT SINNERS

And there shall be those [people on the left] who have lost themselves to evil. Oh, how [unhappy] will be those who lose themselves to evil! (56:9)

The use of the expression maymanah is a metonym for "attaining to what is right", while the term mashamah is used to denote "losing oneself to evil" (e.g., in 90:19). The origin of both these metonyms is based on the belief of the pre-Islamic Arabs that future events could be predicted by observing birds' flight direction at certain times. If they flew to the right, the event was auspicious. If on the left, the reverse is true. Linguistic usage gradually absorbed this ancient belief, so that "right" and "left" became synonymous with "auspicious" and "inauspicious". In the Quran, these two concepts have been transformed into "righteousness" and "unrighteousness".

THOSE WHO PERSEVERED IN EVIL

But as for those who have persevered in evil - what of those who have persevered in evil? [They will find themselves] amid scorching winds, and black smoke shadows neither cooling nor soothing. For, behold, in times passed by, they abandoned themselves wholly to pleasure pursuit, and persist in heinous sin, and say, "What! After we have died and turned into dust and bones, shall we, forsooth, be raised from the dead and perhaps, too, our forebears of old?"

Say: "Verily, those of olden times and those of later times will indeed be gathered together at an appointed time on a Day known [only to God]. O you who have gone astray and called the truth a lie, you will indeed have to taste the tree of deadly fruit and will have to fill your bellies therewith. Whereupon you must drink [many a draught] of burning despair - drink it as the most insatiably thirsty camel drinks!" Such will be their welcome on Judgment Day! (56:41-56)

They persevered in evil until their death. Literally, the phrase reads, "those on the left hand" (see note on verse 9 above).] Their priority in life was the pursuit of pleasure to exclude all moral considerations.

DAY DEVOID OF HOPE

Those bent on denying the truth will not cease to be in doubt about Him until the Last Hour comes suddenly upon them, and [supreme] suffering befalls them on a Day void of all hope. (22:55); And do not think God is unaware of what evildoers are doing. He grants them respite until the Day when their eyes stare in horror, running confusedly to and fro, with their heads raised [in supplication]. They are unable to look away from what they shall behold, and their hearts are an abysmal void. (14:42)

SHRINK IN TERROR AND NOWHERE TO ESCAPE

If thou couldst but see [how the deniers of the truth will fare on resurrection Day] when they will shrink in terror, with nowhere to escape. They will have been seized from so close by and will cry, "We do [now] believe in it!" But how can they [hope to] attain [to salvation] from so far away [from their utterly different past life on earth]. Seeing that they had been bent on denying the truth, and casting scorn, from far away, on something beyond human perception? And so, a barrier will be set between them and all that they have ever desired. Same will be done to those of their kind who lived before their time. For, behold, they were lost in doubt, amounting to suspicion. (34:51-54)

The expression "seized from close by" means from within their own selves because of the burden of sins which they carry. They will not attain salvation because of their utterly different past lives and their denial of life after death. The expression "from far away" is used in a sense similar to sayings like "far off the mark". Man's fate in the hereafter will be a consequence of his spiritual attitude and the manner of his life during the earthly stage of his existence. The barrier represents the impossibility of fulfilling any of their desires of the damned in the life to come. They were lost in suspicions that all moral postulates were meant to deprive them of what they considered the legitimate advantages of life in this world.

TWICE BIRTH AND DEATH

[But] behold, as for those bent on denying the truth—[on that same Day] a voice will call out to them. "Indeed, greater than your

[present] loathing of yourselves was God's loathing of you [at the time] when you were called unto faith but you went on denying the truth!" [Whereupon] they will exclaim: "O our Sustainer! Twice hast Thou caused us to die, twice hast Thou brought us to life! But now that we have acknowledged our sins, is there any way out [of this second death]?" [And they will be told]: "This [has befallen you] because, whenever the One God was invoked, you denied this truth. When divinity was ascribed to aught beside Him, you believed [in it]! But all judgment rests with God, the Exalted, the Great!" (40:10-12)

This relates to the sinner's self-loathing when realizing his past sinfulness. Since it is impossible to attribute to God a purely human emotion, "God's loathing" of those sinners is a metonym for His rejection of them. Thou hast brought us to life on earth, and then caused us to die; then Thou resurrected us and now condemns us to spiritual death in consequence of our willful spiritual blindness on earth.

BLINDNESS IN THE HEREAFTER

For whoever is blind [of heart] in this [world] will be blind in the life to come [as well], and still farther astray from the path [of truth]. (17:72) But as for him who turns away from remembering Me, his life shall be of narrow scope. On the Day of Resurrection, We shall raise him up blind. [The sinner] will ask: "O my Sustainer! Why hast Thou raised me up blind, whereas [on earth] I was endowed with sight?" [God] will reply: "Thus it is there came unto you My messages, but you were oblivious to them, and thus today you shall be consigned to oblivion!" For, thus shall We recompense him who wastes his own self and does not believe in his Sustainer's messages. Indeed, the suffering [of such sinners] in the life to come shall be most severe and enduring! (20:124-127)

A life of narrow perspective is sterile and spiritually hollow, without real meaning or purpose. As indicated in the subsequent clause, will be a source of their suffering in the hereafter.

THE DAY OF LOSS AND GAIN

[Think of] the time when He gathers you all together on the Day of the [Last] Gathering—that Day of Loss and Gain! (64:9) Woe, then, on that Day to all who give the lie to the truth. All those who [throughout their lives] idly played with vain things. (52:11-12) Nay, but [most of] you love this fleeting life and give no thought to the life to come [and to Judgment Day]! (75:20) He who denied the truth will have to bear [the burden of] his denial. Verily, He [God] does not love those who refuse to acknowledge the truth. (30:44-45)

WISH TO AVOID JUDGMENT DAY AS LONG AS POSSIBLE

On the Day when every human being will find himself faced with all the good and evil that he has done, [many a one] will wish that there was a long span of time between himself and that [Day]. Hence, God warns you to beware of Him; but God is most compassionate towards His creatures. (3:30)

GOOD DEEDS SCATTERED LIKE DUST

[Yet] on that Day—the Day on which they shall see the angels—there will be no glad tidings for those who were lost in sin; and they will exclaim, "By a forbidding ban [are we from God's grace debarred]!" For We shall have turned towards all the [supposedly good] deeds they ever wrought and transformed them into scattered dust. (25:22-23)

Sinners' good deeds will be negligible compared to their evil acts.

CHAPTER 15
THE DAY OF REGRETS AND RANSOM OFFER BY UNREPENTANT SINNERS

Hence, those who deny the truth will face a Day of distress. The evildoer will bite his hands [in despair], exclaiming: "Oh, if I had followed the path shown to me by the apostle! Oh, woe is me! I had not taken so-and-so for a friend! Indeed, he led me astray from remembrance [of God] after it had come unto me!" For [thus it is] Satan is ever a betrayer of man. (25:26-29)

The terms "the apostle" and "the evildoer" are here used in their generic sense, applying to all of God's apostles and all who consciously reject their guidance. Similarly, the expression "so-and-so," occurring in the next verse, refers to any person or personified influence responsible for leading a human being astray.

REGRETS OF PAST LIFE AND REQUEST FOR A SECOND CHANCE

Follow the most goodly [teaching] revealed to you by your Sustainer, lest any human being says [on Judgment Day]: "Alas for me for having been negligent in what is due to God, and for having been indeed one of those who scoffed [at the truth]!" Or lest he should say, "If God had but guided me, I would surely have been among those who are conscious of Him!" Or lest he should add, when he becomes aware of the suffering [that awaits him], "Would that I had a second chance [in life], so that I could be among the doers of good!" [But God will reply]: "Yea, indeed! My messages came to you, but you gave them the lie. You were filled with false pride, and among those who denied the truth!" (39:55-59)

APOSTLES HAVE TOLD US THE TRUTH

Are [unbelievers] waiting for the final meaning of that [Day of Judgment] to unfold? [But] on the Day when its final meaning is unfolded, those who were oblivious thereof will say: "Our Sustainer's apostles have indeed told us the truth? Then, are there any intercessors who could intercede for us? Or could we be brought back [to life] so we act differently than we used to?" (7:53)

The Day of Judgment will fulfill the Quran's warnings. In this sense, it connotes the "unfolding of its final meaning."

GRANT US A RESPITE

Hence, warn men of the Day when this suffering may befall them. When those who did wrong [in their lifetime] exclaim: "O our Sustainer! Grant us respite for a short while, so that we might respond to Thy call and follow the apostles!" [But God will answer]: "Why did you previously deny that resurrection and retribution awaited you? And yet, you dwelt in the dwelling places of those who had sinned against their own selves [before your time], and it was made obvious to you how We had dealt with them. We have explained to you many parables [of sin, resurrection, and divine retribution]. (14:43-45)

God grants respite to evildoers for their lifetime. The wrongdoers mentioned here are those who believe there are other powers that rival God and thus commit the unforgivable sin of idol worship. They also denied the afterlife, attended by God's sin retribution, and God's ultimate judgment. They lived on the same earth and in basically the same human environment, as those earlier generations who offended all ethical values and brought destruction upon themselves. Their tragic fate should have been a warning to them. Arabs were well acquainted with stories of earlier generations, such as Pharaoh's enslavement of Israelites, Noah's people, tribes of Ad and Thamud, etc., who offended all moral values.

SUFFERING WILL NOT BE LIGHTENED

We shall take to task, through suffering, those lost in pleasures-they cry out in [belated] supplication. [They will be told]: "Cry not today for you shall not be succored by Us! (23:64-65) They who were bent on evildoing will behold the suffering [that awaits them, they will realize that] it will not be lightened for them [by virtue of their pleading] and neither will they be granted respite. (16:85)

The "taking to task through suffering" spoken of here may refer to the Day of Judgment or to the inevitable social ruin that wrong beliefs and actions bring into this world.

IGNOMINY AND MISERY

And then, on resurrection Day, He will cover them [all] with ignominy, and will say: "Where now, are those beings to whom you ascribed a share in My divinity, [and] for whose sake you cut yourselves off [from My guidance]?" Those who [in their lifetime] were endowed with knowledge will say: "Ignominy and misery [have fallen] this day upon those who have been denying the truth—those whom the angels have gathered in death while they were still sinning against themselves!" (16:27-28)

God will cover them with ignominy, or disgrace, for only on the Day of resurrection will they be repaid for everything they have done (3:185). Those "endowed with knowledge" of good and evil, which God offers mankind through His prophets.

RANSOM FOR SUFFERINGS

OFFER OF ALL EARTH'S TREASURES

And some people [agnostics] ask thee, "Is all this true?" Say: "Yea, by my Sustainer! It is most certainly true, and you cannot elude [the final reckoning]!" And all human beings that have done evil would surely, if they possessed all that is on earth, offer it as a ransom [on Judgment Day]. When they see the suffering [in front of them], they will be unable to express their remorse. But judgment will be passed on them in all equity, and they will not be wronged. God's promise always comes true—but most of them know it not! (10:53-55)

The above phrase "unable to express their remorse" is sinners' inability to express their full remorse.

OFFER OF TWICE THE TREASURES OF EARTH

But if those who are bent on evildoing possessed all that is on earth, and twice as much, they would surely offer it as a ransom for the awful suffering [that will befall them] on the Day of resurrection. For something they had not considered before will [by then] made obvious to them by God. To them, what is obvious will become the evil they wrought [in life]. They will be overwhelmed by the very truth they used to scoff at. (39:47-48)

The ransom offer is metaphorical. God makes it obvious that man's attitude and actions in this world determine his fate in the hereafter. They will be completely overwhelmed by the reality of life after death and the spiritual truths preached by God's prophets.

OFFER OF FAMILY AS A RANSOM IN UTTER DESPERATION

[For] everyone lost in sin will on that Day desire to ransom himself from suffering at the price of his own children, his spouse, his

brother, all the kinsfolk whoever sheltered him, and of whoever [else] lives on earth, all of them—so that he could save himself. (70:11-14)

PARABLE OF SCUM OVER CLEAR WATER

[Whenever] He sends down water from the sky, and [once dry] riverbeds run high according to their measure, the stream carries scum on its surface, [while the water beneath is clear]. Likewise, from that [metal] which they smelt in the fire to make ornaments or utensils, [there rises] scum. In this way, God reveals the parable of truth and falsehood. As far as scum is concerned, it passes away as [does all] dross. What is beneficial to man abides on earth. In this way does God set forth the parables of those who responded to their Sustainer with a goodly response, and of those who did not respond to Him. [As for the latter] if they possessed all that is on earth, and twice as much, they would surely offer it as a ransom [on the Day of Judgment]. A most evil reckoning awaits them, and their goal is hell and how evil a resting place! Can, then, he who knows that whatever has been bestowed from on high upon you by thy Sustainer is the truth be deemed equal to the blind? Only those endowed with insight keep this in mind. (13:17-19)

The scum represents falsehood, and the clear water is truth. The scum of the flood and the minerals smelted pass away as dross, useless refuse. However, that which is of use to mankind, in the form of water and minerals, remains. Likewise, falsehood wanes and is eventually eliminated, even if it prevails over truth briefly. Truth, on the other hand, is established and endures.

CHAPTER 16
RECORD OF UNREPENTANT SINNERS

RECORD OF DEEDS ON EARTH

Verily, We shall indeed bring the dead back to life. We shall record whatever [deeds] they have sent ahead, and the traces [of good and evil] they have left behind. For of all things, We do take account in a clear record. (36:12) On that Day all men will come forward, cut off from one another, to be shown their [past] deeds. And so, he who does an atom's weight of good shall behold it and he who does an atom's weight of evil shall behold it. (99:6-8) On the Day, when everyone will be faced with all the good and evil that he has done. (3:30) Man will be judged on that Day, for what he has done and what he has left undone. (75:13)

EVIL RECORD OF SINNERS

And [on that Day] you will see all people kneeling [in humility]. They will be called upon to [face] their record: "Today you shall be requited for all that you ever did! This Our record speaks of you in all truth. We have caused to be recorded all that you ever did!" (45:28-29) But as for him whose record shall be placed in his left hand, he will exclaim: "Oh, would that I had never been shown this my record, and neither knew this my account! Oh, would this [death] have been the end of me! Of no avail to me is all that I have [ever] possessed, [and] all my power of argument has died away from me!" (69:25-29)

The record placed in his left hand signifies that he was unrighteous in his earthly life. Today, the power of argument against life after death and divine judgment has died away from me.

EVERLASTING RECORD OF THE WICKED

Verily, the record of the wicked has indeed [set down] in a mode inescapable! And what could make you conceive what that mode inescapable will be? A record [everlastingly] inscribed! Woe on that Day unto those who give the lie to the truth who also tell the lie to the [coming of] Judgment Day. For, none gives the lie to it but those who transgress against all that is right [and are] immersed in sin. Whenever Our messages are conveyed to them, they but say, "Fables of ancient times!" Nay, but their hearts are corroded by all [the evil] that they did! From [the grace of] their Sustainer shall they on that Day be debarred. Then, behold, they shall enter the blazing fire and be told: "This is the [very thing] to which you used to give the lie!" (83:7-17)

The term *sijjin* signifies "a prison." Its metaphorical application to a sinner's record is to stress its contents were permanently imprisoned, with no possibility of escaping. The denial of ultimate responsibility before God—and, hence, of His judgment—is invariably conducive to sinning and transgression against all moral imperatives. Their persistence in wrongdoing has gradually deprived them of moral responsibility and the ability to visualize God's ultimate judgment.

MEN CHOOSE THEIR OWN DESTINY

And every human being's destiny We have tied to his neck; and on the Day of Resurrection, We shall bring forth for him a record which he will find wide open; [and he will be told]: "Read this your record! Sufficient is your own self today to make out your account!" (17:13-14)

The Quranic concept of "destiny" relates not so much to the external circumstances of and events in man's life as, rather, to the direction that this life takes because of one's moral choices. It relates to man's inclinations, attitudes, and conscious actions. Man's spiritual fate depends on, and God has made man responsible for, his behavior on earth. He speaks of Himself as having "tied every human being's destiny to his neck." The record and the subsequent account represent man's total comprehension, on Judgment Day, of all his past life. (See 50:22—"Now We have lifted from you your veil, and sharp is your sight today!").

Behold, they were not expecting to be called to account, having given the lie to Our messages one and all. We have placed on record everything [of what they did]. [And so, We shall say]: "Taste, then, [the fruit of your evil doings] for now We shall bestow on you nothing but more and more suffering!" (78:27-30)

SINNERS' REACTION TO THEIR RECORD

And the record [of everyone's deeds] will be laid open. You will see the guilty filled with dread at what [they see] therein and they will exclaim: "Oh, woe unto us! What a record is this! It leaves out nothing, be it small or great, but takes everything into account!" For they will find all that they ever wrought [now] facing them, and [will know that] thy Sustainer does not wrong anyone. (18:49)

HORROR AT HIS RECORD

But as for him whose record shall be given to him behind his back, he will pray for utter destruction, but he will enter the blazing flame. Behold, [in his earthly life] *he lived joyfully among people of his own kind* (people of the same sinful inclinations) *for, behold, he never thought that he would have to return [to God]. Yes indeed! His Sustainer did see all that was in him! (84:10-15)*

The record given "behind his back" alludes to the sinner's horror at his record and his wish to never have been shown it.

I WISH I WAS MERE DUST

Verily, We have warned you of suffering near at hand—[suffering] on the Day when man shall see [clearly] what his hands have sent ahead, and when he who has denied the truth shall say, "Oh, would that I was mere dust!" (78:40)

FACES WILL BE HUMBLED

And [on that Day] all faces will be humbled before the Ever-Living, the Self-Subsistent Fount of All Being; and undone shall be he who bears [a burden of] evildoing. (20:111)

SEND US BACK TO DO GOOD DEEDS

If you could see [how it will be on Judgment Day], when those who are lost in sin will hang their heads before their Sustainer, [saying]: "O our Sustainer! [Now] we have seen and heard! Return us, then, [to our earthly life] that we may do good deeds: for [now], we are certain [of the truth]!" "Most certainly will I fill hell with invisible beings and humans, all together!" (32:12-13)

WEIGHT LIGHT IN THE BALANCE SCALE

We shall set up just balance-scales on resurrection Day, and no human being shall be wronged in the least. For there will be [in him] the weight of a mustard seed [of good or evil], We shall bring it forth, and no one can count as We do! (21:47) And true will be the weighing on that Day, whereas those whose weight is light in the balance—it is they who will have squandered their own selves by their willful rejection of Our messages! (7:8-9) Whereas whose weight is light in the balance—it is they who will have squandered their own selves, [destined] to abide in hell (23:103) engulfed by an abyss. And what could make you conceive what that [abyss] will be? A fire hotly burning! (101:10-11) And there shall be such as will have lost themselves in evil: oh, how [unhappy] will be they who have lost themselves in evil! (56:9) And thus shall thy Sustainer's word come true against all who are bent on denying the truth: they shall find themselves in the fire [of hell]. (40:6)

COMMISSION OF EVIL AND OMISSION OF GOOD

When all human beings are linked [to their deeds]. (81:7) When the scrolls [of men's deeds] are unfolded, and when heaven is laid bare, and when the blazing fire [of hell] is kindled bright. (81:10-12) On that Day Hell will be brought [within sight] and man will remember [all that he did and failed to do]. But what will that remembrance avail him? He will say, "Oh, would that I had provided beforehand for my life [to come]!" For, none can make suffer as He will make suffer [the sinners] on that Day. (89:23-25)

When men are coupled with their deeds, none can divest himself of responsibility for his past deeds. In balance, the weight of his sins will be light because his evils exceed his good deeds, and he will reach an abyss of suffering and despair.

CHAPTER 17
SEPARATION FROM FRIENDS AND LOVED ONES
AND
WITNESS AGAINST THEMSELVES

On resurrection Day, sinners will be irretrievably separated from all whom they loved and were close to them in their earthly life.

LOSS OF SELF, AND KITH AND KIN

When the trumpet [of resurrection] is blown, no ties of kinship will prevail among them, and neither will they ask about one another. (23:101) Say: "Behold, the [true] losers will be they who lose their own selves and their kith and kin on the resurrection Day: for is not this, the [most] obvious loss?" (39:15)

The "loss of one's own self" signifies the destruction of one's identity and uniqueness as a human being. This is the most obvious loss a sinner suffers in life to come.

WHEN NO HUMAN BEINGS WILL HELP

And what could make you conceive that Judgment Day will be? And again: What could make you conceive that Judgment Day will be? [It will be] a Day when no human being shall be of least avail to another person. On that Day [it will become manifest that] all sovereignty is God's alone. (82:17-19)

The repetition of this rhetorical question (What could make you conceive …?) is meant to indicate that man's intellect and imagination cannot answer it. We cannot conceptualize the Day of Judgment, which will usher in reality that is outside our human experience. Only allegory and our emotional response to it can give us an inkling of that reality.

WHEN PARENTS WILL BE UNAVAILABLE

O men! Be conscious of your Sustainer and stand in awe of the Day on which no parent will be of any avail to his child, nor will a child be of any help to his parent! Verily, God's promise [of resurrection] is real indeed. Let not, then, the life of this world deludes you, and [your own] deceptive thoughts about God deceive you! (31:33-34)

The term *gharur* denotes "anything that deludes" a person in the moral sense, whether it be Satan, another human being, an abstract concept, or wishful thinking—For instance, the self-deluding expectation that God will forgive you, while you are deliberately committing a sin.

WHEN FRIENDS ARE OF NO AVAIL

Verily, the Day of Distinction [between the true and the false] is the term appointed for all of them. The Day when no friend shall be of the least avail to his friend, and when none shall be succored save those upon whom God will have bestowed His grace and mercy: for, verily, He alone is almighty, a dispenser of grace. (44:40-42) And [when] no friend will ask about his friend, though they may be in one another's sight. (70:10-11) And so, when the piercing call [of resurrection] is heard on a Day when everyone will [want to] flee from his brother, mother, father, spouse, and his children. On that Day, to every one of them will his own state be of sufficient concern. (80:33-37)

NO ESCAPE FROM THE FINAL JUDGMENT

Never can they elude [their final reckoning, even if they remain unscathed] on earth. They will never find anyone who protects them from God. [In the life to come] double suffering will be imposed on them for having lost the ability to hear [the truth] and failed to see [it]. It is they who have squandered their own selves—for [on the Day of Resurrection] all their false imagery will have forsaken them: truly it is they, they who in the life to come shall be the losers! (11:20-22)

God's punishment may or may not befall sinners during their life on earth; it will certainly befall them in the hereafter.

NO ONE CAN ELUDE GOD

[One Day] We shall take you to the task, O you sin-laden two! [Men and women] Which, then, of your Sustainer's powers can you disavow? O you who live in close communion with [evil] invisible beings and humans! If you [think that you] can pass beyond the regions of the heavens and the earth, pass beyond them! [To escape God's judgment and chastisement] [But] you cannot pass beyond them, save by a sanction [from God]! (Unless He wills to reprieve you.) *(55:31-34)*

THE END OF JOURNEY

On that Day man will exclaim, "Whither to flee?" But nay: no refuge [for you, O man]! With thy Sustainer, on that Day, the journey's end will be! (75:10-12) Verily, it is We who grant life and deal death, and with Us will be all journeys' end. (50:43-44)

MAN WILL BE EYEWITNESS AGAINST HIMSELF

On that Day neither man nor invisible being will be asked about his sins. (55:39) Nay, but man shall be an eyewitness against himself, even though he may veil himself in excuses. (75:14-15) On that Day We shall set a seal on their mouths—but their hands will speak unto Us, and their feet will bear witness to whatever they have earned [in life]. (36:65) On the Day when their own tongues, hands and feet will bear witness against them by [recalling] all that they did! (24:24)

"We shall set a seal on their mouths" is a metaphor for their being unable to excuse or defend their past actions and attitudes.

SKIN WILL BEAR WITNESS

The Day when the enemies of God shall be gathered before the fire, and then shall be driven onward, till when they come close to it, their hearing, sight and [very] skins will bear witness against them, speaking of what they were doing [on earth]. And they will ask their skins, "Why did you bear witness against us?" [And] these will reply: "God, who gives speech to all things, has given speech to us [as well]. He [it is who] has created you in the first instance—and unto Him you are [now] brought back. And you did not try to hide [your sins] lest your hearing, sight or your skins bear witness against you. Nay, but you thought that God did not know much of what you were doing. (41:19-22)

The sinners will find all that they ever wrought now facing them, and their own tongues and hands and feet will bear witness against them by recalling all that they did.

EARTH TO BEAR WITNESS OF MAN'S DOINGS

When the earthquakes with her [last] mighty quaking, and [when] the earth yields up her burdens, and man cries out, "What has happened to her?" On that Day will she recount all her tidings, as thy Sustainer will have inspired her to do. (99:1-5) Now, [as for the deaf and blind of heart] when the word [of truth] stands revealed against them, We shall bring forth unto them out of the earth a creature, which will tell them that humanity had no real faith in Our messages. (27:82)

Many inanimate objects will assume a different identity. The earth will acquire the ability to recount all the tragic events it witnessed caused by man. The "creature," parabolically, tells men that their submergence in exclusively materialistic values—and, hence, their approaching self-destruction—is an outcome of their lack of belief in God.

And one part of him will say: "This has been ever-present with me!" (50:23) Man's other self will say: "O our Sustainer! It was not I that led his conscious mind into evil—nay, but it had gone far astray [of its own accord]! [And] He will say: "Contend not before Me, [O you sinners], for I gave you a forewarning [of this Day of Reckoning]. The judgment passed by Me shall not be altered but never do I do the least wrong unto My creatures!" (50:27-29)

Inner urges and primal desires drive him into unrestrained self-indulgence and, thus, into sin. The "conscious mind" alludes here to the awakening of deeper layers of man's consciousness, leading to a sudden perception of his own moral reality. The lifting of the veil forces him to "bear witness" against himself. The awakened moral consciousness of the sinner will plead that he had always been conscious. He was perhaps even critical of the urges and appetites that drove him into evildoing. But, as is shown in the sequence, this belated and therefore morally ineffective rationale does not diminish but rather enhances the burden of man's guilt.

Man's other self is the complex of the sinner's instinctive urges and inordinate, unrestrained appetites summarized in the term *shaytan* ("Satan" or "satanic force"). Man's evil impulses and appetites cannot gain ascendancy unless his conscious mind goes astray from moral verities.

CHAPTER 18
COMING FACE TO FACE WITH GOD FOR FINAL JUDGMENT

Islamic ethics follows mankind's special status and responsibility on earth. God will judge the quality of earthly lives. There will be subsequent recompense carried out with absolute justice through God's merciful will. To face justice, everyone will come forward alone or as a separate entity.

The final Judgment of all human beings will occur after the destruction of the cosmos and subsequent resurrection of all humans. Why is the Judgment after the end of the world and not after death? The Prophet answered this question: "Whoever calls others to the right way shall have a reward equal to the combined rewards of all who may follow him until resurrection Day, without anything being lessened of their rewards. Whoever calls to the way of error will have to bear a sin equal to the combined sins of all who may follow him until resurrection Day, without anything being lessened of their sins." Since man's actions in this life may continue to accrue both rewards and sins after his earthly demise, man will be judged on the Day of Judgment rather than after death. The possible exceptions are the martyrs who made an ultimate sacrifice by giving their lives for God's cause; they may enter paradise soon after death. After judgment day, their spirits are sent to either the garden or the fire

ANGELS SURROUNDING THE ALMIGHTINESS THRONE

On the Day when the skies, together with the clouds, shall burst asunder, and the angels shall descend in a mighty descent. On that Day [it will become obvious to all that] true sovereignty belongs to the Most Gracious [alone]. (25:25-26) The sky will rent asunder, for frail it will have become on that Day. The angels [will appear] at its ends, and, above them, eight will bear aloft on that Day the throne of thy Sustainer's almightiness. (69:16-17) When the earth is shattered with crushing upon crushing, and [the majesty of] thy Sustainer stands revealed, and [the true nature of] the angels, rank upon rank? (89:21-22) O man, you have been toiling towards thy Sustainer in painful toil—then you shall meet Him! (84:6) Oh, verily, they doubt whether they will meet their Sustainer [on Judgment Day]! Oh, verily, He encompasses everything! (41:54)

Since God is infinite in space and time, His "throne" has a purely metaphorical connotation, His absolute, unfathomable sway over all that exists (see 7:54). The "bearing aloft" of His almightiness's throne also symbolizes the full manifestation of that almightiness on the Day of Judgment. Quranic passages do not mention who or what the "eight" are. Some speculate that they are eight angels. It is believed by others that there are eight ranks of angels. Some admit that it is impossible to say whether "eight" or "eight thousand" is meant. The Quran states elsewhere, "None save God knows its final meaning" (see 3:7).

In man's life-whether one is consciously aware of it or not—sorrow, pain, drudgery, and worry outweigh the rare moments of true happiness and satisfaction. Thus, the human condition is described as "painful toiling towards the Sustainer" when God reveals His transcendental majesty.

ONE WHO HOLDS ABSOLUTE SWAY OVER EVERYTHING

What do they ask one another [most often]? They utterly disagree about the awesome tidings [of the resurrection]. But in time they will understand [it]! And again, in time they will understand! (78:1-5) High above all orders [of being] is He, enthroned in almightiness. By His Own will He inspires whomever of His servants. To warn [all human beings of the coming] of the Day when they shall meet Him. The Day when they come forth [from death], with nothing hidden from God. With whom all sovereignty rests on that Day? With God, the One who holds absolute sway over all that exists! (40:15-16)

DESTINED TO MEET THEIR SUSTAINER

Not one of all [the beings] in the heavens or on earth appears before the Most Gracious except as a servant. Indeed, He has full cognizance of them, and has numbered them with an [unfailing] system. They will appear before Him on resurrection Day alone. (19:93-95) [On that Day] We will [resurrect the dead and] gather them all together, leaving none behind. And they will be lined up before thy Sustainer, [and He will say]: [To those *who* denied the truth of resurrection] *"Now, indeed, you have come to Us [in a lonely state], even as We created you in the first instance. Although you used to assert that We would never appoint a meeting [with Us]! (18:47-48) [And God shall say]: "And now, indeed, you have come unto Us in a lonely state, even as We created you in the first instance." (6:94)*

These passages stress everyone's individual, nontransferable responsibility.

Unto Him you shall return and never—not on earth and not in the skies—you can elude Him. You have none to protect you from God, and none to bring you succor. [As a result], they who deny the truth of God's messages or of their [ultimate] meeting with Him abandon all hope of My grace and mercy. Grievous suffering awaits them [in the life to come]. (29:21-23) He alone grants life and deals death, and to Him you all must return. (10:56)

Those who deny God deprive themselves of God's grace and mercy. In other words, belief in God or one's readiness to believe in Him is, in and by itself, already an outcome of His grace and mercy. Just as suffering in the hereafter is an outcome of being "bent on denying the truth." By implication, they, who reject the resurrection, reject God's existence. They deceive themselves by asserting that they believe in God and, at the same time, reject life after death.

NONE WILL SPEAK WITHOUT GOD'S LEAVE

On that Day, all will follow the summoning Voice from which there will be no escape. All sounds will be hushed before the Most Gracious, and you will hear nothing but a faint sough in the air. (20:108) None shall have it in their power to raise their voices unto Him on the Day when all [human] souls and all the angels will stand up in ranks. None will speak but he to whom the Most Gracious will give leave, and all will speak [only] what is right. That will be the Day of Ultimate Truth. (78:37-39)

The statement that he whom God will allow to speak "will say only what is right" implies the impossibility of anyone being untruthful on Judgment Day. It will be the moment when the ultimate reality of human life and its purpose becomes fully accessible to man's understanding.

FACES OVERCAST WITH DESPAIR

When that Day comes, not a soul will speak, unless by His leave. Those who are [gathered together], some will be wretched and some happy. (11:105) And some faces will on that Day be covered with dust, with darkness overspread, with despair, knowing that a crushing calamity is about to befall them. They denied the truth and were immersed in iniquity! (80:40-42) Before Us will all of them be arraigned [and told]: "Today, then, no human being shall be wronged in the least, nor shall you be requited for aught but what you were doing [on earth]." (36:53-54)

PLACING DISPUTES BEFORE GOD FOR JUDGMENT

Yet, you are bound to die, [O Muhammad] and they, too, are bound to die. Then, on resurrection, you will all bring your dispute before your Sustainer. It is Thou who will judge between Thy servants [on resurrection Day] regarding all on which they differ!" (39:30-31) Oh, verily, unto God belongs all that is in the heavens and on earth. He knows exactly where you stand and what you aim for! And one day, all [who have ever lived] will be brought back to Him, and then He will make them [truly] understand all that they were doing [in life]. God has full knowledge of everything. (24:64)

TESTIMONIES OF PROPHETS AND SATAN

PROPHET MUHAMMAD AS A WITNESS

How, then, [will the sinners fare on Judgment Day] when We shall bring forward witnesses from within every community, and bring thee [O Prophet] as a witness against them? Those who were bent on denying the truth and paid no heed to the Apostle, wish the earth would swallow them on that Day. They shall not conceal from God anything that has happened. (4:41-42)

On the Day of Judgment, the prophets whom God has called forth within every community will symbolically testify that they delivered God's message and explained to them the meaning of right and wrong.

And when all the apostles are called together at a time appointed. (77:11) Thus, [on Judgment Day] We shall most certainly call to account all those to whom the [divine] message was sent and call to account the message-bearers [themselves]. Thereupon We shall most certainly reveal to them Our knowledge [of their actions], for We have never been absent from them at any time. (7:6-7) But one Day, We shall raise up a witness out of every community. They who were bent on denying the truth will not be allowed to plead [ignorance], and neither will they be allowed to make amends. (16:84)

The term "the apostle" is used here in its generic sense and refers to all the apostles who preached God's message. "Witnesses from within every community" refers to the earlier apostles, of whom every community or civilization had a share. The prophets will bear witness for or against those to whom they conveyed God's message. Sinners will be denied the right to plead ignorance, depriving them of any subsequent excuse.

And the record [of everyone's deeds] will be laid bare. All the prophets will be brought forward as witnesses, and judgment will be passed on them all in justice. And they will not be wronged, for everyone will be repaid in full for whatever [good or evil] he has done. He is fully aware of all that they do. (39:69-70)

ASKING SINNERS FOR THEIR RESPONSE TO MESSAGE-BEARERS

And on that Day, He will call unto them, [Those who rejected the *message*-bearers], *and ask: "How did you respond to My message bearers?" But all arguments and excuses will have already been erased from their minds. They will not [be able to] obtain any [helpful] answer from one another. (28:65-66)*

TESTIMONIALS AGAINST OUR OWN SELVES

And in this manner do We cause evildoers to seduce one another by their [evil] doings. [And thus, God will continue]: "O you who have lived in close communion with [evil] invisible beings and [like-minded] humans! Have there not come unto you apostles from among yourselves, who conveyed My message and warned you of the coming of this Day [of Judgment]?" They will answer: "We do bear witness against ourselves!" For the life of this world beguiled them: and so, they will bear witness against themselves that they denied the truth. (6:129-130)

Man's newly awakened consciousness will compel him to bear witness against himself on Judgment Day. The expression "in this manner," which introduces the above sentence, is an allusion to the way the evil ones "whisper unto one another glittering half-truths meant to delude the mind" (6:112).

TESTIMONY OF SATAN: I DECEIVED YOU

And when everything has been decided, Satan will say: "Behold, God promised you something that was bound to come true! I too made [all manner of] promises to you—but I deceived you. Yet I had no power over you. I called you and you responded to me. Hence, blame not me, but blame yourselves. It is not for me to respond to your cry, nor for you to react to mine. I have [always] refused to admit that there was any truth in your erstwhile belief that I had a share in God's divinity. (14:22)

Through insinuations, Satan reaches the soul of the sinner. These satanic insinuations would have had no effect if not for an already existing evil disposition due to lust, anger, superstition, or fanciful ideas.

Satan will reply that he cannot respond to your call for help, just as you should not have, in your lifetime, responded to his call. While leading men astray, Satan never claims to be God's equal. Satan, rather, tries to make men's sinful actions "seem good to them," i.e., he persuades them that it is morally justifiable to follow one's fancies and selfish desires without restraint.

Satan has made all their own doings seem good to them. He is [as] close to them today [as he was to past sinners]. Hence, grievous suffering awaits them. (16:63)

While Satan himself does not claim equality with God, the sinner who submits to Satan's blandishments attributes him thereby, "a share in God's divinity."

RENDERING OF PERFECT JUSTICE

Their spiritual journey will continue with suffering on Judgment Day. During the agonizing wait after the resurrection, sinners will be given ample opportunity to contemplate the imminent punishment for their past deeds. All those lost in sin in their worldly life will undergo catharsis or soul-cleansing through spiritual punishment. On the Day of Judgment, the unrepentant sinners fall into two categories:

(a) LESSER GUILTY AMONG UNREPENTANT SINNERS

Those who were less guilty among unrepentant sinners will suffer the agony and intense fear of the Day of Judgment. God will spare them from the ultimate punishment of the fire of Hell. The Prophet said, "As for those who have been unjust to themselves (by sinning), they are detained throughout the long resurrection period. Then God shall cover them with His mercy, and they will say, 'Thanks to God Who has removed sorrow from us!'"

(b) HARDENED CRIMINALS AND TRULY GUILTY

Hardened criminals and the truly guilty will be driven toward Hell as a thirsty herd. They will be gathered on their knees, around Hell. Even some among this group of vile sinners who vaguely knew God would be spared from the fire. This is because God's mercy prevails over His wrath. In the end, those who have been most determined in their disdainful rebellion against the Most Gracious will suffer from Hellfire.

GOD IS THE MOST JUST OF JUDGES

And [as for thyself, O Muhammad] follow what is revealed to thee and be patient in adversity, until God gives His judgment. He is the best of all judges. (10:109) He [God] cannot be called to account for whatever He does, whereas they will be called to account. Yet, they choose to worship [imaginary] deities instead of Him! (21:23-24) And with Him rest all judgment and to Him shall you all be brought back. (28:70) What, then, [O man], could cause you to give the lie to this moral law? Is not God the most just of judges? (95:7-8)

The above rhetorical question has this implication: Since the moral law referred to here and stressed in the teachings of all monotheistic religions, its truth ought to be self-evident to any unprejudiced mind. The rejection of the moral law negates justice on God's part the most just of all judges.

SINNERS GROUPED ACCORDING TO THE GRAVITY OF SINS

And on that Day, We shall gather from within every community a host of those who gave the lie to Our messages. They will be grouped [according to the gravity of their sins] until they shall come [to be judged]. He will say: "Did you give the lie to My messages even though you failed to encompass them with knowledge? [Or without understanding them.] *Or what was it that [you thought] you were doing?" And the word [of truth] will stand revealed against them in the face of all the wrong they had committed, and they will not [be able to] utter a single word [of excuse]. (27:83-85)*

The phrase "the word [of truth] will stand revealed against them" refers to the truth becoming obvious to them against all their expectations and that will confound them utterly at the approach of the Last Hour, resurrection, and God's Judgment, all of which they regarded as "fables of ancient times." Alternatively, the phrase may be understood as when the sentence of doom is passed on them at the approach of the Last Hour when it will be too late for repentance.

THE FINAL JUDGMENT OF UNREPENTANT SINNERS

On that Day, all dominion shall [visibly] belong to God. He shall judge [all men and distinguish] between them. Shameful suffering awaits all those who deny the truth and gave the lie to Our messages. (22:56-57) And there shall be those who have lost themselves to evil. Oh, how [unhappy] they will be who have lost themselves to evil! (56:9) Those [who have died] are brought before God, their true Lord Supreme. Oh, verily, His alone is all judgment and He is the swiftest of all reckoners! (6:62)

There will be no hope on the Day of Judgment for those who failed to realize God's existence or to submit to His guidance. The God of the Quran is Omnibenevolent, and the strong emphasis on God's mercy should not conjure up a permissive deity. God's mercy exists in dialectical tension with His justice. God's perfect justice is based on the belief that He knows and sees all.

SINNERS DRIVEN CLOSE TO HELL

On that day when We shall drive those who were lost in sin to hell as a thirsty herd is driven to a well. (19:85-86). Hence, [warn all men of] the Day when the enemies of God shall be gathered before the fire, and then shall be driven onward, (till, when they come close to it, their hearing and their sight and their [very] skins will bear witness against them, speaking of what they were doing [on earth]. And they will ask their skins, "Why did you bear witness against us?" [And] these will reply: "God, who gives speech to all things, has given speech to us [as well]. For He [it is who] has created you in the first instance - and unto Him you are [now] brought back. And you did not try to hide [your sins] lest your hearing or your sight or your skins bear witness against you: nay, but you thought that God did not know much of what you were doing. That very thought about your Sustainer has brought you to perdition, and so now you find yourselves among the lost!" And then, [even] if they endure [their lot] in patience, the fire will still be their abode; **and if they pray to be allowed to make amends, they will not be allowed to do so.** *(41:19-24)* [Lit., "they will not be of those who are allowed to make amends": an allusion to the request of the doomed, on the Day of Judgment, to be granted a "second chance" on earth, and to God's refusal of this request (cf. 6:27-28 and 32:12).

MOST DETERMINED AND HARDENED SINNERS

And so, by thy Sustainer, [on Judgment Day] We shall bring them forth together with the satanic forces [which impelled them in life]. We shall gather them on their knees, around hell. Thereupon We shall, indeed, draw forth from every group [of sinners] the ones that were most determined in their disdainful rebellion against the Most Gracious. For, indeed, We know best which of them is most deserving of hellfire. And every one of you [who refuses to believe in the resurrection] *will come within sight of it. This is, with thy Sustainer, a decree that must be fulfilled. And once again, We shall save [from hell] those who have been conscious of Us but We shall leave the evildoers on their knees. (19:68-72)*

Sinners will be symbolically linked to the satanic forces that motivated them throughout their lives. Only those hardened and most determined sinners who have consciously and deliberately rejected the idea of man's responsibility to God. They have thus led their weaker, less-conscious fellow men astray and will be consigned to the deepest suffering in the hereafter. They will be utterly humbled and crushed by their belated realization of God's judgment and ethical truths, which they had arrogantly neglected in life. As the last sentence above indicates, not every one of the sinners will be irrevocably consigned to the suffering described in the Quran as hell. God's mercy will prevail over His wrath against those sinners who were vaguely conscious of Him. In the end, only the most hardened sinners will enter hell.

SINS ATONED BY COMMENSURATE SUFFERING

Those who have done evil deeds—the recompense of an evil deed shall be the like thereof. They will have none to defend them against God—ignominy will overshadow them as though their faces were veiled by the night's own darkness. It is they who are destined for fire, therein to abide. (10:27)

When divine justice prevails on the Day of Judgment, retribution will correspond in direct proportion to the degree of one's guilt. There will be corresponding suffering for unatoned sins in the hereafter. Hell is, therefore, the continuation of earthly life, not arbitrary punishment.

THE MYTH OF INTERCESSION

GOD'S OMNISCIENCE PRECLUDES INTERCESSION

Say: "Do you [think you could] inform God of anything in the heavens or on earth that He does not know?" (10:18) You have none to protect you from God, and none to intercede for you [on Judgment Day]. Will you not, then, bethink yourselves? (32:4) Hence, warn them of that Day which draws ever nearer, when the hearts will chokingly come up to the throats. Evildoers will have no loving friend, nor intercessor who will listen to them. [For] He is aware of the stealthiest glance, and of all that hearts would conceal. (40:18-19)

God's omniscience is the reason why there can be no intercession with Him since He knows the secrets of the heart and even the stealthiest glances. The belief in the efficacy of anyone's unqualified intercession with God, or mediation between man and Him, is equated with a denial of God's omniscience (all-knowing), which takes all the circumstances of the sinner and his sin into consideration. Thus, the Quran rejects the popular but false belief among Muslims in unqualified "intercession" by living or dead saints or prophets.

SYMBOLIC INTERCESSION FOR GREAT SINNERS
(Exception)

Who could intercede with Him, unless by His leave? (2:255) There is none that could intercede with Him unless He grants permission to do so. (10:3) [On that Day] none will have [the benefit of] intercession unless he has [in his lifetime] entered in a bond with the Most Gracious. (19:87) On that Day, intercession shall be of no avail [to any] save him in whose case the Most Gracious will have granted leave, therefore, and whose word [of faith] He will have accepted. [For] He knows all that lies open before men and all that is hidden from them, whereas they cannot encompass Him with their knowledge. (20:109-110)

God will grant His prophets on Judgment Day the permission to "intercede," **symbolically**, for those sinners who have already achieved His redemptive acceptance by their repentance or basic goodness. In other words, the right of intercession thus granted to the prophets will be an expression of God's approval of sinners' salvation.

The "bond with God" refers to the sinner's realization that God is one and unique. Even great sinners may hope for God's forgiveness, symbolically expressed by the right of "intercession," which will be granted to the prophets on Judgment Day provided that, during their life on earth, sinners accepted God's existence and oneness.

CHAPTER 21
THE FIRE OF HELL

(THE FIRST SYMBOL OF TORMENT)

WHY HELL IS NECESSARY?

If hell does not exist, then famous tyrants such as Hitler, Stalin, and countless cruel rulers throughout history—criminals who got away with murder, rape, and the oppression of other human beings—will have the same end as the righteous. If that is true, then God either does not exist or is unjust for granting free will to men to commit evil deeds. He is then not holding them responsible for their acts.

Hell's portrayal is very graphic with its account of molten metal, boiling liquids, and fire that splits everything. Imagine the greatest suffering, bodily and spiritual, that a man may experience. This suffering is burning with fire, utter loneliness, and bitter desolation, the torment of unceasing frustration, a condition of neither living nor dying. Imagine this pain, this darkness, and this despair, intensified beyond anything ever seen in this world and entirely different from anything imaginable. You will know, however vaguely, what hell is.

FOUR SYMBOLS OF TORMENT OF HELL

And leave Me alone [to deal] with those who give the lie to the truth—those who enjoy the blessings of life [without any thought of God] for, behold, heavy fetters [await them] with Us, and a blazing fire, and food that chokes, and grievous suffering. (73:11-13)

These four conditions are symbolic of torment in the hereafter, denoting the spiritual consequences of one's actions in life. All descriptions of otherworldly suffering or "hell" will be utterly dissimilar to all earthly experiences, including its immeasurable intensity. Similarly, all Quranic descriptions of a sinner suffering in the hereafter are metaphors or allegories relating to situations and conditions. These metaphors can be understood only using comparisons with physical phenomena that fall within human experience. Explaining this symbolism of torment in the hereafter, Razi says: "These four conditions may well be understood as denoting the spiritual consequences (of one's doings in life).

3. Thereupon (the sinner) tries to swallow the choking agony of deprivation and the pain of separation (from the objects of his desire): and this is the meaning of the words, 'and **food that chokes**'.

HELLFIRE THE FIRST SYMBOL

Those spiritual shackles generate spiritual 'fires,' because one's strong inclination towards bodily concerns, together with the impossibility of attaining to them, give rise, spiritually, to (a sensation of) severe burning, and this is (the meaning of) 'the **blazing fire**' (al-jahim). Blazing fire is one of the symbols of hell's torment. Fire purifies the soul. The concept of fire of hell is referred to in the Quran under different names, namely *nar* (fire), *jahim* (blazing fire), *sair* (blazing flame), *saqar* (hellfire), *laza* (raging flame), and *hutamah* (crushing torment).

THE OUTCOME OF YOUR ACTIONS

We shall make him taste suffering through fire [and he shall be told]: "This is an outcome of what your own hands have wrought—for, never does God do the least wrong to His creatures!" (22:9-10) [But] behold, they who are lost in sin shall abide in the suffering of hell. It will not be made lighter for them, and they will be lost in hopeless despair. And it is not We who will do wrong to them, but it is they who will have wronged themselves. (43:74-76)

The expression "they shall abide (khalidun) in the suffering of hell" indicates only a limited period but does not convey the meaning of perpetuity.

OBLIVIOUS OF GOD

[And He will say unto the sinners]: "Taste, then, [the penalty] for you been oblivious of the coming of this your Day [of Judgment]— for, verily, We are [now] oblivious to you. Taste, then, [this] abiding suffering for all [the evil] that you did!" (32:14) And on that Day, We shall place hell, for all to see, before those who denied the truth. Their eyes had been veiled against any remembrance of Me because they could not bear to listen [to the voice of truth]! Do they who are bent on denying the truth think, perhaps, that they could take [any of] My creatures as protectors against Me? We have ready hell to welcome all those who deny the truth! (18:100-102) Behold, the wicked will, indeed, be in a blazing fire - [a fire] which they shall enter on Judgment Day, and which they shall not [be able to] escape. (82:13-16)

WORSHIP OTHER THAN GOD

The blazing fire will be laid open before those lost in grievous error. They will be asked: "Where is now all that you worshipped instead of God? Can these [things and beings] be of any help to you?" (26:91-93) On the Day when those who were bent on denying the truth will be brought within sight of the fire [and will be asked], "Is not this the truth?" They will answer, "Yea, by Our Sustainer!" [And] He will say: "Taste, then, this suffering as an outcome of your denial of the truth!" (46:34)

FOLLOWERS OF SATAN DESTINED FOR THE BLAZING FLAME

Satan is a foe to you; therefore, treat him as a foe. He calls on his followers to the end that they might find themselves among those who are destined for blazing flame. [Seeing that] for those who deny the truth, severe suffering awaits. (35:6-7)

BLAZING FIRE

And so, when the mighty, overwhelming event [of resurrection] comes to pass, on that Day man will [clearly] remember all that he has ever toiled over. The blazing fire [of hell] will be laid open before all who [are destined to] see it. For him who transgressed the bounds of what is right and preferred the life of this world [to the good of his soul], that blazing fire will truly be the goal! (79:34-39) Therefore, I will make him endure hellfire [in the life to come]! And what could make thee think what hellfire is? It does not allow you to live, and neither does it let you die, rendering [all truth] visible to mortal men. (74:26-29)

The term "Hellfire" is one of the seven names given in the Quran to the concept of suffering in the hereafter, which man brings upon himself by sinning. "Rendering [all truth] visible to mortals" refers to the sinner's belated cognition of the truth, as well as to his distressing insight into his personal nature, past failings, and deliberate wrongdoings. He now realizes his responsibility for the suffering in store for him: a state neither of life nor of death.

Consider the moon! Consider the night when it departs, and the morning when it dawns! That [hellfire] is indeed one of the great [forewarnings] to mortal man—to everyone, whether he chooses to come forward or hang back! [On the Day of Judgment] every human being will be held in a pledge for whatever [evil] he has wrought. (74:32-38)

Just as the changing phases of the moon and the alternation of night and day are the outcomes of God-given, natural laws, so, too, a sinner's suffering in the hereafter is but a natural consequence of his deliberate wrongdoing in this world. The Hellfire is an awesome forewarning regardless of whether one has chosen to come forward and follow or to disregard and hang back from the divine call, implying that even true believers may stumble into sinning, and hence need to be warned.

If they only knew those bent on denying the truth— [that there will come] a time when they will not be able to ward off the fire from their faces, nor from their backs, and will not find any succor! (21:38-39)

On the Day when they shall be thrust into the fire with [an irresistible] thrust, [and will be told]: "This is the fire which you used to call a lie! Was it, then, a delusion—or did you fail to see [its truth]? Endure it [now]! But [whether you] bear with patience or not, it will be the same for you. You are being requited for what you did." (52:13-16) When they are cast into that [hell], they will hear its breath gurgling as it boils up, well-nigh bursting with fury. Every time a host [of such sinners] is flung into it, its keepers will ask them, "Has no warner ever come to you?" They will reply: "Yea, a warner did indeed come to us, but we gave him the lie and said, 'Never has God sent down anything [by way of revelation]! You [self-styled warners] are lost in a great delusion!'" And they will add: "Had we listened [to those warnings], or [at least] used our own reason, we would not [now] be among those who are destined for the blazing flame!" Thus, they will come to realize their sins but [by that time] remote will have become all good from those who are destined for the blazing flame. (67:7-11)

Reason, properly used, must lead man to a cognition of God's existence and, thus, of the fact that a definite plan underlies all His creation. A logical concomitant of that cognition is the realization that certain aspects of the divine plan touching upon human life—in particular, the distinction between right and wrong—are being continuously disclosed to man through revelation, which God bestows on His chosen message-bearers, the prophets. This innate "bond with God" (referred to in 2:27) may be broken only at the expense of man's spiritual future, with suffering in the life to come as the inevitable alternative.

SPIRITUAL DISGRACE

Limitless art Thou in Thy glory! Keep us safe, then, from suffering through fire! "O our Sustainer! Whomsoever Thou shall commit to the Fire, him, verily, wilt Thou have brought to disgrace [in this world], and such evildoers will have none to succor them. (3:192)

The suffering which a sinner will have to undergo in the life to come will be a consequence of the spiritual disgrace which he has already brought upon himself by his actions **in this world.**

UNREPENTANT SINNERS IN THE FIRE

On the other hand, could one on whom [God's] sentence of suffering has been passed [be rescued by man]? Could you, perhaps, save one who is in the fire? (39:19)

God always accepts sinners' sincere repentance, provided it is proffered before death. The "sentence of suffering" refers to those who die without repentance. After death, they become aware of the coming punishment, so they find themselves, as it were, "already in the fire."

SPARKS FROM GIANT BURNING LOGS

Woe on that Day to those who give the lie to the truth! Go on towards the [resurrection] which you called a lie! Continue towards the threefold shadow that will offer no [cooling] shade and be of no avail against the flame which beholds! - will throw up sparks like [burning] logs, like giant fiery ropes! (77:28-33) For those who give the lie to [the announcement of] the Last Hour We have readied a blazing flame. When it faces them from afar, they will hear its angry roar and hiss. When they are flung, linked [all] together, into a tight space within, they will pray for extinction there and then! [But they will be told]: "Pray not today for one single extinction but pray for many extinctions!" (25:11-14)

The "tight space" into which they will be thrown refers to distress accompanied by a feeling of constriction. Although the concept of "extinction" implies finality and is, therefore, unrepeatable, the sinners' praying for "many extinctions" is used here as a metonym for their indescribable suffering and a desire for a final escape.

THROWN BACK INTO FIRE

As for those who are lost in iniquity—their goal is the Fire: as often as they try to come out of it, they will be thrown back into it; and they will be told, "Taste [now] this suffering through the fire which you use were wont to call a lie!" (32:20) A flash of fire will be let loose upon you, and smoke, and you will be left without succor! ((55:35)

NEITHER ALIVE NOR DEAD

Remind, then, [others of the truth, regardless of] whether this reminding [would be of use [or not]. He who stands in awe of God will keep it in mind. (the Divine reminder) *Aloof from it* (the Divine reminder) *will remain that most hapless wretch—he who [in the life to come] shall have to endure the great fire wherein he will neither die nor remain alive. (87:9-13)*

BURNING DESPAIR

If one happens to be of those who call the truth a lie, and [thus] turn astray, a welcome of burning despair [awaits him in the life to come] and the heat of a blazing fire! This is indeed the truth of truth. [Or the truth most certain] *(56:92-96) Are you not aware of those who have preferred a denial of the truth to God's blessings, and [thereby] invited their people to alight in that abode of utter desolation—hell—which they [themselves] will have to endure? And how vile a state to settle in! For, they claimed that powers rival God, and so they strayed from His path. Say: "Enjoy yourselves [in this world], but, verily, fire will be your journey's end!" (14:28-30)*

"Those who have preferred a denial of the truth" is an allusion to the relationship between the arrogant leaders of thought and their weak followers, who have exchanged God's blessings for a denial of the truth.

FACES TOSSED AROUND IN BLAZING FIRE

Verily, God has rejected the deniers of the truth, and has prepared for them a blazing fire, to abide beyond the count of time. No protectors will they find, and none to bring them succor. On the Day when their faces shall be tossed about in the fire, they will exclaim, "Oh, would that we had paid heed unto God, and paid heed unto the Apostle!" (33:64-66) They who shall come with evil deeds—their faces will be thrust into the fire, [and they will be asked]: "Is this aught but a just requital for what you were doing [in life]?" (27:90)

Those who did only evil, or whose evil deeds outnumber their righteous deeds, are annihilated and reduced to utter passivity in the fire.

PRONE ON THEIR FACES, BLIND, DEAF, AND DUMB

We shall gather them together on the resurrection day. [They will lie] prone upon their faces, blind, dumb and deaf, with hell as their goal. Every time [the fire] subsides, We will intensify its flame for them. Such will be their requital for having rejected Our messages and having said, "After we have become bones and dust, shall we, forsooth, be raised from the dead in a new act of creation?" (17:97-98)

The denial of God's power to resurrect the dead is equivalent to a denial of His almightiness and Being. All of which is characterized by the words "blind, deaf, and dumb" in the preceding verse. God can resurrect them individually, each having the same identity (or "likeness") before death.

GARMENTS OF FIRE

But [thus it is] as for those who are bent on denying the truth, garments of fire shall be cut out for them [in the life to come]. Burning despair will be poured over their heads, causing all that is within their bodies, and skins, to melt away. And they shall be held [in this state as if] by iron grips; and every time they try in their anguish to come out of it, they shall be returned and [be told]: "Taste suffering through fire [to the fullest]!" (22:19-22)

The allegorical descriptions of the suffering that will befall sinners in the hereafter, cause their inner and outer personalities to disintegrate. "They shall be held in the iron grip" denotes the inescapability of the suffering in the hereafter to which "they who are bent on denying the truth" condemn themselves.

BURNT SKIN REPLACED OVER AND OVER AGAIN

And nothing could be as burning as [intensely as the fire of] hell. Those who are bent on denying the truth of Our messages We shall, in time, cause to endure fire. Every time their skins are burned off, We shall replace them with new skins, so that they may taste suffering [in full]. Verily, God is almighty and wise. (4:55-56) And [on that Day] the evil of their doings will become obvious to them, and they will be overwhelmed by the very thing they used to deride. And [the word] will be spoken: "Today, We shall be oblivious to you as you were oblivious of the coming of this your Day [of Judgment], and so your goal is the fire, and you shall have none to succor you. This is because you made God's messages the target of your mockery, having allowed the life of this world to beguile you!" On that Day, therefore, they will not be brought out of the fire, nor will they be allowed to make amends. (45:33-35)

SINNERS FUEL OF THE FIRE

"O our Sustainer! Verily, Thou wilt gather humanity together to witness the Day [the coming of] which there is no doubt: verily, God never fails to fulfill His promise. Behold, as for those who are bent on denying the truth, neither their worldly possessions nor their offspring will in the least avail them against God; and it is they, they who shall be the fuel of the fire! (3:9-10)

BLIND IMITATION OF ERRING PREDECESSORS

And once again, the blazing fire is their ultimate goal. For, they found their forebears on the wrong path, and [now] they make haste to follow in their footsteps! Thus, indeed, most of the people of old went astray before them, although, We had sent warners unto them: and what happened in the end to those that had been warned [to no avail]! Except for God's true servants, [most people are apt to go astray.] (37:68-74)

"Follow in their footsteps," or blind imitation of the absurd beliefs, valuations, and customs of one's erring predecessors, and disregard of all evidence of the truth supplied by both reason and divine revelation is here shown to be the principal cause of the suffering.

GROUPED TOGETHER WITH SINNERS OF OLDEN TIMES

Woe on that Day unto those who give the lie to the truth— that Day on which they will [unable to] utter a word, nor be allowed to make excuses! (77:34-36) Woe on that Day to those who give the lie to the truth—that Day of Distinction [between the true and the false, when they will be told]: "We have brought you together with those [sinners] of olden times; and if you [think you] have a trick left, try to outwit Me!" (77:34-40)

ICY-COLD DARKNESS

Verily, the most evil of all goals awaits those who are wont to transgress the bounds of what is right: hell will they have to endure - and how vile a resting place! This, [then, for them so let them taste it: burning despair and ice-cold darkness and coupled with it, further [suffering] of a similar nature. [And they will say to one another: "Do you see] this crowd of people who rushed headlong [into sin] with you? [I.e., "people whom you had seduced, and who thereupon blindly followed you": an apostrophe stressing the double responsibility of the seducers.] **No welcome to them! Verily, they [too] shall have to endure the fire!"** *(38:56-59)* [In Arabic usage, the phrase "no welcome to them" or "to you" (la marhaban bihim, resp.bikum) is equivalent to a curse. In this context - carried on into the next verse - it expresses a mutual disavowal of the seducers and the seduced.]

DISOWNED BY FALSELY ADORED PERSONALITIES

[On that Day] it will come to pass that those who were [falsely] adored [saints or alleged divine personalities] *shall reject their followers. The latter shall see the suffering [that awaits them], with all their hopes* [of salvation] *cut to pieces! And then those followers shall say: "Would that we had a second chance [in life], so that we could disown them as they have disowned us!" Thus, God will show them their works [in a manner that will cause them] bitter regrets; but they will not come out of the fire. (2:166-167)*

SUFFERING ACCORDING TO THE WORST DEEDS

But We shall most certainly give those who are [thus] bent on denying the truth a taste of suffering severe. We shall repay them according to their worst deeds! That punishment of God's enemies will be fire [of the hereafter]. In it will they have an abode of immeasurable duration as a result of knowingly rejected Our messages. And they who [in their life on earth] were bent on denying the truth will exclaim: "O our Sustainer! Show us those invisible beings and humans that have led us astray: we shall trample them underfoot, so that they are the lowest of all!" (41:27-29)

See Surah 6:112: "Against every prophet We have set up as enemies the evil forces [*shayatin*) from among humans and invisible beings."

PUNISHMENT FOR DENYING RESURRECTION

The true promise [of resurrection] draws close [to its fulfillment]. But then, lo! The eyes of those who [in their lifetime] were bent on denying the truth will stare in horror, [and they will exclaim]: "Oh, woe unto us! We were indeed heedless of this [promise of resurrection]! We were [bent on] doing evil!" [Then they will be told]: "You and all that you worshipped instead of God are but the fuel of hell: that is what you are destined for. If those [false objects of your worship] had truly been divine, they would not have been destined for it: but [as it is, you] all shall abide therein!" Moaning will be their lot therein, and nothing [else] will they hear therein. (21:97-100)

But they answer: "When will that final decision take place, if what you [believers] say is true?" Say: "On the Day of the Final Decision, their [newly found] faith will be of no use to those who [in their lifetime] were bent on denying the truth, nor will they be granted respite!" And then leave them alone and wait [for the truth to unfold as] they are waiting. (32:28-30)

They who blunder along, and are lost in ignorance, they who ask mockingly: "When is that Day of Judgment to be?" [It will be] a Day when they will be sorely tried by fire, [and will be told:] "Taste, this is your trial! It is this that you so hastily ask for!" (51:11-14)

GOOD DEEDS ARE OUTWEIGHED BY DENYING RESURRECTION

"As for those who care for [no more than] the life of this world and its bounties, We shall repay them in full for all that they did in this [life], and they shall not be deprived of their just due therein." [Yet] it is they who, in the life to come, shall have nothing but the fire—for in vain shall be all that they wrought in this [world], and worthless all that they ever did!" Can, then, [he who cares for no more than the life of this world be compared with] one who takes his stand on clear evidence from his Sustainer, conveyed through [this] testimony from Him, as was the revelation vouchsafed to Moses aforetime—[a divine writ ordained by Him] to be a guidance and grace [unto man]? They [who understand this message—it is they alone who truly] believe in it. Oh, verily, God's rejection is the due of all evildoers who turn others away from God's path and try to make it appear crooked—since it is they, they who refuse to acknowledge the truth of the life to come! (11:15-19)

Although their good deeds will be taken fully into account on Judgment Day, they will be outweighed by the sinner's refusal to believe in the resurrection and the life to come. Their refusal to believe in life after death is the ultimate cause of their wrongdoing. In other words, belief in the resurrection, God's judgment, and life in the hereafter are postulated as the only valid and lasting source of human morality.

But what about a person who leads a comfortable, even rich life but also one of virtue and generosity? He hopes the afterlife promise is true, but who can't believe it? Is this person still condemned to hell's fire? See Chapter, "Accounting of the Righteous among Nonbelievers and Those in Limbo." Accounting of the Righteous among nonbelievers and those in limbo" for an answer.

CHAPTER 20
HEAVY FETTERS

(THE SECOND SYMBOL OF TORMENT)

Heavy fetters are a symbol of the soul's remaining shackled to its (erstwhile) physical attachments and bodily pleasures and now that their realization has become impossible, those fetters and shackles prevent the (resurrected) human personality (an-nafs) from attaining the realm of the spirit and of purity.

SINNERS LINKED TOGETHER IN FETTERS

[Thereupon the command will go forth]: "Lay hold of him, and shackle him, and then let him enter hell, and then thrust him into a chain [of other sinners like him—a chain] of seventy cubits. For, behold, he did not believe in God, the Tremendous, and did not feel any urge to feed the needy: and so, no friend has he here today, nor any food save the filth which none but the sinners eat!" (69:30-37)

A fetter is a shackle or chain attached to someone's ankles to restrict their movement. All who were lost in sin were linked together in fetters. The chain is exceedingly long. The number "seventy" is often used in classical Arabic for "very many." Only God knows the length. The term "filth" refers to the devouring of all that is abominable in the spiritual sense. None but the only sinners metaphorically eat in this world and, consequently, in the hereafter.

SINNERS LINKED TOGETHER IN CHAINS

On that Day you will see all who were lost in sin linked together in fetters, clothed in garments of black pitch, with fire veiling their faces. [And all shall be judged on that Day] so that God may repay every human being for all that he has earned [in life]: verily, God is swift in reckoning! This is a message unto all mankind. Hence, let them be warned thereby, and let them know that He is the One and Only God; and let those who are endowed with insight take this to heart! (14:49-52)

The fact that sinners are chained together in fetters is indicative of the utter despair common to them all in the hereafter. It may also be an allusion to the chain reaction, which every evil deed sets in motion on earth, one evil unavoidably begetting another. The "garments of black pitch" and the "fire veiling their faces" are metaphors for the inexpressible suffering and loathsome horror that will engulf the sinners' souls on the Day of Judgment.

SHACKLES AND CHAINS AROUND THEIR NECK

Are you not aware of how far they who call God's messages in question have lost sight of the truth? They give the lie to this divine writ and [thus] to all [the messages] with which We sent forth Our apostles [of old]. (40:69-70)

Since, as the Quran so often points out, the fundamental truths outlined in all divine revelations are the same. Therefore, a rejection of the last amounts to a rejection of all the preceding ones.

But in time they will come to know [how blind they have been. They will know it on Judgment Day], when they shall have to carry the shackles and chains [of their own making] around their necks and are dragged into burning despair, and in the end become fuel for the fire [of hell]. (40:70-72)

The metaphor of "the shackles and chains" represents man's willful self-abandonment to false values and evil ways and the resulting enslavement of the spirit.

And then they will be asked: "Where now are those [powers] to which you ascribed divinity side by side with God?" They will answer: "They have forsaken us or, rather, what we invoked aforetime did not exist at all!" [And they will be told]: "It is thus that God lets the deniers of the truth go astray. This is an outcome of your arrogant exultation on earth without any [concern for what is] right, and you been so full of self-conceit! Enter [now] the gates of hell, where you will live, and how vile an abode for all who are given to false pride!" (40:73-76)

"What we invoked aforetime did not exist at all," thus reflecting, belatedly, the intrinsic nothingness of all those imaginary powers and values—including the belief in man's alleged self-sufficiency and greatness—to which they paid homage in life. They allowed themselves to pursue illusions and foolish fancies due to their unwillingness to acknowledge the self-evident truth of God's existence and uniqueness and of man's utter dependence on Him.

Hence, thou remain patient in adversity—for, verily, God's promise always comes true. And whether We show thee [in this world] something of what We hold in store for those [who deny the truth] or We cause thee to die [before that retribution takes place], know that, in the end, it is unto Us that they will be brought back. (40:77)

SHACKLES OF THEIR OWN MAKING

But if thou art amazed [at the marvels of God's Creation], astonishing, too, is their saying, "What? After we have become dust, shall we resurrect in a new act of creation?" It is they, who [thus show that they] are bent on denying their Sustainer. It is they who carry the shackles [of their own making] around their necks; and it is they who are destined for the fire, therein to stay. (13:5)

It is incredibly surprising that one can refuse to believe in God. This is despite all the evidence, accessible to human observation, of the existence of a definite purpose in all life-related phenomena, and thus of the existence of a conscious Creative Power.

It is no less amazing to see people who, while vaguely believing in God, refuse to believe in individual resurrection. If God has created the universe and life, He obviously has the power to re-create life and its requisite physical vehicle—in a new act of creation. By denying the possibility of resurrection, people implicitly deny God's almightiness, and thus His reality. Carrying shackles around their necks is a metaphor for man's willful self-abandonment of false values and evil ways and of the resulting enslavement of the spirit.

SINNERS DRAGGED BY THEIR FORELOCKS

All who were lost in sin shall by their marks be known and shall by their forelocks and their feet be seized! Which, then, of your Sustainer's powers can you disavow? This will be the hell which those who are lost in sin [now] call a lie: between it and [their own] burning-hot despair will they wander to and fro! (55:42-44)

"Dragged by their forelocks," alludes to their utter humiliation and disgrace. When the ancient Arabs wanted to stress someone's subjection to another person, they would say, "His forelock is in the hand of so-and-so." The allegorical nature of all Quranic descriptions of "rewards" and "punishments" in the hereafter is hinted at in the phrasing of the above verse, which speaks of sinners "wandering to and fro" between hell and burning despair-i.e., tossed between factual suffering and the despair of vain regrets.

CHAPTER 21
CHOKING FOOD

(THE THIRD SYMBOL OF TORMENT)

THE TREE OF ZAQQUM

Choking food is the third symbol of Hell's torment The sinner tries to swallow the choking agony of deprivation and the pain of separation (from the objects of his desire): and this is the meaning of the words, 'food that chokes.'

The lote tree at the boundary of paradise is paralleled by the tree of Zaqqum in the pit of hell, with its bitter smell and flowers like demon heads. As regards "the tree cursed in this Quran," it is the tree of deadly fruit spoken of in 37:62 and 44:43 as one of hell's manifestations. Quranic references to hell and paradise are allegorical. Therefore, they are liable to be grossly misunderstood if one takes them in their literal sense and arbitrarily interprets them.

And lo! We said unto thee, [O Prophet], "Behold, thy Sustainer encompasses all mankind [within His knowledge and might]. So, We have ordained that the vision We have shown thee and the tree [of hell] cursed in this Quran shall be a trial for men. Now [by Our mentioning hell] We convey a warning to them. But [for those bent on denying the truth] this [warning] only increases their gross, overweening arrogance. (17:60)

The [hellish] tree of deadly fruit, We have made it a trial for evildoers. It is a tree that grows in the heart of [hell's] blazing fire. Its fruit is [as repulsive] as Satan's heads. They [who are lost in evil] are indeed bound to eat thereof and fill their bellies therewith. And, above all this, they will be overwhelmed by burning despair! (37:62-67)

The "**vision**" is the Prophet's experience of the Ascension, preceded by the Night Journey. As this experience was and is open to conflicting interpretations and hence may give rise to doubts regarding its objective reality, it becomes—as stated in the sequence— "a trial for men." The weak of faith are shaken in their belief in Prophet Muhammad's veracity and, thus, in his prophethood. Those who firmly believe in God see in it extraordinary evidence of His spiritual grace on His chosen ones. They are, therefore, strengthened in their faith in the message of the Quran.

The "**tree of deadly fruit**"—one of the metaphors for sinners' suffering in the hereafter—has become "a trial for evildoers." It's described as "cursed" since it symbolizes hell itself and is specifically mentioned here as a warning.

"**Deadly food**," a symbol of hell, symbolizes the fact that the otherworldly sufferings that the Quran describes as "hell" are the fruit or consequence of evil deeds done on earth.

"Fruit as repulsive as Satan's head" is a purely verbal metaphor meant to express the ultimate in repulsiveness and ugliness, as Satan is the epitome of all that is evil.

EATING FROM THE TREE OF DEADLY FRUITS

[In life to come] the tree of deadly fruit will be the food of the sinful. Like molten lead, it boils in the belly, like burning despair. [And the word will be spoken]: "Seize him, [O you forces of hell] and drag him into the midst of the blazing fire. Then pour over his head anguish of burning despair! Taste it—you who [on earth] consider yourself so mighty, so noble! This is the very thing you [deniers of the truth] called in question!" (44:43-50)

INSATIABLE THIRST AND HUNGER

But as for those who persevered in evil—what of those who persevered in evil? [They will find themselves] in the midst of scorching winds, burning despair, and the shadows of black smoke, neither cooling nor soothing. For in times gone by, they abandoned themselves wholly to the pursuit of pleasures and persisted in heinous sin. They would say, "What?" After we have died and dissolved into dust and bones, shall we, forsooth, be raised from the dead? And perhaps, too, our forebears of old?" Say: "Those [sinners] of olden times and later times will indeed be gathered together at an appointed time on a Day known [only to God]. And then, O you who have gone astray and called the truth a lie, you will indeed have to taste the tree of deadly fruit. You will have to fill your bellies with it and consume [many a draught] of burning despair—drink it as the most insatiably thirsty camels' drink!" Such will be their welcome on Judgment Day! (56:41-56)

DRINKING WATERS OF BITTER DISTRESS

And [thus it is], every arrogant enemy of the truth shall be undone [in the life to come], with hell awaiting him. He shall be made to drink water of most bitter distress, gulping it [constantly], little by little, and yet hardly able to swallow it. And death will beset him from every quarter—but he shall not die for [yet more] severe suffering lies ahead of him. (14:15-17) [The parable of the recompense for sinners] is to abide in the fire and be given waters of burning despair to drink, so that it tears their bowels asunder? (47:15)

The word *sadid* signifies anything repulsive; it is also used to describe the pus that flows from wounds or the viscous liquid that oozes from corpses. The expression *ma sadid* is used here metaphorically and should be understood as "waters of most bitter distress"—a metaphor for the boundless suffering and bitter frustration that, in the life to come, awaits those who during their life in this world denied all spiritual truths.

BOILING SPRINGS AND BITTER DRY THORNS

Has there come unto you the tiding of the Overshadowing event? [On the Day of resurrection], *some faces will be downcast, toiling [under the burdens of sin], worn out [by fear], about to enter a glowing fire, given to drink from a boiling spring. No food for them, save the bitterness of dry thorns, which gives no strength and neither stills hunger. (88:1-7)*

The noun *dari* is a bitter, thorny plant in its dried state. It signifies "he became abject" or "abased," hence the rendering of this metaphorical expression as "the bitterness of dry thorns." A similarly metaphorical meaning also applies to the expression "a boiling spring."

WATER HOT LIKE MOLTEN LEAD

All who sin against themselves [by rejecting Our truth], We have prepared a fire whose billowing folds will encompass them from all sides. If they beg for water, they will be given hot water like molten lead, which will scald their faces: how dreadful a drink, and how evil a place to rest! (18:29)

The expression "billowing folds" literally denotes an awning or the outer covering of a tent. It alludes here to the billowing "walls of smoke" that will surround sinners, a symbol meant to stress the inescapability of their suffering in the hereafter.

GRIEVOUS SUFFERING
THE FOURTH SYMBOL OF TORMENT

Sinners remain deprived of all illumination by God's light, and of communion with the blessed one: and this is the meaning of the words 'grievous suffering.'

They who have bought a denial of the truth at the price of faith can never harm God, whereas grievous suffering awaits them. (3:177) But remind [them] herewith that [in the life to come] every human being shall be held in pledge for whatever wrong he has done, and shall have none to protect him from God, and none to intercede for him. Though he offers any conceivable ransom, it shall not be accepted from him. It is [people such as] these that shall be held accountable for the wrong they have done. For them, there is [in the life to come] a draught of burning despair and grievous suffering awaits them because of their persistent refusal to acknowledge the truth. (6:70)

In the Quranic eschatology, "burning despair" invariably refers to intense heat and painful cold, the allegorical suffering of sinners in the life to come. After the resurrection, the sinner might offer any atonement for his past sins, but it will not be accepted.

GOLD AS RANSOM

Those who are bent on denying the truth and die as deniers of the truth—not all the gold on earth could ever be their ransom. It is they for whom grievous suffering is in store and they shall have none to succor them. (3:90-91)

The meaning of this sentence is metaphorical; but due to the mention of ransom, some commentators believe what is meant here are otherwise good actions in this world (and efforts and possessions spent helping one's fellow men). On the strength of which such stubborn deniers of the truth might plead for God's clemency on the Day of Judgment—a plea that would be rejected for their deliberate denial of fundamental truths.

CHAPTER 22
ANGELS GUARDIANS OF HELL

And what could make you conceive what Hellfire is? It does not allow living, and neither [to die], making [all truth] visible to mortal man. Over it, there are nineteen [powers]. For We have caused none but angelic powers to lord over the fire [of hell]. We have not caused their number to be aught but a trial for those bent on denying the truth. (74-31)

The allegorical figure of nineteen represents the angels who act as keepers or guardians of hell.

AWESOME ANGELIC POWERS OVER HELL

O you who have attained faith! Ward off yourselves and those close to you that fire [of the hereafter] whose fuel is human beings and stones. [Lording] over it are angelic powers awesome [and] severe. They do not disobey God whatever He has commanded them, but [always] do what they are bidden to do. [Hence] O you bent on denying the truth, make no [empty] excuses today. [In the life to come] you shall be recompensed for what you did [in this world]. (66:6-7)

GATEKEEPERS OF HELL

And those bent on denying the truth will be urged on in throngs towards hell till, when they reach it. Its gates will be opened, and its keepers will ask them, "Have there not come to you apostles from among yourselves, who conveyed to you your Sustainer's messages and warned you of the coming of this your Day [of Judgment]?" They will answer: "Yes, indeed!" But the sentence of suffering will [already] have fallen due upon the deniers of the truth. They will be told, *"Enter the gates of hell, to abide!" And how vile an abode for those who have false pride! (39:71-72)*

As a result of their unrepentant sin, they have been subjected to suffering. Due to false pride, they refused to submit to God's apostles' guidance (see 96:6-7: "man becomes grossly overweening whenever he believes himself to be self-sufficient.").

SEVEN GATES OF HELL

And for all [those lost in grievous error], hell is the promised goal, with seven gates leading into it, each gate receiving its allotted share of sinners. (15:43-44) On that Day, We will ask Hell, "Art thou filled?" And it will answer, "[Nay] are there any more [for me]?" (50:30)

We may assume that the "seven gates of hell" signify seven approaches or ways to hell. In classical Arabic, the number "seven" is often used in the sense of "several" or "various," and so the above Quranic phrase may well mean "various ways leading to hell"—in other words.

INTERCEDE WITH GOD TO LIGHTEN SUFFERING OR CAUSE US TO DIE

And they who are in the fire will say to the keepers of hell, "Pray unto your Sustainer that He lighten, [though it is] for one day [only], this suffering of ours!" [But the keepers of hell] will ask, "Is it not [true] that your apostles came unto you with all evidence of the truth?" Those [in the fire] will reply, "Yea, indeed." [And the keepers of hell] will say, "Pray, then!" For the prayer of those who deny the truth cannot lead to aught but delusion.) (40:4749-50) And they will cry: "O you [angel] who rule [over hell]! Let thy Sustainer end us!" He will reply: "You must live on [in this state]." (43:77)

The answer that the prayers of those who deny the truth lead to delusion implies a refusal on the part of the "keepers of hell" to intercede for doomed sinners. The alternate explanation may be: Pray now to those imaginary powers to which you ascribed a share of God's divinity and see whether they can help you.

CHAPTER 23
DIALOGUE BETWEEN THE RIGHTEOUS AND THE UNREPENTANT SINNERS

WHAT HAS BROUGHT YOU INTO THE HELLFIRE?

Those who have attained righteousness [dwelling] in gardens [of paradise], they will inquire of those who were lost in sin: "What has brought you into hellfire?" They will answer: "We were not among those who prayed neither we fed the needy, and we indulged in sinning together with all [the others] who indulged in it. The Day of Judgment we called a lie— until certainty came upon us [in death]." And so, of no benefit to them could be the intercession of any that would intercede for them. (74:39-48)

For those who have attained righteousness, their conduct in life will have earned them God's forgiveness of whatever sins they may have committed. "We were not among those who prayed." At the time of this revelation, canonical prayer was not yet obligatory for followers of the Quran. It is reasonable to assume that this term is used in its broadest sense, namely, conscious belief in God. Until God grants His permission, no one will intercede for them.

GIVE US SOME OF PARADISE'S GOODIES

And the inmates of the fire will call out to the inmates of paradise: "Pour some water upon us, or some of the sustenance [of paradise] which God has provided for you!" [The inmates of paradise] will reply: "God has denied those who denied the truth and were seduced by the life of this world and made a play and passing delight of their religion!" (7:50-51)

GOOD FORTUNE TO THE BLESSED VS. THEIR MOCKERS

Those who abandoned themselves to sin and laugh at those who have attained faith and whenever they pass by them, they wink at one another [derisively]. When they returned to people of their own kind, they were full of jest. Whenever they see those [who believe] they say, "these [people] have indeed gone astray!" They have no call to watch over [the beliefs of] others. But on the Day [of Judgment], those who have attained faith will [be able to] laugh at the [erstwhile] deniers of the truth. [For resting in paradise] on couches, they will look on [and say to themselves]: "Are these deniers of the truth being [thus] paid back for what they were accustomed to do?" (83:29-36)

Those without faith have no right to criticize or watch over others' faith. Speaking of the righteous, the Quran repeatedly stresses that on the Day of Judgment, God shall have removed whatever unworthy thoughts or feelings may have been (lingering) in their bosoms. (7:42-43). Since an expression of vengeful joy on the part of the blessed at the calamity, which in the hereafter will befall the erstwhile sinners, would certainly fall into the category of unworthy feelings, their "laughing" can only have a realization of their own good fortune.

OUR SUSTAINER'S PROMISE HAS COME TRUE

And the inhabitants of paradise will call out to the fire inmates: "Now we have found that what our Sustainer promised us has proven true. Have you, too, found that what your Sustainer promised you has also come true?" [The others] will answer, "Yes!" Whereupon from their midst a voice will loudly proclaim: "God's rejection is the due of the evildoers who turn others away from God's path and try to make it appear crooked, and who refuse to acknowledge the truth of the life to come!" And between the two there will be a barrier. (7:44-46)

There will be a barrier between hell's fire and the gardens of paradise. This barrier is symbolic of the division of humanity based on the recompense meted out for actions in this world. The word *hijab* denotes anything that serves as an obstacle between things or conceals something from another. It is used in both an abstract and concrete sense. However, paradise and hell inhabitants still can communicate, as shown in the verses above.

DISPUTES AND CONTENTION AMONG THE DAMNED

MUTUAL REPROACHES OF SINNERS

On that Day, they would willingly surrender [to God] but [since it will be too late,] they will turn upon one another, demanding of each other [to relieve them of the burden of their past sins]. Some [of them] will say: "You approached us [deceptively] from the right!" [To which] the others will reply: "No, you yourselves were bereft of all faith! Moreover, we had no power over you, and you were people filled with overweening arrogance! The word of our Sustainer has now come true against us [as well]. We are bound to taste [the fruit of our sins]. So then, [if it is true that] we have caused you to err grievously—we ourselves were lost in grievous error!" On that Day they all will share in their common suffering. We will deal with all lost in sin. (37:2426-34)

The idiomatic phrase "approaching one from the right" is synonymous with pretending to give morally good advice, as well as approaching another person from a position of power and influence.

RELIEVE US FROM THIS FIRE

And lo! They [who in life denied the truth] will contend with one another in the fire [of the hereafter]. Then the weak will say to those who gloried in their arrogance, "We were your followers. Can you, then, relieve us of some [of our] share of this fire?" [To which] they who were *[once]* arrogant will reply, "We are all in it *[together]*! God judges between His creatures!" (40:47-48)

DISPUTES BETWEEN THE PEOPLE OF THE FIRE

[They will say to one another: "Do you see] this crowd of people who rushed headlong [into sin] with you? No welcome to them! They [too] shall have to endure the fire!" [They [who had been seduced] will exclaim: "No, but it is you! No welcome to you! It is you who have prepared this for us: and how vile a state to abide in!" [And] they will pray: "O our Sustainer! Whoever prepared this for us, double his suffering in the fire!" And they will add: "How is it that we do not see [here any of the] men whom we counted among the wicked, [and] whom we made the target of our derision? Or is it that [they are here, and] our eyes have missed them?" Such will be the [confusion and] mutual wrangling of the people of the fire! (38:59-64)

If the leader seduces his followers, and they follow him blindly, his responsibility would double. The phrase "no welcome to them" is equivalent to a curse; carried on into the next verse, it expresses a mutual disavowal of the seducers and the seduced. The target of their derision were the prophets and the righteous, who—as the Quran points out in many places—have always been derided by people enamored of the life of this world and, therefore, who are averse to all moral exhortation.

CONDEMNING THEIR LEADERS AND FELLOW HOST

And they will say: "O our Sustainer! We paid heed to our leaders and our great men, and it is they who have led us astray from the right path! O our Sustainer! Give them double suffering and banish them utterly from Thy grace!" (33:67-68) [And God] will say: "Join those hosts of invisible beings and humans who have gone before you into the fire!" [And] every time a host enters [the fire], it will curse its fellow hosts so much so that, when they all pass into it, one after another, the last of them will speak [thus] of the first of them: "O our Sustainer! They have led us astray. Give them double suffering through fire!" He will reply: "Every one of you deserves double suffering—but you know it not." And the first of them will say unto the last of them: "So you were not superior to us! Taste, then, this suffering for all [the evil] you did!" (7:38-39)

The first and last refer here either to a sequence in time, those who came earlier and those who came later, or to status, leaders, and followers. In both cases, they relate, as the next sentence indicates, to the evil influence the former exerted on the latter during their lifetime. This was either directly, as leaders of thought and persons of distinction, or indirectly, as forerunners in time, whose example was followed by later generations. There will be double suffering for going astray and leading others astray. See 16:25; on resurrection Day, they shall bear the full weight of their own burdens, as well as some of the burdens of those ignorant ones whom they have led astray. And the first of them will say that you are not superior to us because you chose the wrong way, as we did, out of your own free will. You bear the same responsibility as we do.

CHAPTER 24
BEGGING FOR GOD'S CLEMENCY
AND
PARDON OF ALL SINNERS

GIVE US A SECOND CHANCE IN LIFE

O our Sustainer! Cause us to come out of this [suffering]—and then, if we ever revert [to sinning], may we truly be [deemed] evildoers!" Would that we had a second chance [in life] to be among the believers!" [But] He will say: "Away with you from this [ignominy]! And speak no more unto Me!" (23:107-108) Would that we had a second chance [in life], so that we could be among the believers!" In all this, behold, there is a message [to men], even though most of them will not believe [in it]. But, verily, thy Sustainer—He alone—is almighty, a dispenser of grace! (26:102-104)

ERRORS OF OUR WAYS IN THE PAST LIFE

And on the day when He gathers them [all] together, [He will say]: "O you who have lived in intimate communion with the [evil] invisible beings! A great many [other] human beings have you ensnared!" And the humans who were close to them will say: "O our Sustainer! We enjoyed one another's fellowship [in life]; [being close to the evil invisible beings], but [now that] we have reached the end of our term—the term which Thou hast laid down for us—[we see the error of our ways]!" (6: 127-128)

EXCUSE OF BAD LUCK

The fire will scorch their faces, and they will stay with their lips distorted in pain. [And God will say:] "Were not My messages conveyed unto you, and you gave them the lie?" They will exclaim:

"O our Sustainer! Our bad luck overwhelmed us, and so we wandered astray! (23:104-106)

This dialogue is meant to bring out the futile excuse characteristic of so many sinners who attribute their failings to abstract "bad luck." It stresses the element of free will—and, therefore, of responsibility—in man's actions and behavior.

WE DID NOT MEAN TO DO EVIL

Then they will [who are thus arraigned] proffer their submission, [saying]: "We did not [meant to] do any evil!" [But they will be answered]: "Yea, God has full knowledge of all that you were doing! Hence, enter the gates of hell, and dwell therein! Evil, indeed, shall be the state of all who are given to false pride! (16:28-29)

"God has full knowledge," and He will judge you based on your motivation. Their plea of ignorance is rejected because they were offered God's guidance through His revealed messages, which they deliberately scorned in their false pride and dismissed out of hand as "fables of ancient times." (46:17-19).

WE SHALL BE OBLIVIOUS OF THEM AS THEY WERE OBLIVIOUS OF US

[And God will say], "And so We shall be oblivious of them today as they were oblivious of the coming of this Day [of Judgment], and as Our messages they denied. For, indeed, We conveyed a divine writ which We clearly, and wisely, spelled out—a guidance and grace unto those who will believe. (7:51-52)

BEGGING FOR MERCY

Those who are bent on denying the truth, the fire of hell awaits them. No end shall be put to their lives so that they could die, nor shall the suffering caused by that [fire] be lightened for them. We will repay all who are without gratitude. And in [hell], they will cry aloud: "O our Sustainer! Bring us out of this suffering! We shall [henceforth] do good deeds, not as we did [aforetime]!" [But We shall answer]: "Did We not grant you a life long enough so that whoever was willing to reflect and bethink himself? And a warner came to you! Taste, then, [the fruit of your evil deeds]. For evildoers shall have none to succor them!" God knows the hidden reality of the heavens and the earth. He has full knowledge of what is in the hearts [of men]. He made you inherit the earth. (35:36-39)

SUFFERING LIMITED BY GOD'S MERCY

Now as for those who [by their deeds] brought wretchedness upon themselves, [they shall live] in the fire, where they will have [nothing but] moans and sobs [to relieve their pain], therein to abide as long as the heavens and the earth endure. Unless thy Sustainer wills it otherwise: for, thy Sustainer is a sovereign doer of whatever He desires. (11:106-107) [But] He [God] will say: "The fire shall be your abode, to stay, unless God wills it otherwise. Thy Sustainer is wise, all-knowing. (6:128) For, whenever Our messages are conveyed to such a one, he turns away in his arrogance as though he had not heard them—as though his ears were deaf. Give him, then, the tidings of grievous suffering [in the life to come]. [As against this], those who attain to faith and do righteous deeds shall have gardens of bliss, to abide therein in accordance with God's true promise: for He alone is almighty, truly wise. (31:7-9)

The expressions "as long as the **heavens and the earth endure**," were used in the sense of "time beyond count." The fire of hell will be their abode unless God wills to reprieve them and grace them with His mercy. Hell's otherworldly suffering will not last forever. The deliberate contrast between the plural in the promise of "gardens (*jannat*) of bliss" and the singular in that of "suffering" (*adhab*) is meant to show that God's grace surpasses His wrath (see 6:12). The use of the expression "to abide therein" in connection with the mention of paradise only, and not otherworldly suffering (or hell), is an indication that whereas the enjoyment of the former will be unlimited in duration, suffering in what is described as "hell" will be limited.

The following is a parabolic saying of the Prophet: "On the Day of Judgment, those who deserve Paradise will enter Paradise, and those who deserve fire, the fire. Thereupon God, the Sublimely Exalted, will say, 'Take out of the fire everyone in whose heart there was as much faith [or, in some versions, "as much of good"] as a grain of mustard seed!' And so, they will be taken out of it, already blackened, and thrown into the River of Life. Then they will come alive [literally, as a herb sprouts] by the side of a stream: and did you not see how it turn yellow and budding?" The description of "yellow and budding"—i.e., tender and of light color—indicates the freshness of renewal of life in the pardoned sinner.

Considering the above and the similar phrase appearing in 11:107, and several well-authenticated sayings of the Prophet, some of the great Muslim theologians conclude that sinners will go through limited suffering in hell. The fury of Hell's fire will subside after a given duration. In the end, forgiven sinners will enter paradise and live in God's presence.

(2)
ACCOUNTING OF SINNERS WHO REPENTED AND ATTAINED RIGHTEOUSNESS

CHAPTER 25
SINNERS ASCENDING TO RIGHTEOUSNESS THROUGH REPENTANCE

THOSE WHO ATTAINED FAITH AFTER ERRING

And when the Last Hour dawns on that Day, all [men] will be sorted out. As for those who have attained faith and done righteous deeds, they shall be happy in a garden of delight. (30:14-15) There shall be those who attain what is right. O, how [happy] will be those who have attained to what is right! (56:8) Now as for those who have attained to righteousness - what of those who have ascended to righteousness? [They, too, will find themselves] amidst fruit-laden lote trees, and acacias flower-clad, and shade extended. (56:27-30)

After the resurrection, all human beings will be gathered for the final judgment. There are roughly three groups of humanity: the first group is the unrepentant sinners discussed previously. The second group will be those who were not always "foremost in faith and righteous works." After erring and sinning, they realize their moral failure in this life. They gradually attained righteousness through true repentance mended their ways and finally achieved excellence in conduct or righteousness. God will exempt those who have attained faith after sinning from the supreme awesomeness of the Day of Judgment. They will undergo light accounting and enter paradise.

The Prophet said, "Those who excel in good works and are the foremost in faith shall enter paradise without being held accountable for their actions. Those who follow the middle course (attain righteousness after sinning) shall be subjected to light accountability." Though they may not have been as perfect in life as the "foremost," their ultimate achievement brings them to the same state of spiritual fulfillment as those others.

GRANT OF RESPITE

WHAT IF THE PUNISHMENT FOR SINS IS IMMEDIATE?

Now were it not for a decree from thy Sustainer, setting a term [for each sinner's repentance], it would inescapably follow [that all who sin must be doomed at once]. (20:129) Yet, thy Sustainer is the truly forgiving One, limitless in His grace. If He took them [at once] to task for whatever [wrong] they committed, He would bring about their speedy punishment [then and there]. They have a time limit beyond which they find no redemption. (18:58) Man is created weak (4:28) **and prone to sin, but** *God "has willed upon Himself the law of grace and mercy" (6:12).*

Since man is created weak by nature and prone to sin. All of us are sinners and have fallen short of God's glory. God grants sinners respite in their lives on earth, during which they may reflect, repent, and mend their ways. All people have a life term decreed by God, during which they are at liberty to accept or reject the guidance offered to them through revelation. God does not punish sinners without considering all their circumstances. The "time limit" signifies the end of sinners' lives on earth - the "point of no return" beyond which God does not accept repentance.

GRANTING OF RESPITE BEFORE THE DYING HOUR

For all people a term has been set. When [the end of] their term approaches, they can neither delay it by a single moment, nor hasten it. (7:34)

God's acceptance of repentance relates only to those who do evil out of ignorance and then repent before their time runs out: [before the actual approach of death] *and it is they to whom God will turn again in His mercy - for God is all-knowing, wise. (4:17)*

REPENTANCE

Repentance and atonement for sins are essential parts of salvation. One can stop sinning, repent, and live a virtuous life to receive Divine mercy.

DEFINITION OF REPENTANCE

Repentance is remembering or returning to God's path, Islam's straight path. When Ali ibn Talib was asked what true repentance meant, he replied,

1. "Repentance must be genuine, and you should feel penitent for the wrong you have done."
2. "Compensate the victims for your evil deeds. Carry out the duties you have ignored, restore the rights you have usurped."
3. Ask forgiveness of those you wronged and God's forgiveness.
4. "Resolve not to repeat the sin again."
5. "Dedicate yourself to God and perform righteous deeds."

And [always], O you believers - all of you - turn unto God in repentance, so that you might attain a happy state! (24:31) [It is a triumph for] those who turn [unto God] in repentance [whenever they have sinned], who worship and praise [Him], and continue on and on [seeking His goodly acceptance], bow down [before Him] and prostrate themselves in adoration. They enjoin the doing of what is right and forbid the doing of what is wrong and keep within the bounds set by God. And you give [O Prophet] glad tidings [of God's promise] to all believers. (9:112)

GOODLY ENJOYMENT OF LIFE

[Say, O Prophet]: "I come to you from Him [as] a warner and a bearer of glad tidings. Ask your Sustainer to forgive your sins, and then turn towards Him in repentance. [Whereupon] He will grant you full enjoyment of life [in this world] until a term set [by Him is

fulfilled], and [in the life to come] He will bestow upon everyone possessed of merit [a full reward for] his merit." (11:2-4)

In Islam, it is not a sin to enjoy life within the bounds set by God. God, in His unfathomable wisdom, does not always grant worldly happiness and material benefits to everyone who believes in Him and lives righteously. The good enjoyments of life in this world promised in the above sentence relates to the community of believers, and not necessarily to individuals. God will, in the life to come, bestow the full measure of His favor upon everyone who has acquired merit by virtue of his faith and righteousness.

ONLY GOD CAN ACCEPT REPENTANCE

Do they not know that only God accepts the repentance of his servants? He is the [true] recipient of whatever is offered for His sake. (9:102-104)

No human being, not even the Prophet, can absolve a sinner of his guilt. A prophet can only pray to God to forgive sinners.

SINS AGAINST GOD

Failure to fulfill God's duties constitutes a sin. God being an almighty and independent entity, does not need defenders or human worship. God's rights are a private matter between humans and God. There is no punishment ordained in the Quran for sins of omission in this life, however, God will render judgment for violation of God's rights (Huquq Ullah) in the afterlife. If a Muslim repents and asks God's forgiveness during his lifetime, God being merciful and loving can forgive any indiscretion, since man is created weak.

SINS AGAINST FELLOW MAN

Sins committed against fellow men must be atoned for by compensating the victims of your evil deeds. If the injury is to another human being, it is no longer a private matter between man and

God. The victim will also have a seat in God's court on the Day of Judgment.

The following is the Prophet's saying that emphasizes the importance of avoiding human rights abuses: "In my community, the poorest is he who will appear before God on the Day of Resurrection with his acts of prayer, fasting, and charity. While he abused someone, usurped property, shed blood, or struck someone else. Then his virtuous deeds were given over to each of his victims, and when nothing was left of his good deeds to pay compensation, some of the sins of the wronged one were transferred to him, and he shall be cast into Hell." When human rights are violated, asking God for forgiveness will not suffice.

CHAPTER 26
FORGIVENESS OF SINS ATONEMENT OR MITIGATION OF SINFUL DEEDS

Religious acts of atonement are an effort to make up for wrongdoings. When you apologize for doing something wrong, that's an act of atonement. Many religions have atonement rituals, such as Yom Kippur, the Day of Atonement, on which Jewish people repent of their sins.

LAW OF GRACE AND MERCY

Say: "[Thus speaks God]: O you servants of Mine who have transgressed against your own selves! Despair not of God's mercy. God forgives all sins—for He alone is much-forgiving, a dispenser of grace!" Hence, turn towards your Sustainer [alone] and surrender yourselves unto Him before the suffering [of death and resurrection] comes upon you, for then you will not be succored. (39:53-54) And when those who believe in Our messages come unto thee, say: "Peace be upon you. Your Sustainer has willed upon Himself the law of grace and mercy. So, that if any of you does an evil deed out of ignorance, and repents and lives righteously, He shall be [found] much-forgiving, a dispenser of grace." (6:54)

God "has willed upon Himself the law of grace and mercy" and, consequently, does not punish sinners without taking all their circumstances into consideration. In the Quran, divine mercy is of paramount importance, without which repentance would be meaningless. Several factors can mitigate sinful action effects:

1. Charity
2. Forgiving begets forgiveness

3. Striving for God's cause
4. Pain and sorrow
5. Avoiding heinous and grave sins
6. Effacing bad deeds through good deeds.

ASK GOD'S FORGIVENESS

Yet he who does evil or [otherwise] sins against himself, and then prays to God to forgive him, shall find God much-forgiving, a dispenser of grace. He who commits a sin, commits it only to his own hurt, and God is indeed all-knowing, wise. (4:110-111)

CHARITY AND FORGIVENESS OF SINS

If you do charity deeds openly, it is well and good; but if you bestow it upon the needy in secret, it will be even better for you, and it will atone for some of your sinful deeds. And God knows all that you do. (2:271) Be conscious of God as best you can, and listen [to Him], and pay heed. And spend in charity for your own good and save from their own covetousness. They shall attain happy state! If you offer God a generous loan, He will amply repay you for it and forgive you of your sins; for God is ever responsive to gratitude. (64:16-18)

BARGAIN THAT NEVER FAILS

[It is] they who [truly] follow God's revelation, are constant in prayer, and spend on others, secretly and openly, out of what We provide for them as sustenance. It is they who may look forward to a bargain that can never fail since He will grant them their just rewards and give them yet more out of His bounty. For He is ever-forgiving, responsive to gratitude. (35:29:31)

FORGIVENESS BEGET FORGIVENESS

We have ordained for them in that [Torah]: A life for a life, an eye for an eye, a nose for a nose, an ear for an ear, a tooth for a tooth, and [similar] retribution for wounds. He who forgoes it out of charity will atone for some of his past sins. (5:45)

When they are wronged human beings naturally respond with anger, hold grudges, and seek revenge. Victims of wrongdoing usually do all three. The act of forgiveness is good for the body and soul. Unforgiving hearts have serious mental, emotional, and physical consequences.

Scientific studies have linked forgiveness to a reduction in back pain, depression, and stress hormone levels. People without faith may have difficulty forgiving. However, forgiveness has its limits, and one should not condemn those who refuse to forgive. Forgiveness will bring closure, but also seeing that offenders get what they deserve can bring closure. One of the criteria for heaven is for a victim to forgive others for their sins.

THOSE WHO STRIVE IN GOD'S CAUSE

Thy Sustainer [grants His forgiveness] unto those who forsake the domain of evil after succumbing to its temptation, and who thenceforth strive hard [in God's cause] and are patient in adversity: after such [repentance] Thy Sustainer is indeed much-forgiving, a dispenser of grace! (16:110)

PAIN AND SORROW

In God's sight, the unhappiness caused by unjust persecution confers—as does every undeserved and patiently endured suffering, spiritual merit on the person thus afflicted. The Prophet said, "Whenever a believer is stricken with any hardship, or pain, anxiety, sorrow, harm, or distress—even if it be a thorn that has hurt him—God redeems some of his failings."

According to another well-authenticated Hadith, if a person dies a violent death not caused, directly or indirectly, by his sinful actions, and since he had no time to repent his previous sins will be forgiven. In cases of unprovoked murder, the murderer is burdened—in addition to the sin of murder—with the sins his innocent victim might have committed in the past and of which he (the victim) is now absolved.

RIGHTEOUS LIVING

For all men and women who surrender to God, truly devout men and women who are true to their word. They are patient in adversity, humble themselves [before God], and give in charity. All self-denying men and women, who remember God unceasingly. For [all] God has promised forgiveness of sins and a mighty reward. (33:35) Those who stand in awe of God, knowing He is beyond their perception. Forgiveness is in store and an excellent reward. (67:12)

Islam does not offer easy salvation paths. Evangelical Christians claim that salvation is free, but in Islam salvation must be earned, by avoidance of evils and doing righteous works. Leading a righteous life exemplifies a good faith effort on the part of the believer. Good deeds alone will not save you if sins exceed good deeds. In the end, God's mercy is the key to salvation. All human beings including the highly exalted Prophets need God's forgiveness. The Prophet said, "Act and try to act as righteously as you possibly can but know that a person's action alone will not make him enter Paradise." When asked what about your actions? He replied, "Yes, even I will not make it to paradise on the strength of my actions unless my Lord covers me up in His mercy.

FAITH, GOOD WORKS, AND EFFACING SINS

Those who have attained faith and do righteous deeds and have come to believe in what has been bestowed from on high on Muhammad – for it is the truth from their Sustainer – [shall attain to God's grace]. He will erase their sinister deeds and set their hearts at rest. This is because they who are bent on denying the truth pursue falsehood, whereas they who have attained faith pursue [but] the truth [that flows] from their Sustainer. In this way, God reveals to man the parables of their true state. (47:2-3)

The "going to waste" refers to their good deeds Ie of their deliberate "pursuance of falsehood" of those who deny the truth, as well as the "effacement of the bad deeds" of the true believers, in consequence, of their "pursuance of the truth." The "true state" relates to the parabolic expressions relating to man's spiritual conditions and destinies in this world as well as in the life to come.

He who brings the truth and wholeheartedly accepts It as true - it is they who are [truly] conscious of Him! All they have ever yearned for awaits them with their Sustainer. Such will be the reward for those who do good. And to this end, God will erase their worst acts. He will reward them for the best they ever did [in life]. (39:33-35)

AVOIDANCE OF HEINOUS SINS

If you avoid the grave sins, which you have been enjoined to shun, We shall wipe away your [minor] wrongful deeds. We shall cause you to enter an abode of glory. [paradise] (4:31) As for those who avoid [truly] grave sins and shameful deeds—even though they may sometimes stumble—behold, thy Sustainer abounds in forgiveness. (53:32) And [remember] whatever you are given [now] is but for the [passing] enjoyment of life in this world – whereas that which is with God is far better and more enduring. [It shall be given] to all who attain to faith and in their Sustainer place their trust; and who shun the more heinous sins and abominations; and who, whenever they are moved to anger, readily forgive. (42:36-37)

All those evil acts, which will lead to grievous sufferings on the Day of Judgment or ultimate punishment in Hell, are considered major sins. If one avoids major sins, God forgives minor sins. God will forgive an occasional stumble into sin followed by sincere repentance because of man's inborn weakness—an implied echo of the statement that "man has been created weak" (4:28) and, therefore, liable to stumble into sin.

SHUN EVIL

O you servants of Mine! Be, then, conscious of Me—seeing that for those who shun the powers of evil, lest they [be tempted to] worship them, and turn unto God instead, there is the glad tiding [of happiness in the life to come]. (39:16-17)

Power of evil is the term that circumscribes the seductive force of certain evil ambitions or desires—like striving after power for its own sake, acquisition of wealth by exploiting one's fellow beings, social advancement by all manners of immoral means, addiction to sex, drugs, pornography, gambling and so forth. Any of which may cause a man to lose all spiritual orientations and be enslaved by his passions.

GOOD DEEDS ARE REWARDED TEN TIMES

Indeed, to God belongs all that is in the heavens and on earth. He will reward those who do evil for what they did and those who do good with ultimate good. (53:31-32) Whoever shall come [before God] with a good deed will gain ten times the like thereof; but whoever shall come with an evil deed will be requited with no more than the like thereof; and none shall be wronged. (6:160)

God's mercy rewards good deeds with far more than their merits warrant, whereas bad deeds will be recompensed with no more than their equivalent. Why? God wants to encourage humans to perform charitable deeds which in turn makes the world a better place. In the afterlife, God does not want to punish his Own creation and will give all the advantage to prevent the suffering of hell.

TRANSFORMING BAD DEEDS INTO GOOD DEEDS

The exception, however, will be those who repent and attain faith and do righteous deeds. For it is they whose [previous] bad deeds God will transform into good ones – seeing that God is indeed much-forgiving, a dispenser of grace. He who repents and [then] does what is right has truly turned unto God by [this very act of] repentance. But [the abiding truth of man's condition will become fully apparent] in the life to come [either] severe suffering or God's forgiveness and His goodly acceptance. (57:20)

OVERLOOK BAD DEEDS

"Unto Thee have I turned in repentance: for I am of those who have surrendered themselves unto Thee!" It is [such as] these from whom We shall accept the best that they ever did, and whose bad deeds We shall overlook: [they will find themselves] among those who are destined for paradise, in fulfillment of the true promise which they were given [in this world]. (46:15-16)

REWARD IN THE AFTERLIFE

God has full knowledge of what is in [men's] hearts, and it is He who accepts repentance from His servants, and pardons bad deeds. He knows all that you do and responds to all who attain faith and do righteous deeds. [It is He who, in the life to come], will give them, out of His bounty, far more [than they will have deserved]. (42:24-26) "Unto Thee have I turned in repentance. I am of those who have surrendered themselves to Thee!" It is [such as] these from whom We shall accept the best they ever did, and whose bad deeds We shall overlook. [They will find themselves] among those destined for paradise, in fulfillment of the true promise they were given [in this world]. (46:15-16)

MARTYR'S DESTINED FOR PARADISE

"O our Sustainer! Whomsoever Thou shalt commit to the fire, him, verily, wilt Thou have brought to disgrace and such evildoers will have none to succor them. "O our Sustainer! Behold, we heard a voice call [us] unto faith, 'Believe in your Sustainer!' – And so we believed. O our Sustainer! Forgive us, then, our sins, and wash away our wrongdoing deeds; and let us die the death of the truly virtuous!" And, O our Sustainer, grant us that which Thou hast promised us through Thy apostles, and disgrace us not on Resurrection Day! Verily, Thou never fail to fulfill Thy promise!" And thus, does their Sustainer answer their prayer: "I shall not lose sight of the labor of any of you who labor [in My way], be it man or woman: each of you is an issue of the other. Hence, as for those who forsake the domain of evil, and are driven from their homelands, and suffer hurt in My cause, and fight [for it], and are slain – I shall most certainly efface their bad deeds and shall most certainly bring them into gardens through which running waters flow, as a reward from God: for with God is the most beauteous of rewards." (3:192-195)

GOD'S FORGIVENESS AND PARADISE

The life of this world is nothing but an enjoyment of self-delusion. [Hence], vie with one another in seeking your Sustainer's forgiveness, and [thus] to a paradise as vast as the heavens and the earth, which has been prepared for those who have attained faith in God and His Apostle. Such is God's bounty, which He grants unto whomever He wills – for God is limitless in His vast bounty. (57:20-21)

And pay heed to God and the Apostle, so that you might be graced with mercy. And vie with one another to attain to your Sustainer's forgiveness and to a paradise as vast as the heavens and the earth. This paradise has been made ready for the God-conscious who spend [in His way] in times of plenty and hardship, and hold in check their anger, and pardon their fellowmen because God loves the doers of good. When they have committed a shameful deed or sinned against themselves, remember God and pray that their sins be forgiven. Who but God could forgive sins? And do not knowingly persist in doing whatever [wrong] they have done. These it is who shall have as their reward forgiveness from their Sustainer, and gardens through which running waters flow, therein to abide and how excellent a reward for those who labor! (3:132-136) But unto him who shall have stood in fear of his Sustainer's Presence, and held back his inner self from base desires, paradise will truly be the goal! (79:40-41)

Vie with one another for God's forgiveness rather than striving for glory and worldly possessions. This is because no man is free from faults and sins, so everyone needs God's forgiveness.

PRAYERS FOR FORGIVENESS

BESTOW THY MERCY

"O our Sustainer! Take us not to task if we forget or unwittingly do wrong! And Thou will efface our sins, grant us forgiveness, and bestow mercy upon us! Thou art our Lord Supreme: succor us, then, against those who deny the truth!" (2:286)

PRAYER OF ANGELS FOR MAN'S FORGIVENESS

He is all that is in the heavens and on earth. It is He who is most exalted and tremendous. The uppermost heavens are well-nigh rent asunder [by His awe], and the angels extol their Sustainer's limitless glory and praise and ask forgiveness for all on earth. Oh, God alone is truly forgiving, a dispenser of grace! (42:4-5)

The implication is that whereas all humans - whether believers or unbelievers - are liable to err and sin, God is full of forgiveness for men despite all their evil doings.

KEEP US SAFE FROM FIRE

God sees all that is in [the hearts of] His servants - those who say, "O our Sustainer! We believe [in Thee]; forgive us, then, our sins, and keep us safe from suffering through the fire." Those who are patient in adversity, and true to their word, and truly devout, and who spend [in God's way], and pray for forgiveness from their innermost hearts. (3:15-17)

CHAPTER 27
EASY ACCOUNTING OF THOSE WHO ATTAINED RIGHTEOUSNESS

SECURE FROM JUDGMENT DAY TERROR

[On that Day] the trumpet [of judgment] will be sounded, and all [creatures] in the heavens and on earth will fall senseless unless they are such as God wills [to exempt]. (39:68) For those [the decree of] ultimate good has already gone forth from Us, they will be kept far away from that [hell], and no sound will they hear. They will abide in all that their souls have ever desired. The supreme awesomeness [of the Day of Resurrection] will cause them no grief since the angels will receive them with a greeting: "This is your Day [of triumph— the Day] you were promised!" (21:101-103) Whoever shall come [before Him] with a good deed will gain [further] good therefrom; and they will be secure from the terror of that Day. (27:89)

After the ultimate desolation of the earth and the extinction of all living things, we have God's final proclamation of His absolute and omnipotent oneness. This is in accord with repeated Quranic statements that all living creatures will taste death. God will exempt the righteous from the supreme awesomeness of the resurrection Day. The terror and tribulations of Resurrection Day will not grieve the righteous. This is an allusion to the unbroken spiritual life in this world—and, therefore, happiness in the hereafter—of those who have attained faith and done good deeds.

RECORD OF THE RIGHTEOUS

We shall summon all human beings [and judge them] according to their conscious disposition, which governed their deeds [in life]. They whose record shall be placed at their right hand are the ones who will read their record [with happiness]. Yet none shall be wronged by a hair's breadth. (17:71) Even the most hidden of your deeds will not remain hidden. Now as for him whose record shall be placed in his right hand, he will exclaim: "Come you all! Read this my record! Behold, I knew [one day] I would have to face my account!" (69:18-20)

"They whose record shall be placed at their right hand" had always been conscious of resurrection and judgment, and tried to behave accordingly, and his record shows that he was righteous in his life on Earth. This is a symbolic expression of "right" and "left" as "righteous" and "unrighteous."

EASY ACCOUNTING FOR THOSE WHO ATTAINED FAITH

And as for him whose record shall be placed in his right hand, he will in time be called to account with easy accounting. He will [be able to] turn joyfully to those of his own kind. [Who were righteous in life]. *(84:7-9) Thus, there shall be those who will have attained to what is right: oh, how [happy] will be they who have attained to what is right! (56:8) Their Sustainer will admit them to His grace and that will be [their] manifest triumph! (45:30) All who did what is right and just made goodly provision for themselves, so that He might reward, out of His bounty, those who have attained to faith and done righteous deeds. (30:44-45)*

RECORD OF VIRTUOUS WITNESSED BY PROPHETS, SAINTS AND ANGELS

Nay, verily, the record of the truly virtuous is [set down] in a mode most lofty! And what could make you imagine what that most lofty mode would be? A record engraved in [indelible ink], witnessed by all who are close to God. (83:18-21).

The record of the virtuous will be witnessed by "all who are close to God," such as prophets, saints, and angels.

THE WEIGHT OF RIGHTEOUSNESS IS HEAVY IN BALANCE

Whose weight [of righteousness] is heavy in the balance—it is they who will attain a happy state. (23:102) Whereas anyone—be it man or woman—who does [whatever he/she can] of good deeds and is a believer, shall enter paradise, and not be wronged by as much as [would fill] the groove of a date-stone. (4:124) Behold, [only] those who attain to faith, do righteous deeds and humble themselves before their Sustainer—[only] they are destined for paradise, and there shall they abide. (11:23)

FORGIVENESS OF SINS

Whereas anyone who did [whatever he could] of righteous deeds, and was a believer, need have no fear of being wronged or deprived [of any of his merit]. (20:112) God has promised those who attain to faith and do good works, theirs shall be forgiveness of sins, and a mighty reward. (5:9) We shall most certainly erase their [previous] bad deeds and reward them for the best they ever did. (29:7)

Those who did righteous deeds need not fear punishment for any sin they may have committed nor diminution of their merit. The righteous shall be recompensed in the hereafter for the best they ever did, and God will wipe away their bad deeds.

GOOD DEEDS AND HEAVEN

O you who have attained faith! Remain conscious of God. Let every human being look to what he sent ahead for the tomorrow! And [once again]: Remain conscious of God, for God is fully aware of all that you do. (59:18) Those who are destined for paradise—it is they, [alone] who shall triumph [on Judgment Day]! (59:20) Those who have attained faith and done righteous deeds, We shall most certainly cause them to join the righteous [in the hereafter as well]. (29:9)

CHAPTER 28
ACCOUNTING OF THE RIGHTEOUS OF OTHER MONOTHEISTIC FAITHS

Islam is the only major religion that categorically states that followers of other faiths can also attain salvation in the afterlife. This is an ultimate example of not only tolerance of other faiths but equality of all God's religions. (See also Volume Two of this series, under Salvation of Jews and Christians.)

EXCLUSIVE SALVATION

If, for example, only Judaism followers are worthy of salvation, as some Jews believe, then out of seven billion humans, only a few million will enter paradise. If Christian fundamentalists are correct, and only they will go to Heaven, then six and a half billion humans are hell-bound. If only Muslims go to heaven, five and a half billion humans are condemned.

This claim of exclusive salvation is even more controversial because it is not exactly by choice that most human beings adopt a particular religion. For example, a child born into a Hindu family will most likely grow up to follow Hinduism. Similarly, a child born into a Jewish family will probably grow up to follow Judaism, etc. The randomness of birth and parental/societal influences usually determine the future religious preference. Across all cultures, most believers take much pride in the religious traditions of their ancestors, and therefore conversion to another religion is rare.

The obvious question is how a loving God can knowingly create all these souls as fodder for Hell. It does not portray God as loving or merciful. The Quran solves this dilemma by declaring that all righteous people regardless of their denomination are eligible for salvation.

SPIRITUAL ARROGANCE

The claim of exclusive salvation amounts to spiritual arrogance and self-righteousness, which causes many evils. Such narcissism dehumanizes anyone belonging to a different religious group. The process of denigration leads to discrimination, and if taken to the extreme, can result in violence and genocide. Listed below are some examples where religious affiliations of the victim or the perpetrator were a key motivating factor for violence:

- Jewish Holocaust during the second world war by German Nazis predominantly Christian.

- Massacre of Hindus, Muslims, and Sikhs at independence and partition of India.

- Bosnian Muslims were massacred by Christian Serbs during the 1992–1995 Bosnian War.

- The Rohingya Muslim genocide by Buddhist fanatics of Myanmar.

- Genocide of Palestinian Muslims in Gaza by supremacist Jews supported by fanatic Evangelical Christians in 2024.

TIMELESS DOCTRINE OF SALVATION

Those who have attained faith [in this divine writ] **[Muslims]**, *those who follow the Jewish faith, the Christians, and the Sabians–all who believe in God and the Last Day and do righteous deeds—shall have their reward with their Sustainer. No fear should they have, and neither shall they grieve. (2:62) Those who have attained faith [in this divine writ], those who follow the Jewish faith, the Sabians, and* *the Christians—all who believe in God and the Last Day and do righteous deeds. No fear should they have, neither shall they grieve. (5:69)*

The Quranic passages teach a fundamental doctrine of salvation, transcending all religious affiliations. It is of timeless import, as it applies to Adam down to the last human on this earth. With a breadth of vision unparalleled in any other religious faith, salvation is granted by God's grace for having faith, belief in Judgment Day, and doing righteous works. This is done while avoiding major sins. If good deeds exceed sins, salvation will be granted through God's grace regardless of denomination.

PARADISE FOR THE RIGHTEOUS OF ALL DENOMINATION

They claim, "None shall ever enter paradise unless he is a Jew" or "a Christian." Such are their wishful beliefs! Say: "Produce a shred of evidence for what you are claiming, if what you say is true!" [From your own scriptures] *Yes, indeed everyone who surrenders his whole being unto God, and does good, shall have his reward with his Sustainer. They should have no fear, nor shall they grieve. Furthermore, the Jews assert, "The Christians have no well-founded valid ground for their beliefs," while the Christians assert, "The Jews have no valid ground for their beliefs." Both quote the divine writ! Those who were devoid of knowledge (pagans) say the same about people of faith. It is God who will judge between them on resurrection Day regarding on what they differ. (2:111-113)*

Definition of Islam: The expression, "Who self-surrender unto God," repeatedly in the Quran provides a perfect definition of Islam. It is derived from the root verb *aslama*, "he surrendered himself" which means "self-surrender to God," and it is in this sense that the terms Islam and Muslim are used throughout the Quran.

Salvation is open to all and not reserved for any denomination. It is open to everyone who consciously realizes God's oneness, surrenders himself to His will, and by living righteously, gives practical effect to this spiritual attitude. Such are their wishful beliefs, who assert that only followers of their own denomination shall partake of God's grace in the hereafter.

God will Judge between you: God will confirm the truth of what was true in their respective beliefs and show the falseness of what was false therein. The Quran maintains throughout that there is a substantial element of truth in all faiths based on divine revelation. Their subsequent divergence was the result of "wishful beliefs" (2:111) and gradual alterations of the original teachings. (22:67-69.)

GOD WILL GRANT A MIGHTY REWARD

But as for those among them [Jews] who are deeply rooted in knowledge, and the believers [Muslims] who believe in what has been bestowed upon thee from on high and that what was bestowed from on high before thee? Those who are [especially] constant in prayer, spend in charity, believe in God and the Last Day-to whom We grant a mighty reward. (4:162)

Those Jews who are deeply rooted in knowledge do not content themselves with mere observance of rituals but try to penetrate the deepest meaning of faith. In reference to "Those who are [especially] constant in prayer," the construction of the sentence is such that it is meant to stress the special, praiseworthy quality attached to prayer and to those who are devoted to it.

ZOROASTRIANISM

Zoroastrianism is one of the world's oldest religions, older than Judaism and Christianity. Magians were members of the Zoroastrian priestly caste of the Medes and Persians. Zoroastrians are not fire-worshippers, a common misconception, and for them, fire is a symbol of God's light or wisdom. The Prophet Zoroaster (or Zarathustra) founded this religion in ancient Iran approximately 3,500 years ago. For 1,000 years, Zoroastrianism was one of the most powerful religions in the world. It was the official religion of Persia (Iran) from 600 BCE to 650 CE. Now, its followers are a small minority. They are represented today by the Gabrs of Iran and, more prominently, by the Parsis of India and Pakistan.

Dualism: Zoroastrians believe there is one God called ***Ahura Mazda*** (Wise or good Lord) who created the world. Dualism in Zoroastrianism is the existence of, yet complete separation of, good and evil. This is recognized in two interconnected ways:

(1) **Cosmic Dualism** refers to the ongoing battle between the God of good (***Ahura Mazda***) and the Evil God (***Angra Mainyu***) within the universe. The ***Angra Mainyu*** is destructive energy that opposes God's creative energy.

(2) **Moral Dualism** refers to the opposition of good and evil in mankind. God's gift to man was free will. Man has the choice to follow evil or righteousness. Evil leads to misery and ultimately Hell. The path of righteousness leads to peace and everlasting happiness in Heaven. Belief in the existence of evil that is completely independent of ***Ahura Mazda*** denies God's omnipotence and cannot be categorized as pure monotheism. Zoroastrianism combines cosmogonic dualism and eschatological monotheism in a manner unique among the major religions of the world.

SABIANS

The Sabians seem to have been a monotheistic religious group intermediate between Judaism and Christianity. Their name was probably derived from the Aramaic verb *tsebha*, "he immersed himself in water." They were followers of John the Baptist—in which case they could be identified with the Mandaeans community, which is still found in Iraq. They are not to be confused with the so-called "Sabians of Harran," a Gnostic sect that still existed in the early centuries of Islam and which may have deliberately adopted the name of the true Sabians to obtain the advantages accorded by Muslims to followers of every monotheistic faith.

CHRISTIANITY

Some Muslims erroneously argue that the Quranic verses above refer to the early Christians who were true Unitarians. Continuing the argument, salvation requires faith in one God. Trinitarian Christians commit associationism by raising Jesus Christ to the Godhead, forfeiting their salvation. Just as some Christians believe that all non-Christians are damned, so do many Muslims believe the same myth about non-Muslims. The Quran does not differentiate between Unitarian and Trinitarian Christians in salvation. If strict monotheism is essential for salvation, then why do dualist Persians go to heaven?

PARADISE FOR RIGHTEOUS CHRISTIANS

Thou will surely find that those who say, "We are Christians," come closest to feeling affection for those who believe [in this divine writ]. This is because there are priests and monks among them, and they are not given to arrogance. For, when they understand what has been bestowed from on high upon this Apostle, thou can see their eyes overflow with tears. They recognize something of its truth, [and] they say: "O our Sustainer! We believe, so make us one with all who bear witness to the truth. And how could we fail to believe in God and in whatever truth has come unto us, when we so fervently desire that our Sustainer counts us among the righteous?" And for this belief God will reward them with gardens through which running waters flow, therein to abide for such is the requital of good doers. (5:82-85) As for those who have attained faith [in this divine writ] [such as Muslims], *and those who follow the Jewish faith, the Sabians, the Christians, and the Magians, [on the one hand[, and those who are bent on ascribing divinity to aught but God, [on the other] verily, God will decide between them on Resurrection Day: for, behold, God is the witness unto everything. (22:17)*

Zoroaster's followers (Magians) and Christians are included in the Unitarian faith, along with Jews, Muslims, and Sabians in verse 22:16. It is noteworthy that the Quran does not include Christians and Magians among those who attribute divinity to anything besides God. However, Christians and Magians attribute divine qualities to other beings besides God. On the other hand, "those who deliberately ascribe divinity to beings other than God" reject the principle of His oneness and uniqueness (22:17). God will decide their destiny with justice on the resurrection, and they will not be arbitrarily condemned.

WHY ARE THE MAGIANS AND CHRISTIANS INCLUDED IN THE UNITARIAN FAITH?

Intentions behind actions: Christians regard those beings, fundamentally, as no more than manifestations—or incarnations—of the One God, thus persuading themselves that they worship one God alone. Their actions can only be interpreted based on their intentions. Islam bases moral judgment on intention. Similar arguments can be applied to other religions. The Prophet's saying is thus: "The reward of deeds depends upon intentions, and everyone will get the reward according to what he intended."

The element of intent is expressed in the past tense. This is because although by their deification of Jesus, they are guilty of the sin of "shirks" (the ascribing of divinity to anyone or anything besides God), Christians do not consciously worship a plurality of deities. Theoretically, their theology postulates belief in the One God, who manifests Himself in a trinity of aspects, or "persons," of whom Jesus is supposed to be one. Their worship of Jesus is not based on conscious intent but rather flows from their overstepping the bounds of truth in their veneration of Jesus (see 4:171, 5:77).

PREDICTION OF BYZANTINES VICTORY OVER PERSIANS

In the verses below, God favors Christians over Persians. This irrefutable argument is supported by the prediction of the Quran of the victory of Byzantines, who believed in the Trinity as a depiction (adulterated version) of monotheism, over Persian dualists, indicating God's favor for Christianity over Zoroastrianism.

Defeated have been the Byzantines in the lands close-by; yet it is they who, notwithstanding this defeat, shall be victorious within a few years: [for] with God rests all power of decision, first and last. (30:2-4)

The Thirtieth Surah, (The Byzantines), revealed during the Mecca period about six or seven years before the *Hijrah*, takes its designation from the prophetic reference to the Byzantines in the opening verses. It is an unequivocal prediction of events that at the time of its revelation were still shrouded in the mists of the future.

The defeats and victories spoken of above relate to the centuries-long struggle between the Byzantine and Persian Empires. In the early seventh century, the Persians conquered parts of Syria and Anatolia, "the lands close-by," i.e., near the heartland of the Byzantine Empire; later they took Damascus, Jerusalem, and Egypt, and they laid siege to Constantinople itself. At the time of this surah's revelation, the Byzantine Empire seemed on the brink of destruction. The few Muslims around the Prophet were despondent upon hearing the news of the utter discomfiture of the Byzantine Christians. The pagan Quraysh, on the other hand, sympathized with the Persians who, they thought, would vindicate their own opposition to the One-God idea. When the Prophet enunciated the above Quran verses predicting a Byzantine victory "within a few years," the Quraysh received this prophecy with derision. The term "a few" in Arabic denotes any number between three and ten. In 622—i.e., six or seven years after the Quranic prediction—the tide turned in favor of the Byzantines. In that year, Emperor Heraclius defeated the Persians and drove them out of Asia Minor. By 626, the Persian armies were completely routed by the Byzantines.

CHAPTER 29
PAUL/AUGUSTINE'S SALVATION THEOLOGY

In this section, three different points of view are presented concerning salvation theology: How Paul/Augustine, Jesus, and the Quran describe salvation.

JESUS DIED FOR OUR SINS

In Romans 5:12-19, Paul establishes a parallel between Adam and Christ. He states that whereas sin and death entered the world through Adam, grace and eternal life came in greater abundance through Christ. Paul said that Jesus suffered and "died for our sins." Paul and the other New Testament writers never attempted a precise, definitive explanation of salvation. There were no detailed theories about the crucifixion as an atonement for Adam's "original sin" in the early Church. This theology did not emerge until the fourth century.

ST. AUGUSTINE'S EXPLANATION

One of the decisive developments in Western philosophy was the widespread merging of Greek philosophy with Judeo-Christian religious traditions. Augustine (354 – 430 CE) became one of the main figures through whom Greek philosophy was merged.

Augustine is the founder of the Western spirit. No other theologian, apart from St. Paul, has been more influential in the West. Although raised as a Catholic, Augustine left the Church to follow the Manichaean religion, much to his mother's despair. As a youth, Augustine lived a hedonistic lifestyle for a time. In Carthage, he developed a relationship with a woman who became his concubine for thirteen years and gave birth to his son. Later in life, Augustine reverted to Catholicism.

INHERITANCE OF THE ORIGINAL SIN

St. Augustine believed God condemned humanity to eternal damnation due to Adam's one sin. It is called the condition or state of sin. Every human being is born because of the first man, Adam, who disobeyed God by eating the forbidden fruit (of knowledge of good and evil), thus transmitting his sin and guilt by heredity to his descendants. Human beings are predestined to go to hell. Even at birth, a child is already deserving of God's wrath for its share of the original sin of mankind, and before it acquires the guilt of its actual sin.

DIVINE WRATH IS UPON MANKIND?

The first Adam was the representative of fallen humanity in whose transgression we all sinned and came under the penalty of death (Rom. 5:12). Sin was a violation of divine honor. God was supposedly so angry at man's sinfulness that only the sacrifice of His only begotten Son would have pacified His anger. Only a Savior who is both truly God and true man can secure man's salvation. Jesus was such a Savior who was 100% human and 100% divine, both coexisting within him. In other words, a life truly human and yet with infinite worth would have been enough to satisfy God's honor on behalf of the entire human race.

Christ was the sacrificial lamb, offered up to God to still divine anger. By his own volition and effort, no person can save himself but must depend absolutely on Christ's saving grace. Christ's crucifixion was a vicarious sacrifice offered to God as propitiation or atonement for human sin. Alternatively, it was the price paid to redeem man from the devil. Therefore, Christ was the second Adam, creating a second human race. His death shows how much God loves humanity.

APPEASING SINNERS WITHOUT REFORMATION

Catholic salvation is different from evangelical Christianity. Catholics believe they are saved by God's grace alone, but both faith and works are necessary. Protestants assert that the only response necessary is faith. Evangelical Christians are conservative Protestants who believe in the free gift of salvation. This is if one accepts that Jesus died on the cross for humanity's sins.

In short, God was so angry at man's sinfulness, which He created in the first place, that He sent his only begotten son on a suicide mission to save humanity. A sinner's behavioral change to become a better human being is negated by the emphasis on receiving a "free gift" of salvation. There is no Biblical verse or passage to support the above salvation position. The whole concept is man-made without Jesus' support. Jesus never claimed he would die on the cross for man's sins.

BERNARD SHAW

Bernard Shaw in *Androcles and the Lion* said about the Christian concept of salvation: "There is no record of Christ having ever said to any man: 'Go and sin as much as you like: you can put it all on me.' He said, 'Sin no more,' and insisted that he was putting up the standard of conduct, not debasing it and that the righteousness of his followers must exceed that of the Scribe and Pharisee. The notion that he was shedding his blood so that every petty cheat and adulterator and libertine might wallow in it and come out whiter than snow cannot be imputed to him on his own authority."

CHAPTER 30
WHAT DID JESUS SAY ABOUT SALVATION?

UNIVERSAL SALVATION

In the Gospels, Jesus lays down the principles of universal salvation based on good deeds, repentance, and sin forgiveness. Salvation is not restricted to denominations or religious affiliations.

LORD'S PRAYER: FORGIVENESS BEGETS FORGIVENESS

Our Father in Heaven, hallowed be your name, your kingdom come, your will be done, on earth as it is in heaven. Today, give us our daily bread and forgive us our sins, as we have forgiven those who sin against us. And don't let us yield to temptation but rescue us from the evil one. If you forgive others when they sin against you, your heavenly Father will also forgive you. But if you refuse to forgive others, your Father will not forgive your sins. (Matthew 6:5-15)

Forgiveness is the central theme of the Lord's prayer. God will then forgive our sins as we forgive others who sin against us. The concept is identical to the Quran's teachings. *We ordained for them in that [Torah]: A life for a life, and an eye for an eye, and a nose for a nose, and an ear for an ear, and a tooth for a tooth, and [similar] retribution for wounds. He who forgoes it out of charity will atone for some of his past sins. (Quran 5:45)*

THE SALVATION OF THE POOR AND THE WEALTHY

According to Jesus, the meek, the poor, those who thirst after righteousness, those who are persecuted for righteousness, those who are pure of heart, merciful, peacemakers, etc., will enter the Kingdom of God. Contrast that with what Jesus said about the salvation of the wealthy. (See next).

DIALOGUE WITH A WEALTHY YOUNG MAN

As Jesus walked, a man ran up to him and fell on his knees before him. "Good teacher," he asked, "what must I do to inherit eternal life?" "Why do you call me good?" Jesus answered. "No one is good—except God alone." "You know the commandment: 'You shall not murder, you shall not commit adultery, you shall not steal, you shall not give false testimony, you shall not defraud, honor your father and mother. "Teacher," he declared, "all these I have kept since I was a boy." Jesus looked at him and loved him. "One thing you lack is," He said, "Go sell everything you have and give to the poor, and you will have treasure in heaven. Then come, follow me." At this, the man's face fell. He walked away disappointed because he had substantial wealth.

"Why do you call me good? Only God is good." Jesus emphasizes his humanness and vulnerability. Jesus only mentioned commandments relating to fellow men's rights (Huquq al Abad), stressing orthopraxy (deeds) over orthodoxy (correct beliefs). Some Biblical commentators condemn the rich man for not giving up all his wealth. If this test is applied today, almost all of us will react the same as the rich man. In Islam, one has the right to keep his wealth earned through honest means after paying the poor tax or zakah. This is equal to 2.5 percent of his net worth annually.

Jesus looked around and said to his disciples, "How arduous it is for the rich to enter the kingdom of God!" The disciples were amazed at his words. But Jesus said again, "Children, how arduous it is to enter God's kingdom! It is easier for a camel **(rope in some translations)** *to go through the eye of a needle than for someone rich to enter the kingdom of God." The disciples were even more amazed and questioned, "Who then can be saved?" Jesus looked at them and* answered, *"With man, this is impossible, but not with God; all things are possible with God." (Mark 10:17-31)*

Leading a righteous life and doing righteous deeds exemplify good-faith effort. While good deeds alone may not be enough to save people (with man, it's impossible). By God's grace and mercy, eternal life is possible.

REPENTANCE AND RESTORING VICTIMS' USURPED RIGHTS

Jesus entered Jericho and passed through. A man named Zacchaeus was there. He was a chief tax collector and wealthy. He wanted to see who Jesus was, but he could not see through the crowd because he was short. So, he ran ahead and climbed a sycamore fig tree to look at Jesus, who was coming that way. When Jesus came to the place, he looked up and said to him, "Zacchaeus, hurry and come down, for today I must stay at your house." And he hurried and came down and received him gladly. When they saw it, they all began to grumble, saying, "He has gone to be the guest of a man who is a sinner." Zacchaeus stopped and said to Jesus, "Half of my possessions I will give to the poor, and if I have defrauded anyone of anything, I will give back four times as much." And Jesus said to him, "Today salvation has come to this house because he too is a son of Abraham. For the Son of Man has come to seek and save all that was lost." (Luke 19:5-10)

For true repentance of sins against a fellow man, one must restore usurped rights and ask forgiveness from the victim and God. Most importantly, not to repeat the same sin again. This is consistent with the Quran. The goal is to become better by learning from mistakes and being a better person than before.

THE NARROW GATE TO HEAVEN AND THE BROAD WAY TO HELL

You must enter God's kingdom through a narrow gate. The highway to Hell is broad, and its entrance is wide for many who choose that way. But there is a small gate and a narrow road that leads to life, but few find it. (Matthew 7:13-14)

ONLY the righteous can enter through the narrow gate, and only a few will find it. Evil has no boundaries or restraints, and the road to Hell is wide for many.

THE NARROW DOOR IS FOR THE RIGHTEOUS ONLY

He passed through towns and villages, teaching, and journeying toward Jerusalem. And someone said to him, "Lord, will those who are saved be few?" And he said to them, "Strive to enter through the narrow door." I tell you; many will seek to enter and cannot. (Luke 13:22–24)

REPLY TO THE SINNERS: "I DON'T KNOW YOU"

When the master of the house has risen and shut the door, and you stand outside and knock at the door, asking, 'Lord, open the door to us', he will answer you, 'I do not know where you come from.' Then you will say, 'We ate and drank in your presence, and you taught us in our streets.' But he will say, 'I tell you; I do not know where you come from. Depart from me, all you workers of evil!' (Luke 13:25–27)

ALL THE PROPHETS IN THE KINGDOM

In that place, there will be weeping and gnashing of teeth when you see Abraham, Isaac, and Jacob, and all the prophets in the kingdom of God. However, you were cast out. And people will come from east and west, north and south, and sit down at the table in God's kingdom. And behold, some are last who will be first, and some are first who will be last." (Luke 13:28–30)

SIN AND HELL

If your right eye causes you to sin, tear it out and throw it away. For it is better to lose one part than your entire body to Hell. And if your hand—even your strongest hand—causes you to sin, cut it off and throw it away. It is better to lose one part of your body than your whole body to be thrown into Hell. (Matthew 5:29-30)

THE FATE OF THE SHEEP AND THE GOATS

"When the Son of Man comes in his glory, and all the angels are with him, he will sit on his glorious throne. All the nations will be gathered before him, and he will separate the people as a shepherd separates the sheep from the goats. He will put the sheep on his right and the goats on his left.

SHEEP ON THE RIGHT (COMMISSIONS OF GOOD DEEDS)

"Then the King will say to those on his right, 'Come, you who are blessed by my Father; take your inheritance. The kingdom has been prepared for you since the world was created. For I was hungry, and you gave me something to eat. I was thirsty, and you gave me something to drink. I was a stranger, and you invited me in. I needed clothes, and you clothed me. I was sick, and you looked after me. I was in prison, and you visited me.' "Then the righteous will answer him, 'Lord, when did we see you hungry and feed you, or thirsty and give you something to drink? When did we see you as a stranger and invite you in, or need clothes and clothe you? When did we see you sick or in prison and visit you?' "The King will reply, 'Truly I tell you, whatever you did for one of the least of these brothers and sisters of mine, you did for me.'

GOATS ON THE LEFT (OMISSIONS OF GOOD DEEDS)

"Then he will say to those on his left, 'Depart from me, you cursed ones, into the eternal fire prepared for the devil and his angels. For I was hungry, and you gave me nothing to eat, I was thirsty, and you gave me nothing to drink, I was a stranger, and you did not invite me in, I needed clothes, and you did not clothe me, I was sick and in prison, and you did not look after me.' "They also will answer, 'Lord, when did we see you hungry or thirsty or a stranger or needing clothes or sick or in prison, and did not help you?' "He will reply, 'Truly I tell you, whatever you did not do for one of the least of these, you did not do for me.' "Then they will go away to eternal punishment, but the righteous to eternal life." (Matthew 25:31-46)

In this spectacular passage, Jesus makes it crystal clear that people will be saved not because they believe in Christ. They will enter paradise because they helped people in need. Salvation is based on good deeds, not just belief. It is in line with the Quranic teachings. In addition, salvation is not restricted to denominations or religious affiliations. It is the opposite of the Apostle Paul's assertion that salvation could not be earned by doing the things the law required. This is even doing anything at all. Paul says, *"I do not set aside God's grace, for if righteousness could be gained through the law, Christ died for nothing!" (Galatians 2:21).*

The conclusion is that Jesus did not suffer on the cross for humanity's sins, and his crucifixion becomes irrelevant to salvation.

CHAPTER 31
THE ISLAMIC PERSPECTIVE OF SALVATION

THE ORIGINAL SIN

[Satan said]: "O Adam! Shall I lead you to the tree of life eternal and to a kingdom that will never decay?" And so, the two ate [of the fruit] thereof. They became conscious of their nakedness and covered themselves with pieced-together leaves from the garden. [Thus], Adam disobeyed his Sustainer and fell into grievous error. (20:120-121)

The human condition (suffering, death, and a universal tendency toward sin) is accounted for by Adam's Fall in the early chapters of Genesis. However, the Old Testament says nothing about hereditary sin transmission to the entire human race. In the Gospels, Jesus never mentioned the Man's Fall and universal sin. The Quran has a different perspective on the Fall Story.

Sin in Islam is not a state of being. It results from disobedience-failure to do or not do what God commands or prohibits. Human beings are not sinful by nature but instead are created weak and subject to temptation by Satan. Death follows the human condition and is not due to sin or the Fall. Sin's consequences belong to sinners. In the Bible, the fall brings shame, disgrace, and hardship. The Quran teaches that Adam disobeyed God but repented, and God extended mercy and guidance.

PROPORTIONALITY OF PUNISHMENT

Was Adam eating the forbidden fruit truly a grave sin that the whole human race deserves condemnation for? Adam and Eve did not kill, rob, or harm anyone. He and Eve were not punished enough by God by throwing them out of the Garden.

SATAN IS NOT THE PRIMARY CAUSE OF SIN

Satan has no power over those who attain faith and in their Sustainer place their trust. He has power only over those willing to follow him and accord him a share of God's divinity. (16:99-100)

Satan of the Quran is not an all-powerful monster lurking above human beings and forcing them to commit evil. Satan can only tempt man. The power of Satan's negative principle has no intrinsic reality. It becomes real only through men choosing the wrong course of action willfully.

PREDESTINATION IS INCOMPATIBLE WITH FREE WILL

The concept of "inheriting sin" is predestined and incompatible with free will. It negates one of freedom's most fundamental principles: everyone is responsible for his actions.

FROM ANIMAL-LIKE STATE TO MORAL FREE WILL

On the contrary, the original sin had a silver lining. This is because Adam, who lived in an innocent but animal-like state, became conscious of right and wrong, a significant evolutionary step separating human beings from the animal kingdom. It transformed him from a purely instinctive being into a full-fledged human entity as we know it—capable of discerning right from wrong and endowed with moral free will, which distinguishes him from all other sentient beings.

FORGIVING ADAM

Say: "Unto God, who has willed upon Himself the law of grace and mercy." (6:12) "My grace overspreads everything." (7:156) Adam received words [of guidance] from his Sustainer, and He accepted his repentance, for He alone is the acceptor of repentance, the Dispenser of Grace. (2:37)

In the Quranic version, God forgives Adam and Eve for relatively minor acts of sin. In the Christian version, God did not forgive Adam, demanding human sacrifice instead.

VICARIOUS ATONEMENT

No bearer of burdens shall be made to bear another's burden, and if one weighed down by his load calls upon [another] to help him carry it, nothing thereof might be carried [by that other], even if it be one's nearest of kin. (35:18) In time, to your Sustainer, you all must return, and then, He will make you [truly] understand all that you were doing [in life]. He has full knowledge of what is in the hearts [of men]. (39:7)

Thus, any transfer of moral responsibility from one person to another is impossible. All wrongs committed by humans will be judged on Judgment Day. This is one of the metaphorical Quran passages. It doesn't mean that no one can or should help anyone with anything. It refers to moral burdens: you can't ask someone else to absolve you of your sins. You must shoulder them yourself by repenting, repairing the damage you did, and as Jesus might say, "Go, and sin no more." Contrary to Paul's and Augustine's views, the Quranic and Jesus' version of salvation is almost identical.

THE PATH LEADING TO SALVATION

O Bible followers! Now, there has come unto you Our Apostle, to make clear what you have been concealing [from yourselves] in the Bible, and to pardon much. Now there has come unto you from God a light, and a clear divine writ, through which God shows unto all that seek His goodly acceptance of the paths leading to salvation. By His grace, He brings them out of the depths of darkness into the light and guides them onto a straight way. (5:15-16) Oh, Bible followers! Now, after a long time during which no apostles have appeared, there has come unto you [this] Our Apostle to make [the truth] clear to you, lest you say, "No bearer of glad tidings has come unto us, nor any warner." For now, there has come unto you a bearer of glad tidings and a warner—since God has the power to will anything. (5:19)

The verses above are addressed to the Jews and the Christians; the term al-Kitab may suitably be rendered here as "the Bible." The phrase, "There has come unto you Our Apostle to make clear unto you" is the concealing of something from oneself. In other words, it is a reference to the gradual obscuring, by Bible followers, of its original verities which they are now unwilling to admit even to themselves. The word Salam, here rendered as salvation, denotes inner peace, soundness, and security from evil of any kind, both physical and spiritual, and the achievement of what is described as salvation: with the difference that the Christian concept of salvation presupposes the existence of an apriori state of sinfulness, or the doctrine of original sin, not justified in Islam, which does not subscribe to this doctrine. Consequently, the term "salvation"—used here for want of a better word—does not adequately convey Salam's full meaning. Salam expresses spiritual peace and fulfillment without being connected with Christian salvation doctrine.

SALVATION BY THE OBSERVANCE OF THE TORAH AND THE GOSPEL

If the Bible followers attain [true] faith and God-consciousness, We should indeed efface their [previous] evil deeds, and certainly, bring them into gardens of bliss. If they truly observe the Torah, the Gospel and all [the revelation] bestowed from on high upon them by their Sustainer, they will certainly partake of all the blessings of heaven and earth. Some of them pursue the right course, but most of them are Vile! (5:65-66) Say: "O Bible followers! You have no valid ground for your beliefs unless you [truly] observe the Torah and the Gospel, and all that has been bestowed from on high upon you by your Sustainer!" (5:68)

The phrase "if they truly observe the Torah and the Gospel," etc., implies observance of those scriptures in their genuine spirit. This is free of arbitrary distortions such as the concept of the chosen people or the alleged divinity of Jesus and the vicarious redemption of his followers. The expression "partake of all the blessings of heaven and earth" accompanies spiritual truth and social happiness. This is bound to follow an observance of moral principles laid down in the Bible's genuine teachings.

A PARADISE FOR RIGHTEOUS CHRISTIANS

Thou will surely find that, of all people, they who say, "We are Christians," come closest to feeling affection for those who hold faith [in this divine writ]. This is so because there are priests and monks among them, who are not given to arrogance. For, when they understand what has been bestowed from high upon this Apostle, thou canst see their eyes overflow with tears, because they recognize something of its truth [and] they say: "O our Sustainer! We believe; make us one with all who witness the truth. And how could we fail to believe in God and in whatever truth has come unto us when we so fervently desire, our Sustainer counts us among the righteous?" And for this, their belief God will reward them with gardens through which running waters flow, therein to abide for such is the requital of the doers of good. As for those who deny the truth and denigrate Our messages, blazing fire awaits them. (5:82-86)

It is noteworthy that the Quran does not include Christians among those who attribute divinity to anything besides God. The last sentence above clearly states that righteous Christians will enter paradise, unlike idol worshippers who are destined for blazing fire.

THE THREE CRITERIA OF UNIVERSAL SALVATION

Those who have attained faith [in this divine writ], as well as those who follow the Jewish faith, the Christians, and the Sabians—all who believe in God and the last day and do righteous deeds— shall have their reward with their Sustainer; and no fear need they have, and neither shall they grieve. (5:69) For those who have attained faith [in this divine writ], and those who follow the Jewish faith, the Sabians, the Christians—all who believe in God and the Last Day and do righteous deeds—no fear is needed, and neither shall they grieve. (2:62)

The above passages occur in the Quran several times and lay down a fundamental message of pluralism and salvation. Religious pluralism is the state of being where everyone in an ethnically diverse society has the rights, freedoms, and safety to worship, or not to worship, according to their conscience. Salvation is not restricted to Muslims because Islam is not the only way to God. Islam categorically states that people from other faiths will also ascend to heaven. It applies to Adam and the last human on this earth and is therefore of timeless import and transcends all religious affiliations. With a breadth of vision unparalleled in any other religious faith, the idea of Quranic "salvation" is conditional upon the following three factors: belief in God, belief in the Day of Judgment, and above all, righteous actions in this life.

Faith in God is the only objective source of all moral law from which to judge the true and untrue, right and wrong. Therefore, individuals and societies are bound by a standard of ethical valuation.

Judgment Day—Belief in Judgment Day is accepting responsibility for one's actions and an incentive to avoid evil deeds and do virtuous works. Man controls his actions and is entirely responsible for his decisions. For Muslims, life on earth is the seedbed of an eternal future.

It will be followed by a day of reckoning. Depending on how it fares in this accounting, the soul will then go either to Hell or Heaven.

Good Works—The belief in God and Judgment Day is a powerful motivation to do righteous deeds and avoid evil, a major cause of misery in our world. Only through righteous acts can a better and just society be established.

Thomas Carlyle (1795-1881), one of the great literary geniuses of his time, in his essay "The Hero As Prophet," compared Islam and Christianity: "Mahomet's Creed we called a kind of Christianity; and really, if we look at the wild rapt earnestness with which it was believed and laid to heart, I should say a better kind than that of those miserable Syrian sects, with their vain janglings about Homoiousion and Homoousion, the head full of worthless noise, the heart empty and dead! The truth of it is embedded in portentous error and falsehood; but the truth of it makes it be believed, not the falsehood: it succeeded by its truth."

CHAPTER 32
ACCOUNTING OF THE RIGHTEOUS AMONG NONBELIEVERS AND THOSE IN LIMBO

The entire Quran condemns worshipping idols as an unforgivable sin. This is especially true for those who deliberately deny God's oneness after all evidence is given to them. In the pagan society of pre-Islamic Arabia, idolatry had a close association with evils such as sexual immorality, sacrificing children to idols, superstitions, many arbitrary restrictions, and greed in all forms. The severe condemnation of idol worship in the Quran is partly due to the association of Arabian idolatry with all sorts of evil acts. But what about those who worship idols but otherwise live righteously? It is clear from the verses below that one can live righteously while holding erroneous beliefs. This is because most right and wrong reflect universal values.

NO PUNISHMENT FOR ERRONEOUS BELIEFS

For, thy Sustainer will never destroy a community for wrong [beliefs alone] so long as its people behave righteously [towards one another]. (11:117) We would never destroy a community unless its people did wrong [to one another]. (28:59)

In this life, God's chastisement does not afflict any people for holding beliefs amounting to shirk and *kufr*. Instead, *it* afflicts them only if they persistently commit evil in their mutual dealings. They deliberately hurt others, and act tyrannically towards them. The wrong beliefs include denial of the truths revealed by God through His prophets. They also include the refusal to acknowledge His existence or the ascribing of divine powers or qualities to anyone or anything besides Him.

REWARDS FOR GOOD DEEDS OF NONBELIEVERS

The following Quranic verses depict that the final judgment will not be arbitrary and cut and dried. Righteous men and women of all denominations have hope of salvation through God's grace. Even some unrepentant sinners who were confused or sinned out of weakness may also attain salvation.

RECORD OF GOOD WORKS WITH GOD

Unto Him ascend all good words, and He exalts righteous deeds. (35:10) And everything [that man does], whether small or great, is recorded [with God]. (54:53) And [withal] We do not burden any human being with more than he has the capacity to bear. For with Us is a record that speaks the truth [about what men do and can do], and none shall be wronged. (23:62)

ATOM WEIGHT OF GOOD AND EVIL

On that Day all men will come forward, cut off from one another, to be shown their [past] deeds. And so, he who did an atom's weight of good, shall behold it; and he who did an atom's weight of evil, shall see it. (99:6-8) And true will be the weighing on that Day. Those whose weight [of good deeds] is heavy in the balance, they shall attain a happy state. While whose weight is light in the balance, they shall have squandered their own selves by their willful rejection of Our messages. (7:8-9)

Men will come forward alone or as separate entities to face justice. See 6:94: "And now, indeed, you have come to Us in a lonely state, even as We created you in the first instance." Thus, stressing the individual, nontransferable responsibility of every human being.

ARE THOSE WHO WORSHIP IDOLS DOOMED?

In the great dialogue between Pharaoh and Moses, Pharaoh asked about the previous generation, who worshiped many deities. Are they irretrievably doomed?

Said [Pharaoh], "And what of all the generations before?" [Moses] answered: "The knowledge thereof rests with my Sustainer [alone and is laid down] in His decree. My Sustainer does not err, nor does He forget." (20:51-52).

Moses replied that God alone determines their destiny in the life to come. Only He solely knows their motives and understands the cause of their errors, and He alone can appreciate their spiritual merits and demerits. Moses did not declare that they all were doomed.

GOOD AND EVIL DEEDS OF POLYTHEISTS COUNTED EQUALLY

So, [O Prophet] be not in doubt about anything that those [misguided people] worship. They [thoughtlessly] worship as their forefathers worshipped in the past. We shall most certainly give them their full due [for whatever good or evil they have earned], without diminishing anything aught thereof. (11:109)

THE SHINING EXAMPLE OF SIR GANGA RAM

Sir Ganga Ram Agarwal was born on 13 April 1851 to a Punjabi Hindu family of the Agarwal clan. He was an Indian civil engineer and architect. His extensive contributions to the urban fabric of Lahore, then in colonial India and now in modern Pakistan, were described as "the father of modern Lahore." Sir Ganga Ram designed and built the General Post Office, Lahore Museum, Aitchison College, the National College of Arts, Ganga Ram Hospital, Lady Mclagan Girls High School, the chemistry department of the Government College University, the Albert Victor wing of Mayo Hospital, Lahore college for women, Hailey College of Banking and Finance, Ravi Road House for the Disabled, the Ganga Ram Trust Building on "the Mall" and Lady Maynard Industrial School. He also constructed Model Town and Gulberg Town, once Lahore's best localities. This is not an exclusive list of Ganga Ram's achievements. There is much more he did for fellowmen, without considering their race, caste, creed, and religion. Those who have done great deeds, such as Sir Ganga Ram, will enter paradise based on the work they have done for the benefit of other people.

FORGIVE THOSE WHO DENIED THE JUDGMENT DAY

Tell all who have attained faith that they should forgive those who do not believe in the coming of the Days of God, [since it is] for Him [alone] to requite people for whatever they may have earned. (45:14)

THOSE WHO WERE CONFUSED OR WERE HELPLESS

Though We may erase the sins of some of you [referring to hypocrites], *We shall chastise others—seeing that they were lost in sin. (9:66) But excepted shall be the truly helpless—be they men or women or children—who cannot bring forth any strength and have not been shown the right way. As for them, God may well forgive their sins-for God is indeed an absolver of sins, much forgiving. (4:98-99)*

The above Quranic verses express the doctrine that In His final judgment, God will consider all that is in a sinner's heart. Those hypocrites who sinned out of weakness or an inner inability to resolve their doubts, and not out of a conscious inclination to evil, God out of his mercy and grace may wipe away their sins. Forgiveness will also be granted to those who are helplessly confused and have not been adequately informed and explained about Islam's basic demands. Children are considered sinless—i.e., not accountable for their actions—and will, therefore, remain untouched by the ordeals and terrors of the Day of Judgment.

THOSE IN LIMBO AND WAITING FOR JUDGMENT

On Judgment Day, after the unrepentant hardened sinners are punished and the righteous are granted paradise, there is still another group that deserves neither hell nor heaven. In their lifetime they were able to discern between right and wrong but did not strongly favor either path – that is to say, they were indifferent to either. Their lukewarm attitude prevented them from doing good or wrong, resulting in neither paradise nor hell. Below is the dialogue between "the indifferent ones" and the inmates of paradise and hell.

DIALOGUE WITH THE INMATES OF PARADISE AND HELL

And there will be persons who [in life] were endowed with the faculty of discernment. Among them are those who remain halfway between the right and the wrong. And they will call out to the inhabitants of Paradise, "Peace be upon you!" Not having entered it themselves, [but longing for it]. And whenever their eyes are turned towards the inmates of the fire, they will cry: "O our Sustainer! Place us not among the people who have been guilty of evildoing!" And they who [in life] possessed this faculty of discernment [the indifferent ones] will call out to those whom they recognize by their marks [as sinners], saying: "What has your amassing [of wealth] availed you, and all the false pride of your past? Are those [blessed ones] the very same people you once solemnly declared, 'Never will God bestow grace upon them.' [For now they have been told], 'Enter paradise; no fear need you have, and neither shall you grieve!'" (7:46-49)

The expression "you solemnly declared" is a metaphor for the unbelievers' utter conviction in this case, implying either that the believers did not deserve God's grace or that God does not exist. Since only hardened sinners will face Hell's ultimate punishment, in the end,

God's mercy will prevail over His wrath. Those in limbo will also be forgiven.

(3)
THE FOREMOST AMONG THE RIGHTEOUS AND PARADISE

CHAPTER 33
THE FOREMOST IN RIGHTEOUSNESS AND GOOD WORKS

[On that Day] then, you shall be [divided into] three kinds. (56:7) And some who, by God's leave, are foremost in deeds of goodness [and] this, indeed, is a merit most high! (35:32) But the foremost shall be [those who in life] excelled [in faith and good works]. They were [always] drawn close to God! In gardens of bliss [will they dwell] - a good many of those of olden times, but [only] a few of later times. (56:10-14)

"Three kinds" refer to unrepentant sinners, those who sinned but repented and attained righteousness, and the foremost among the righteous. The foremost will be those who excelled in their faith and good works in their earthly life. They kept their covenant with God and man; refrained from doing evil; were truthful, penitent, and contrite of heart; they fed the needy and orphans, and some of them made the ultimate sacrifice in the cause of faith. God will remove all unworthy thoughts or feelings that may have been lingering in the hearts of the righteous, resulting in true inner peace. They will enter paradise without accounting, and this is the highest stage of spiritual development for the soul.

The above emphasis on "many" and "few" alludes to the progressive diminution, in the historical sense, of the element of excellence in men's faith and ethical achievements.

GREETINGS BY THE ANGELS

Good fortunes await, in this world, all who persevere in doing good. However, their ultimate state will be far better still for, how excellent indeed will be the state of the God-conscious [in the life to come]! Thus, God will reward those who are conscious of Him—those whom the angels gather in death while they are in a state of inner purity, greeting them thus: "Peace be upon you!" (16:30-32)

This "good fortune" does not necessarily signify material benefits but refers, to the spiritual satisfaction and inner security resulting from genuine God-consciousness.

NO ACCOUNTING FOR THE FOREMOST

Some faces will on that Day be bright with happiness, looking up to their Sustainer, (75:22-23) laughing, rejoicing at the glad tidings. (80:39) Now if one happens to be drawn close unto God, [the foremost] happiness [awaits him in the life to come], and inner fulfillment, and a garden of bliss. (56:88-89) [But unto the righteous, God will say], "O thou human beings that have attained to inner peace! Return thou unto thy Sustainer, well-pleased [and] pleasing [Him]. Enter, then, together with My [other true] servants—yea, enter thou into My Paradise!" (89:27-30)

GOOD WORKS

Faith in God and observing the five pillars of Islam are a starting point for good deeds for an observing Muslim.

THE FLIGHT OF TIME

The hundred-third surah al-Asr (the flight of time) sums up the importance of faith and virtuous acts.

In the name of Allah, the most gracious, the dispenser of grace. Consider the flight of time! Man is bound to lose himself unless he is of those who attain faith, do good works, and enjoin upon one another to keep to the truth and be patient in adversity. (103:1–3)

Morality is based on God-consciousness in Islam. It is a disposition that follows belief in an all-powerful, omnipresent God who commands obedience. The feeling of indebtedness to existence fosters humility toward God and His creations.

Avoidance of evil: A God-conscious or *"muttaqui"* desires to mold his existence around divine awareness and guard himself against evil. He is morally responsible and accountable to God. Such a believer lives his life mindful of the eternal consequences on Judgment Day.

SAYINGS OF THE PROPHET REGARDING GOOD WORKS

When good deeds are counted tenfold: "God, exalted be He, says: 'If a servant of mine desires merely to do a good deed, I shall regard this [desire] as a virtuous deed, and if he does it, I shall reward it tenfold. If he desires to commit an evil deed but does not commit it, I shall count this as a good deed, for he refrained from it only for my sake.'" Some Christians are taught that even to think of sin is a sin. It's challenging to control what we think, but we can usually control what we do.

Intentions behind the action: The Prophet said, "The reward of deeds depends upon intentions, and everyone will get the reward according to what he intended." For a Muslim, sin or virtue lies in deeds and intentions.

Actions are an integral part of Faith: The emphasis on actions is an essential part of faith and fundamental to the Holy Quran's ethics. There is a frequent juxtaposition of believing and doing good works. This is coupled with the condemnation of all who, while believing, do no good works.

THE CIRCLE OF RIGHTEOUS DEEDS

At the individual level, righteous deeds involve the development of personal morality, and the circle of righteous deeds expands to help family-neighbors, community, and, finally, humanity at large.

(1) PERSONAL MORALITY

A "muttaqui" becomes conscious of personal morality and becomes humble, selfless, truthful, and compassionate. He strives for self-improvement and practices moderation in every action, avoiding extremes in all aspects of life.

COMPASSION

Those who have attained faith and enjoin patience in adversity and compassion have achieved righteousness. (90:17–18)

Moral behavior is based on empathy and compassion.

HUMILITY

For, [true] servants of the Most Gracious are [only] they, who tread gently on the earth, and, whenever the foolish address them, reply with [words of] peace. (25:63) And [who], whenever they pass by [people engaged in] frivolity, pass on with dignity. (25:72)

They act with dignity whenever the foolish address them, intending to ridicule or argue against their beliefs.

KEEP PROMISES AND SPEAK ONLY THE TRUTH

Be true to every promise—for [on Judgment Day], you will be called to account for every promise you have made! (17:34) O you who have attained faith! Remain conscious of Allah, and [always] speak with a will to bring out [only] what is just and true—[whereupon] He will make your deeds virtuous and forgive your sins. (33:70–71)

The expression "a saying that hits the mark" means truthful, relevant, and to the point. It relates to speaking of others without hidden meanings, insinuations, and frivolous suspicions, aiming at no more and no less than the truth.

ENCOURAGE GOOD AND FORBID EVIL

Allah is most powerful, almighty, [aware of] those who, [even] if We firmly establish them on earth, remain constant in prayer, give in charity, and enjoin the doing of what is right and forbid the doing of what is wrong, but with Allah rests the outcome of all events. (22:40-41) [Pray thus] for We can let you witness [the fulfillment, even in this world, of] whatever We promise them! [But whatever they may say or do], repel the evil [which they commit] with something better. We are fully aware of what they attribute [to Us]. (23:95–96)

The ethical principle implied in the injunction is the same evil must not be countered with another evil but instead repelled by goodness.

PATIENCE IN ADVERSITY

You give the glad tidings [of Allah's acceptance] unto all who are humble—all whose hearts tremble with awe whenever Allah is mentioned, who patiently bear whatever ill befalls them, and are constant in prayer and spend on others out of what We provide them with as sustenance. (22:34–35) What is with Allah is the best for you if you know it. All that is with you is bound to end, and what is with Allah is everlasting. And most certainly shall We grant those who are patient in adversity their reward in accordance with the best they ever did. As for anyone— be it man or woman—who does righteous deeds and is a believer, he shall live a worthy life. And we will reward them according to the best they ever did. (16:95–97) No calamity can befall [man] unless it is by Allah's leave. Therefore, whoever believes in Allah guides his [own] heart [toward this truth], and Allah has full knowledge of everything. (64:11)

A good life can be described as the life of a true believer who finds happiness in his God-consciousness, or to the happiness that awaits him hereafter, or to both. Guide your heart toward self-surrender to

God's will, gratitude in times of ease, and patience in times of misfortune.

GRATEFULNESS A VIRTUE

Indeed, We granted this wisdom unto Luqman: "Be grateful unto Allah—for he who is grateful [unto Him] is grateful for his own good. While he who chooses to be ungrateful [ought to know that], Allah is self-sufficient, ever to be praised!" (31:12)

Luqman was a fabled ancient wise man appearing in the Arabic, Persian, and Turkish traditions.

ENLIGHTENMENT THROUGH KNOWLEDGE

The first Quranic revelation started with the word "Read" (96:1), which reminds us that the Islamic faith is founded on knowledge and scholarship. "ILM," the word for knowledge in Arabic, is featured more than any other word in the Holy Quran apart from "Allah."

Allah will exalt by [many] degrees those of you who have attained faith and, [above all] have been vouchsafed [true] knowledge, for Allah is fully aware of all that you do. (58:11)

SCHOLARS EXEMPTED FROM WAR

Not all believers should take to the field [in times of war]. From within every group in their midst, some shall refrain from rushing forth to war and devote themselves [instead] to acquiring a deeper knowledge of the Faith. They shall [thus] teach their homecoming brethren how to guard themselves against evil. (9:122)

Although this verse explicitly mentions religious knowledge, it positively affects all knowledge. This is because the Holy Quran does not draw any dividing line between spiritual and worldly concerns. The Holy Quran calls upon the believer to observe all nature and discern

God's creative activity in its manifold phenomena and laws. The Holy Quran itself is addressed to "those who think." Intellectual activity is a valid way to understand God's will better. Scholars must acquire a more profound knowledge of the Faith and God's works and impart it to their fellow believers in every branch of knowledge.

ACQUISITION OF KNOWLEDGE AND DIVINE REVELATION

We shall teach you, and you will not forget [anything you are taught], save what Allah may will [you to forget]. For Allah [alone] knows all that is open to [man's] perception as well as hidden [from it], and [thus] shall We make easy for you the path toward [ultimate] ease. (87:6–8)

These verses relate to humanity's cumulative acquisition of empirical and rational knowledge, handed down from generation to generation and from civilization to civilization. God may cause men to forget what becomes redundant through his evolving experiences and broader knowledge. Yet all knowledge derived through observation is limited in scope. It does not suffice to give us insight into ultimate truths beyond human perception (al-ghayb). Since human knowledge must forever remain imperfect, man depends on divine revelation, which shows us the path toward peace of the spirit.

ACQUIRING OF KNOWLEDGE AND THE PROPHET'S SAYINGS

The Quranic principle of acquiring knowledge has been emphasized in many well-authenticated sayings of the Prophet. For instance,

- "The scholar's ink is more holy than the martyr's blood."
- "The superiority of a learned man over a (mere) worshipper, i.e., one who merely prays, fasts, etc., is like the superiority of the full moon over all the stars."

- "Go in quest of knowledge even to China."
- "Striving after knowledge is a sacred duty for every man and woman who has surrendered to God."
- "Whoever honors the learned honors me."
- "Seek knowledge from the cradle to the grave."
- Spending more time learning is better than spending more time praying."
- "That person who dies while studying to revive religion knowledge will be only one degree inferior to the prophets."
- "The pursuit of knowledge is a divine commandment for Muslims."
- "He who leaves his home in search of knowledge walks God's path."
- "One hour's meditation on the Creator's work is better than seventy years of prayer."

(2) HELPING FAMILY

Good deeds extend beyond the self to benefit the family as well.

REVERE YOUR PARENTS

Now [among the best deeds] We have enjoined upon man is goodness toward his parents. In pain did his mother bear him, and in pain did she give him birth; her bearing him and his utter dependence on her took thirty months. (46:15) His mother bore him by enduring strain upon strain, and his utter dependence on her lasted two years. [Hence, O man], be grateful toward Me and your parents, [and remember that] with Me is all journeys' end. (31:14)

Child nurture includes conception, gestation, birth, feeding, and weaning in infancy—a child's utter dependence on its mother. Thus, gratitude toward parents, who were instrumental in one's coming to life, corresponds with man's gratitude toward God, the ultimate cause and source of his existence.

GUIDING THE FAMILY

O you who have attained Faith! Protect yourselves and those close to you [your families] against that fire [of the hereafter] whose fuel is human beings and stones. (66:6)

A person's responsibility is not confined to efforts for his salvation. His responsibility includes helping those close to his family to be morally upright. The Prophet said: "Each of you is a shepherd and is responsible for his flock. The ruler is accountable for his subjects; the man is a shepherd of his family and is accountable to them, and the woman is a shepherd of her husband's house and children and is responsible to them."

(3) HELPING THE COMMUNITY AND NEIGHBORS

The circle of virtuous deeds expands to neighbors and the community.

Have We not shown him the two highways [of good and evil]? But he would not ascend the steep uphill road [toward salvation]. And what makes you envision that steep uphill road? [It is] the freeing of one's neck [from slavery], or the feeding, upon a day of [one's own] hunger, of an orphan, near of kin, or a need [stranger] lying in the dust. (90:10–16) Do good to your parents, near kin, orphans, the poor, the neighbor among your people, the neighbor who is a stranger, the friend by your side, the wayfarer, and those you rightfully possess. (4:36)

The expression "your people" refers to the community, not to one's actual relatives. "The friend by your side" is one's wife or husband. "Those whom you rightfully possess" refer to slaves.

TAKING GOOD CARE OF ORPHANS

And they will ask thee about [how to deal with] orphans. Say: "To improve their condition is best." And if you share their life, [remember that] they are your brethren. Allah distinguishes between spoilers and improvers. And had Allah so willed, He would indeed have imposed hardships on you, which you would not have been able to bear: [but], behold, Allah is Almighty, wise! (2:220)

The implication is that if one shares the life of an orphan in his charge, one is permitted to benefit from such a business partnership. This should not harm the orphan's interests in any way.

HELPING WIDOWS

The Prophet said, "The one who looks after a widow or a poor person is like a warrior fighting for God's cause or like a person who fasts during the day and prays all night."

LOVE THY NEIGHBORS

The Prophet often stressed a believer's moral obligation toward his neighbors, whatever their faith. He said: "Whoever believes in God and the Last Day, let him do good unto his neighbor. Gabriel continued to recommend me about treating neighbors kindly and politely, so much so that I thought he would order me to make them my heirs." Such mundane acts, including returning salutations or saying, "God have mercy on you," when someone sneezes, accepting invitations, visiting the sick, following funerals, visiting a family member to preserve the bond of kinship, speaking kindly, and respecting parents, are considered virtuous deeds and recommended by the Prophet. Jesus said similar words, profound yet counterintuitive to our divisive human nature.

"But I say to you, love your enemies, bless anyone who curses you, do good to anyone who hates you, and pray for those who carry you

away by force and persecute you, so that you may become sons of your Father who is in heaven, who causes His sun to shine upon the good and the wicked, and who pours down His rain upon the just and upon the unjust." (Matt. 5:44–48) "You must love your neighbors as yourself." (Mark 12:31)

(4) HELPING HUMANITY

The circle of charitable deeds finally expands to all living creatures and humanity.

Allah enjoins justice, doing good, and generosity toward [one's] fellowmen. (16:90)

The circle of generosity extends to humanity. "Generosity toward [one's] fellowmen" refers to a relationship common to all human beings, the fellowship of men. Care for one another's material and spiritual welfare is a fundamental ethical principle.

GUIDING OTHERS

Now, among those We have created, some people guide [others] in the way of the truth and act justly in its light. (7:181) Say [O Prophet]: "No reward do I ask of you for this [message] other than [that you should] love your fellowmen." For if anyone gains [the merit of] a virtuous deed, We shall grant him an increase of good. Allah is much-forgiving, ever responsive to gratitude. (42:23)

Man's fellowship implies the fundamental ethical postulate to care for one another's material and spiritual welfare.

HELP ENEMIES BECOME FRIENDS

But [since] good and evil cannot be equal, you combat [evil] with something better. Between you and him, what was once enmity may become as though he [always] been close [to you], a true friend! Yet [to achieve] this is not given to anyone but those who are patient in adversity and endowed with the most excellent good fortune! (41:34–35)

STRIVE HARD IN GOD'S CAUSE

Strive strenuously in Allah's cause with all the striving due to Him. It is He who has elected you [to carry His message] and has laid no hardship on you in anything that pertains to religion [and made you follow] Abraham's creed. He named you in bygone times and this [divine writ]—"those who have surrendered themselves to Allah," so that the Apostle might witness the truth before you and that you might bear witness to it before all humanity. Thus, pray constantly, pay your purifying dues, and hold fast to Allah. He is your Lord Supreme, and how excellent is this Lord Supreme and this Giver of Succor! (22:78)

CARE FOR ANIMALS

The Prophet urged the humane treatment of animals in the following parable: He said, "A thirsty man came across a well, got down to it, drank water, and came out. Meanwhile, he noticed a dog licking mud due to excessive thirst. He walked down to the well again and watered the dog. God thanked him for that deed." When asked if there was a reward for serving animals, the Prophet said, "Yes, there is a reward for serving any living being. If any Muslim plants any plant and a human being or an animal eats it, he will be rewarded as if he had given that much charity."

GIFT OF LOVE THROUGH FAITH AND RIGHTEOUS DEEDS

Those who attain Faith and do righteous deeds the Most Gracious endow them with love. Only to this end, We have made this [divine writ] easy to understand, in your tongue, [O Prophet], so that you can convey the glad tiding to the God-conscious and warn those who are engaged in futile contention. (19:96–97) The God-conscious will find themselves in [a paradise of] gardens and running waters, in a seat of truth, in the presence of a Sovereign who determines everything. (54:54–55)

God bestows His love on those who attain Faith. He endows them with the ability to love His creation and be loved by their fellow men. This gift of love is inherent in divine guidance. Since man cannot understand God's "word", it has always been revealed in his human tongue. It has always been explained in terms accessible to the human mind.

RIGHTEOUS STRIVE FOR HERE AND HEREAFTER

But there are among them those who pray, "O our Sustainer! Grant us good in this world and good in the life to come and keep us safe from suffering through fire." It is these that shall have their portion [of happiness] in return for what they have earned. (2:201-202) God is most kind unto His creatures. He provides sustenance for whomever He wills—for He alone is powerful, almighty! To him who desires a harvest in the life to come, We will increase his harvest. (42:19-20)

Those who live righteously and turn their endeavors towards spiritual ends are sure to receive in the hereafter (*akhirah*) more than they hope for. God would have made a clear-cut distinction, in this world, between those who look forward to the hereafter and those who care only about worldly success, by granting unlimited happiness to the former and causing the latter to suffer. Since man's life is only truly fulfilled in the hereafter, God has postponed this distinction until then.

CHAPTER 35
ATTRIBUTES OF THE BLESSED PEOPLE OF PARADISE

Happiness in the afterlife is the result of man's endeavor to attain righteousness and inner illumination. Therefore, every act of good is described as a benefit for oneself because of the reward waiting in the afterlife. Paradise is not an arbitrary reward but a continuation of righteous living into the hereafter. Below are some more examples of the virtuous actions and attributes of the blessed people of Paradise.

KEPT COVENANT WITH GOD AND MAN

They are true to their bond with God and never break their covenant. They keep together what God has intended to be joined and stand in awe of their Sustainer. And who are patient in adversity out of a longing for their Sustainer's countenance. They are constant in prayer, and spend on others, secretly and openly, out of what We provide for them as sustenance, and [who] repel evil with good. (13:20-22)

The "covenant" is the spiritual obligation arising from one's faith in God and the moral and social obligations towards one's fellow men. The phrase "What God has intended to be joined" refers to all ties arising from human relationships—e.g., family bonds, responsibility for orphans and the poor, neighbors' mutual rights and duties. It also applies to the moral and practical bonds between all who belong to Islam's brotherhood (8:75). It includes the moral duty to treat all living beings with love and compassion. They do not repay evil with evil but repel it by doing good. The end result of their patience in adversity will be the attainment of the ultimate abode or life in the hereafter.

STRIVING FOR HERE AND HEREAFTER

But as for those who care for the [good of the] life to come and strive for it as it ought to be striven for and are [true] believers withal— they are the ones whose striving finds favor [with God]! All [of them]—these as well as those—do We freely endow with some of thy Sustainer's gifts, since thy Sustainer's giving is never confined [to one kind of man]. How We bestow [on earth] more bounty on some of them than on others: but [remember that] the life to come will be far higher in degree and far greater in merit and bounty. (17:19-21)

DOING RIGHT, FORBIDDING EVIL, PRAYER, AND CHARITY

And [as for] the believers, both men and women—they are close to one another. They [all] enjoin what is right and forbid what is wrong. They are constant in prayer, render purifying dues, and pay heed to God and His Apostle. It is they upon whom God will bestow His grace: verily, God is almighty, wise! (9:71)

HOLD ANGER IN CHECK, PARDON OTHERS, AND REPENT

But to him who stands in fear of his Sustainer's presence, and held back his inner self from base desires, Paradise will truly be the goal! (79:40-41) And pay heed to God and the Apostle, so that you might be graced with mercy. And vie with one another for their Sustainer's forgiveness. Paradise as vast as the heavens and the earth awaiting for the God-conscious who spend [in His way] in the time of plenty and hardship and hold in check their anger, and pardon their fellow men because God loves the doers of good. (3:132-134)

FEEDING THE HUNGRY WITHOUT RECOMPENSE

[The truly virtuous are] those who fulfill their vows and stand in awe of a Day the woe of which is bound to spread far and wide. They give

food—however great be their own need-to the needy, the orphan, and the captive, [saying in their hearts] "We feed you for the sake of God alone. We desire no recompense from you, nor thanks. We stand in awe of our Sustainer's judgment on a distressful, fateful Day!" And so, God will preserve them from the woes of that Day, and will bestow on them brightness and joy, and will reward them for all their patience in adversity with a garden [of bliss] and with [garments of] silk. (76:7-12)

. The term captive denotes anyone who is literally captive (e.g., a prisoner) or figuratively captive by circumstances. The Prophet said, "Thy debtor is thy captive; be, therefore, truly kind to thy captive." The injunction of kindness towards all who are in need of help—and therefore captive—applies to believers and non-believers alike, and also to animals dependent on man.

PROSTRATE IN ADORATION

Only they [truly] believe in Our messages when conveyed to them, they fall down, prostrating themselves in adoration, and extol their Sustainer's limitless glory and praise. They are never filled with false pride and are impelled to rise from their beds [at night] to call out to their Sustainer in fear and hope. (32:15-16) They would lie asleep only for a small part of the night and pray for forgiveness from their hearts. (51:17-18)

CHARITY

Is he [in his earthly life] a believer to be compared with one who was iniquitous? [No] these two are not equal! As for those who attain faith and do righteous deeds, gardens of rest await them, as a welcome [from God], as a result of what they did. (32:18-19) The God-conscious will find themselves amid gardens and springs, enjoying all that their Sustainer will have granted them because they were doers of good in the past. (51:15-16) They [would assign] out of their possessions a share for those who ask [for help] and suffer privation. (51:19)

This applies to those who suffer from the scarcity of things essential for well-being, such as food and warmth, and to all living creatures, whether human beings or animals, irrespective of whether the need is of a physical or emotional nature.

FAITH, REPENTANCE, AND GOOD DEEDS

O, you who have attained faith! Turn unto God in sincere repentance. It may well be that your Sustainer will erase from you your bad deeds. He will admit you to gardens through which running waters flow, on a Day when God will not shame the Prophet and those who share his faith. Their light will spread rapidly before them, and on their right; [and] they will pray: "O, our Sustainer! Cause this light to shine for us forever, and forgive us our sins: for, verily, Thou hast the power to will anything!" (66:8)

Turn unto God in sincere repentance, since no human being, however imbued with faith, can remain entirely free from faults and temptations. The implication is that He will not only shame the Prophet and his followers but exalt them.

THOSE WHO ACHIEVE A HAPPY STATE

Anyone who repents and attains faith and does righteous deeds may well [hope to] find himself among those who achieve a happy state [in the life to come]. (28:67) They will enter Paradise and will not be wronged in any way. [Theirs will be the] gardens of perpetual bliss which the Most Gracious has promised to His servants, in a realm beyond the reach of human perception: [and] verily, His promise is ever sure of fulfillment! (19:60-63)

FAITH AND DOING WHAT IS JUST AND RIGHT

As for him who shall have believed in God and done what is just and right, He will [on that Day] efface his bad deeds and will admit him into gardens through which running waters flow, therein to abide beyond the count of time: that will be a triumph supreme! (64:9) Thus, there shall be such as will have attained to what is right: oh, how [happy] will be they who have attained to what is right! (56:8)

PEACE BE UNTO YOU

And if one happens to be of those who have attained righteousness, [he, too, will be welcomed into paradise with the words,] "Peace be unto thee [that are art] of those who have attained righteousness!" (56:90-91) Those who attain to faith and do righteous deeds shall have gardens of bliss, to abide therein in accordance with God's true promise: for He alone is almighty, truly wise. (31:8-9)

MARTYRS IN GOD'S CAUSE

Do you think you could enter paradise without suffering like those [believers] who passed away before you? Misfortune and hardship befell them, and so shaken were they that the Apostle, and the believers with him, would exclaim, "When will God's succor come?" Oh, God's succor is [always] near! (2:214)

Intellectual cognition of the truth cannot, by itself, lead to ultimate bliss. It must be complemented by a readiness to sacrifice and spiritual purification through suffering. The term "the apostle" is used here in a generic sense, applying to all apostles.

PERSECUTED AND SLAIN

Hence, as for those who forsake the domain of evil, and are driven from their homelands, and suffer hurt in My cause, and fight [for it], and are slain—I shall most certainly efface their bad deeds and bring them into gardens through which running waters flow, as a reward from God. For with God is the most beautiful of rewards. (3:195) Those who are slain in God's cause, never will He let their deeds go to waste. He will guide them [in the hereafter as well], and will set their hearts at rest, and will admit them to the Paradise which He has promised them. (47:4-6)

SACRIFICED THEIR LIVES AND POSSESSIONS

O you who have attained faith! Shall I point out to you a bargain that will save you from grievous suffering [in this world and in the life to come]? You are to believe in God and His Apostle and to strive hard in God's cause with your possessions and your lives. This is for your own good—if you knew it! [If you do so] He will forgive you your sins, and [in the life to come] will admit you into gardens through which running waters flow, and into goodly mansions in [those] gardens of perpetual bliss: that [will be] the triumph supreme! He will grant you] yet another thing that you dearly love succor from God [in this world], and a victory soon to come: and [thereof, O Prophet,] you will give glad tidings to all who believe. (61:10-13)

The "victory soon to come" relates to a spiritual victory of the Quranic message and its spread among people who had not previously understood it.

CHAPTER 36
THE PROPHET'S NIGHT JOURNEY

After the loss of his uncle and wife, the two pillars upon which the Prophet's personal and emotional security rested, if ever there was a time for a heavenly gift, this was it. Close to the end of the mourning year, the miracle came from a mystical experience.

A GLIMPSE OF HELL AND HEAVEN

While the Allah-conscious will see Paradise on Judgment Day, the Prophet had a glimpse of heaven and hell on the "Night Journey" (*Isra*) from Mecca to Jerusalem and his subsequent "Ascension" (*Miraj*) to heaven. They are two stages of one mystical experience, dating almost exactly one year before the departure to Medina.

PHYSICAL OR SPIRITUAL EXPERIENCE

Since the Prophet himself did not leave any clear-cut explanation for this experience, Muslim thinkers have always widely differed as to its true nature. Many of the Prophet's companions believed that the Night Journey and the Ascension were physical occurrences. The Prophet's widow and most intimate companion of his later years, Aishah, emphatically declared that "he was transported only in his spirit, while his body did not leave its place." No one knows the exact mode of transport and the "how" of this incident. The Prophet probably time-traveled into the future after Judgment Day to see people in the fire or in the gardens of paradise.

THE NIGHT JOURNEY (ISRA) FROM MECCA TO JERUSALEM

Limitless in His glory is He who transported His servant by night from the Inviolable House of Worship [at Mecca] to the Remote

House of Worship [at Jerusalem]—the environs of which We blessed—so that We might show him some of Our symbols: for, verily, He alone is all-hearing, all-seeing. (17:1)

In this otherworldly experience, the Apostle of Allah, accompanied by the Angel Gabriel, was Transported by night to the site of Solomon's Temple in Jerusalem. He led a congregational prayer for many earlier, long-since deceased prophets; some of whom he encountered again in heaven afterward. The expression "some of Our symbols" refers to insight, through symbols, into some of the ultimate truths.

The Inviolable House of Worship (*al-masjid al-haram*) is one of the designations given in the Quran to the Temple of the Kabah, the prototype of which owed its origin to Abraham and was "the first Temple set up for mankind" for the worship of the one Allah.

"The Remote House of Worship" denotes the ancient Temple of Solomon—or, rather, its site—which symbolizes here the long line of Hebrew prophets who preceded the advent of the Prophet Muhammad. These prophets are alluded to by the phrase "the environs of which We blessed."

ISLAM IS NOT THE NEWEST DOCTRINE

The juxtaposition of these two sacred temples is meant to show that the Quran does not inaugurate a "new" religion. Instead, it represents the continuation and ultimate development of the same divine message preached by the prophets of old who had Jerusalem as their spiritual home. It expresses the principle that Islam, as preached by the Prophet Muhammad, is the fulfillment and perfection of humanity's spiritual development. His leading a congregational prayer to earlier prophets symbolizes that Muhammad was the last and greatest message-bearer.

THE ASCENSION

The Prophet's Night Journey from Mecca to Jerusalem, immediately preceding his Ascension, is the second phase of the journey. Gabriel led the Prophet toward the very throne of Allah. Legendary descriptions of the Prophet's excursions follow him through the various levels of heaven, where he meets all the prominent prophetic forebears. However, the Prophet did not see Allah.

Besides heaven's splendor, Gabriel also showed him hell and the horrors of the damned. The tree of Zaqqum is not earthly, found only in the depths of hell with its bitter smell and flowers like the heads of demons, the food of inmates of hell. Ascension is important from Muslim theology's viewpoint. During this experience, the five daily prayers were instituted as an integral part of the Islamic faith by Allah's ordinance.

THE LOTE-TREE SYMBOL OF PARADISE

And indeed, he saw him [Angel] a second time by the lote tree of the farthest limit, near the garden of promise. The lote tree veiled in a veil of nameless splendor. [And withal] the eye did not waver, nor yet did it stray truly did he see some of the most profound of his Sustainer's symbols. (53:13-18)

THE VISION OF ANGEL GABRIEL IN HIS TRUE FORM

The above verses allude to the Prophet's mystic ascension to heaven. He saw the angel Gabriel manifested in his true shape and nature the second time. The Prophet had twice in his lifetime a vision of this angelic force "manifested in its true shape and nature" once after the hiatus of revelation (see Surah 74) and during his mystic vision known as the Ascension.

THE LOTE TREE

The Arabian lote tree, owing to the abundance of leafy shade, symbolizes paradise's spiritual peace and fulfillment. "The lote tree veiled in a veil of nameless splendor" is a phrase deliberately vague. It is indicative of the inconceivable majesty and splendor attached to this symbol of Paradise that no description can picture and no definition can embrace.

The qualifying term "of the **utmost or farthest limit**" indicates that Allah has set a definite limit to all knowledge accessible to created beings. During his mystic experience, the Prophet saw and understood some, but not all, of the ultimate truths. Human wisdom cannot, even in paradise, understand the ultimate reality, which the Creator reserved for Himself.

Chapter 37
PLEASURES OF PARADISE AND THE BEAUTIFUL VISION OF GOD

ANGELS SURROUNDING THE GOD'S THRONE

Behold, [In the life to come] the truly virtuous will indeed be in bliss. [Resting] on couches, they will look up [to God]. Upon their faces, you will see the brightness of bliss. (83:22-24) And you will see the angels surrounding the throne of [God's] almightiness, extolling their Sustainer's glory and praise. And the word will be spoken: "All praise is due to God, the Sustainer of all the worlds!" (39:75)

The throne of God is used to symbolize His absolute dominion over all that exists. This is because God is unlimited, and a throne has physical limitations.

BEATIFIC VISION OF GOD

And [as for all such believers], no human being can imagine what blissful delights, yet hidden, await them [in the life to come] as a reward for all that they did. (32:17)

The expression "what is kept hidden for them" refers to the unknowable—and, therefore, only an allegorically describable quality of life in the hereafter. We are told to envision the most joyous sensations, bodily and emotional, accessible to man, indescribable beauty, love physical and spiritual, the consciousness of fulfillment, perfect peace and harmony. Imagine these sensations intensified beyond anything imaginable in this world— and at the same time entirely different, and you have an inkling, however vague, of what paradise is.

The Prophet in the well-authenticated hadith sums up man's impossibility of imagining paradise. Supporting the non-materialistic and allegorical interpretation of paradise, the Prophet said: "The joy of joys consists in the beatific vision in which the veil, which divides man from God, will be rent forever and His heavenly glory disclosed to the soul untrammeled by its earthly raiment. A similar Prophet's statement for the favored of God is to "see his Lord's face night and morning is a felicity that will surpass all the pleasures of the body, as the ocean surpasses a drop of sweat." The Prophet indicated the essential difference between man's life in this world and in the hereafter in these words: "God says, I have readied for My righteous servants what no eye has ever seen, and no ear has ever heard, and no heart of man has ever conceived."

[On that Day] every human being will know what he has prepared [for himself]. (81:13-14) Every human being shall be recompensed for what he earned, and none shall be wronged. (45:22) And [on that Day] paradise will be brought within the sight of the God-conscious and will no longer be far away. [And they will be told]: "This is what you were promised—[the promise] to everyone who turned to God and kept Him always in mind. [Everyone] who stood in awe of the Most Gracious, even though He is beyond human perception, and who has come [unto Him] with a heart full of contrition, enter this [paradise] in peace; this is the Day when life abiding begins!" (50:31-34)

RIGHTEOUS BROUGHT INTO PARADISE

Every human being is bound to taste death: but only on the Day of Resurrection will you be rewarded in full [for whatever you have done]. Whereupon he that shall be drawn away from the fire and brought into paradise will indeed have gained a triumph: for the life of this world is nothing but an enjoyment of self-delusion. (3:185)

God has promised believers, both men and women, gardens through which running waters flow, where they may abide, and goodly dwellings in gardens of perpetual bliss. God's goodly acceptance is the greatest [bliss of all]—for this, this is the triumph supreme! (9:72)

HONORED GUESTS OF PARADISE

On the Day when We shall gather the God-conscious unto [Us] the Most Gracious, as honored guests. (19:85) Clearly, indeed, We have spelled out these messages unto people who [are willing to] take them to heart! Theirs shall be an abode of peace with their Sustainer, and He shall be near to them because of what they have done.(6:126-127) Say: "Which is better—that, or the paradise of life abiding which has been promised to the God-conscious as their reward and their journey's end—a promise given by thy Sustainer, [always] to be prayed for?" (25:15-16) On that same Day, those who are destined for paradise will be graced with the best of abodes and the fairest place of repose. (25:24)

LIGHT EMANATING FROM BELIEVERS

On the Day when you shall see all believing men and believing women, with their light spreading rapidly before them and on their right, [and with this welcome awaiting them:] "A glad tiding for you today: gardens through which running water flows, therein to abide! This, this is the triumph supreme!" (57:12)

The metaphor of "the right hand" or "right side" is used in the Quran to denote "righteousness" and, therefore, "blessedness." It is symbolized in the present context by the "light spreading rapidly" before and on the right side of the believers as a result of their cognition of God, their high morality, and their freedom from ignorance and blameworthy traits.

FACES SHINING WITH BLISS

[And] some faces will on that Day shine with bliss, well-pleased with [the fruit of] their striving, in a garden sublime, wherein thou will hear no empty talk. Countless springs will flow therein. (88:8-12)

This metaphor of the life-giving element is analogous to that of the "running waters" frequently mentioned in Quranic descriptions of paradise.

WELCOME TO PARADISE

The God-conscious will find themselves [on that Day] in gardens and in bliss, rejoicing in all that their Sustainer has granted them. [And they will be told]: "Eat and drink with good cheer as an outcome of what you did, reclining on couches [of happiness] ranging in rows!" (52:17-20) God has promised believers, both men and women, gardens through which running waters flow, therein to abide and goodly dwellings in gardens of perpetual bliss. (9:72) [And God will say]: "O you servants of Mine! No fear need you have today, and neither shall you grieve. [O you] who have attained faith in Our messages and have surrendered your own selves to Us! Enter paradise, you, and your spouses, with the blessings of happiness!" (43:68-70)

"Reclining on couches" or "on carpets" in paradise is a symbol of inner fulfillment and peace of mind.

But those who were conscious of their Sustainer will be urged on in throngs towards paradise till, when they reach it, they shall find its gates wide-open. Its keepers will say to them, "Peace be upon you! You have done well, enter then, this [paradise], therein to abide!" And they will exclaim: "All praise is due to God, who has made His promise to us come true, and has bestowed upon us this expanse [of bliss] as our portion, so that we may dwell in paradise as we please!"

And how excellent a reward will it be for those who labored [in God's way]! (39:73-74)

They shall find their fulfillment in the hereafter: gardens of perpetual bliss, which they shall enter together with the righteous from among their parents, spouses, and offspring. The angels will come to them from every gate [and will say]: "Peace be upon you because you have persevered!" How excellent, then, is this fulfillment in the hereafter! (13:22-24)

The righteousness of their children increases parents' merit. However, righteous parents cannot absolve their offspring of individual responsibility.

GREETING OF PEACE

Those who have attained faith and do righteous deeds, their Sustainer guides them right through their faith. [In the life to come], running waters will flow at their feet in gardens of bliss. In that [state of happiness] they will call out, "Limitless art Thou in Thy glory, O God!" and will be answered with the greeting, "Peace!" And their call will close with [the words], "All praise is due to God, the Sustainer of all the worlds!" (10:9-10)

Salam implies spiritual soundness and peace, freedom from faults and evils of any kind, and inner contentment. Its closest—though not perfect—equivalent is the French *salut*, in the spiritual sense of that word.

GOD IS TRULY BENIGN AND ULTIMATE LOVE

And they [who are thus blessed] will turn to one another, asking [about their past lives]. They will say: "Behold, aforetime, when we were [still living] in the midst of our kith and kin, we were full of fear [at the thought of God's displeasure]. So, God has graced us with His favor and protected us from scorching winds [of frustration]. Verily, we did invoke Him [alone] before this: [and now He has shown us] that He alone is truly benign, a true dispenser of grace!" (52:25-28)

Symbolically, "asking them about their past lives" illustrates the fact that man's consciousness invariably survives his physical death, and continues unbroken in the afterlife.

CHAPTER 38
INFINITE GARDENS AND
HEAVENLY DRINKS

The conditions of heavenly bliss are described with all the vividness of Eastern imagery for people who lived in an arid climate. Paradise is called gardens, plural. The description of a paradise as vast as "heavens and earth" is the Quranic synonym for the entire created universe. We have the image of gardens abounding with deep rivers of cool, crystal water, milk, honey, and wine. There is neither too much heat in the garden, nor bitter cold. Springs spout everywhere, lush vegetation of wondrous hues, blissful shade, flowering meadows, boundless fertility, and fruits of every kind. At the top of the garden realm, there is a lote tree.

GARDENS THROUGH WHICH RUNNING WATERS FLOW

They who attain faith and do righteous deeds shall [in the life to come] have gardens through which running waters flow - the greatest triumph of all! (85:11)

This is the earliest Quranic reference to "gardens through which running waters flow" as an allegory of the bliss that awaits the righteous in the hereafter.

Those who attain faith and do righteous deeds, We shall bring them into gardens through which running water flows, to abide beyond the count of time. This is, in truth, God's promise—and whose word could be truer than God's? (4:122) Running waters will flow at their feet; [or all blessings will be at their command] *and they will say: "All praise is due to God, who has guided us unto this; for we would certainly not have found the right path unless God guided us! Indeed, our Sustainer's apostles have told us the truth!" And [a voice] will call out to them: "This is the paradise which you have inherited by virtue of your past deeds!" (7:43)*

GOODNESS SUPREME

But when those who are conscious of God are asked, "What is it that your Sustainer has bestowed from on high?" They answer, "Goodness supreme! Gardens of perpetual bliss they will enter through which rushing waters flow–having all that they might desire. (16:30-32)

GARDENS OF WONDROUS HUES, AND ALL VARIETIES OF FRUITS

Those who of their Sustainer's Presence stand in fear, two gardens [of paradise are readied], (55:46) [two gardens] of many wondrous hues. (55:48). In [each of] these two [gardens] two springs will flow. (55:50) In [each of] these two will there be two kinds of every fruit be [found]. Which, then, of your Sustainer's powers can you disavow? (55:52-53) And besides those two will be yet two [other] gardens. (55:62) of the deepest green (55:64). In [each of] these two [gardens] will two springs gush forth. (55:66) In both will be [all kinds of] fruit, and date palms and pomegranates. (55:68-69)

The "two gardens," or two kinds of paradise to be experienced simultaneously, allude to the allegorical character of all descriptions of life to come. In addition, they allude to the inexpressible intensity (or multiplication) of all imaginable and unimaginable sensations in that afterlife. The juxtaposition of "two other gardens" with the "two" previously mentioned is meant to convey the idea of infinity in connection with the concept of paradise as such - gardens beyond gardens in an endless vista, slightly varying in description, but all of them symbols of supreme bliss. The "two springs" and the subsequent descriptions of the joys of paradise must be understood in the same symbolic light.

The adjective "green" is often used in the Quran to indicate ever-fresh life - e.g., the "green garments" the inmates of paradise will wear (18:31 and 76:21), or the "green meadows" upon which they will recline (see 55:76).

FLOWERING MEADOWS

In the flowering meadows of the Gardens [of Paradise thou wilt see] those who have attained faith and done righteous deeds. All they might desire they shall have with their Sustainer. [And] this, this is the great bounty whereof God gives glad tidings to such of His servants as attain faith and do righteous deeds. (42:22-23)

PERFECT ENVIRONMENT OF EASE

In that [garden] they will on couches recline and will know therein neither [burning] the sun nor cold severe, since its [blissful] shades will come down low over them, and low will hang down its clusters of fruit, most easy to reach. (76:13-14)

HEAVENLY DRINKS

[They will be seated] on gold-encrusted thrones of happiness, reclining upon them, facing one another [in love]. Immortal youths will wait upon them with goblets, and ewers, and cups filled with water from unsullied springs by which their minds will not be clouded, and which will not make them drunk, and with fruits of any kind that they may choose, and with the flesh of any fowl that they may desire. (56:15-21)

As regards the reference to "fruit and meat in abundance—whatever they may desire," it represents symbolic "abundance" of sensual satisfaction that will not lead to satiety but, rather, to a pleasurable desire which—contrary to man's lot in this world—can always be gratified. A goblet is a vessel for drinking, usually of glass or metal, with a base and stem but without handles.

RIVERS OF WATER, MILK, HONEY, AND WINE

[And can] the parable of the paradise which the God-conscious are promised—[a paradise] wherein there are rivers of water which time does not corrupt, and rivers of milk the taste never alters, and rivers of wine delightful to those who drink it, and rivers of honey of all impurity cleansed. It is enjoyment of all the fruits [of their good deeds] and of forgiveness from their Sustainer. (47:15)

DRINK FROM UNSULLIED SPRINGS

And in that [paradise] they shall pass on to one another a cup which will not give rise to empty talk, and neither incite to sin. (52:23) A cup will be passed round among them [with a drink] from unsullied springs, clear, delightful to those who drink it. It will not cause headiness, and they will not get drunk from it. (37:45-47) [Whereas] behold, the truly virtuous shall drink from a cup flavored with the calyx of sweet sweet-smelling flowers, a source [of bliss] from which God's servants shall drink, seeing it flow in a flow abundant. (76:5-6)

Lexicologists define kafur in different ways: the calyx (*kimm*) of a grape before flowering; the calyx of any flower; the spathe of a palm tree, etc. And so forth. The meaning of *kafur* in the above context is an allusion to the sweet, extremely delicate fragrance of the symbolic drink of divine knowledge, having it always at their disposal.

SEEK THY WAY

And in that [paradise] they will be given to drink of a cup flavored with ginger, [derived from] a source [to be found] therein, whose name is "Seek Thy Way." (76:17-18)

Namely, "seek thy way" to paradise by doing righteous deeds." It contains the highly allegorical character of the concept of "paradise" as a spiritual consequence of one's positive endeavors in this world. That its delights are not of a material nature is also evident from their varying descriptions—i.e., "a cup flavored with ginger" and "flavored with the calyx of sweet-smelling flowers." Or "they will be waited upon with trays and goblets of gold" and "vessels of silver and goblets that will [seem to] be crystal—crystal-like [but] of silver," and so forth.

DIVINELY DRINK

And their Sustainer will give them to drink of a drink most pure. [And they will be told], "All this is your reward since your endeavor [in life] has met with [God's] goodly acceptance!" (76:21-22)

This implies that God Himself will slake their spiritual thirst by purifying their inner selves of all envy, rancor, malice, and all that leads to harm, and all that is based on man's nature, and by allowing them to drink of His Own Light.

PURE WINE FROM THE FOUNTAIN OF PARADISE

They will be given a drink of pure wine on which the seal [of God] will have been set, pouring forth with a fragrance of musk. To that [wine of paradise], then, let all such aspire as [are willing to] aspire to things of high account: for it is composed of all that is most exalting— a source [of bliss] for those drawn close to God shall drink. (83:25-28)

The pure wine of the hereafter, which, contrary to the wine of this world, will carry "the seal" of God because no headiness will be in it and they will not get drunk thereon. It is another symbol of paradise, by means of comparison with sensations that can be experienced by man. This is in contrast to the otherworldly sensations of joy intensified beyond human imagination in store for the righteous. Some of the great Muslim mystics (e.g., Jalal ad-Din Rumi) see "pure wine" as an allusion to a spiritual vision of God. Most of the classical commentators regard the infinitive noun *tasnim* as the proper name of one of the allegorical "fountains of paradise," flowing with the "wine" of divine knowledge, which is ennobling or exalting.

FRUITS OF PARADISE

RIGHTEOUS DEEDS MIRRORED IN FRUITS OF HEAVEN

The Quran speaks of the blessed in paradise:

Whenever they are granted fruits as their appointed sustenance, they will say, "It is this that in the days of yore was granted to us as our sustenance!" They shall be given something that will recall that [past]? (2:25)

There will be infinitely varied and unending delights, and yet somehow comparable to what may be conceived of as most delightful in this world. These delights will remind you of that past.

God's true servants [in the hereafter] theirs shall be sustenance, which they will recognize as the fruits [of their life on earth]. They shall be honored in gardens of bliss. (37:40-43)

It is this that we were promised during our earthly life as a reward for faith and righteous deeds. In other words, man's actions and attitudes in this world will be reflected in his "fruits," or consequences, in the life to come. They will not be deprived of reward for the least of their good deeds but will be granted blessings far beyond their actual deserts.

EAT AND DRINK IN GOOD CHEER

The God-conscious shall dwell beneath [cool] shades and springs, and [partake of] whatever fruit they desire. [They will be told]: "Eat and drink in good cheer in return for what you did [in life]!" Thus, behold, do We reward the doers of good. (77:41-44) And so, he will find himself in a happy state of life, in a lofty paradise, with its fruits within easy reach. (69:21-23)

EVERLASTING FRUITS

The parable of paradise promised to those conscious of God [is that of a garden] through which running waters flow. [Unlike an earthly garden] its fruits will be everlasting, and its shade will also be everlasting. **[It is the gift of happiness].** *Such will be the destiny of those who remain conscious of God. (13:35)*

FRUITS OF GOOD DEEDS ENDURE FOREVER

And God [alone] determines all things. Wealth and children are the adornments of this world's life. Good deeds, the fruit of which endures forever, are of far superior merit in thy Sustainer's sight, and a far better source of hope. (18:45-46)

The expression "good deeds, whose fruit endures forever" appears twice in the Quran - in the above verse and 19:76.

FRUIT-LADEN LOTE-TREES

And We shall bestow on them fruit and meat in abundance— whatever they desire. (52:22) [They, too, will find themselves] amidst fruit-laden lote trees and acacias flower-clad, and shade extended, and waters gushing, and fruit abounding, never-failing and never out of reach. (56:28-33) And therein shall you abide, [O you who believe] for such will be the paradise you shall inherit by virtue of your past deeds. Fruits [of those deeds] shall you have in abundance, [and] from them shall you partake! (43:71-73)

DELIGHTFUL FOOD

There will be thrones [of happiness] raised high, goblets placed ready, cushions ranging, and carpets spread out. (88:13-16) They will be waited upon with trays and goblets of gold, all the souls might desire, and the eyes might delight in. [Also], vessels of silver and goblets that will [resemble] crystal, or crystal-like, [but] of silver—the measure of which they alone will determine. (76:15-16)

IMMORTAL YOUTH

They will be waited on by [immortal] youths, [as if they were children] of their own, [as pure] as if they were pearls hidden in their shells. (52:24) When you see them, you will deem them to be scattered pearls. When you see [anything that is] there, you will see [only] bliss and a realm transcendent. (76:19-20)

The expression "immortal youth" refers to the imperishable quality (the eternal youthfulness) of all experiences in paradise. Light will emanate from believers because of their freedom from blameworthy traits.

CHAPTER 39
REUNITING WITH FAMILY AND SPOUSES AND PERFECT HAPPINESS

COMPANIONS OF PARADISE

[In such a paradise the blessed will dwell] reclining upon carpets lined with rich brocade. The fruits of both gardens will be within easy reach. (55:54) In these [gardens] will be [all] things most excellent and beautiful. (55:70) [There the blessed will live with their] pure and modest companions in beautiful pavilions. (55:72) [Companions] whom neither man nor invisible beings have touched. (55:74) [In such a paradise they will dwell], reclining upon green meadows and carpets rich in beauty. (55:76) Hallowed be thy Sustainer's name, full of majesty and glory! (55:78) For the God-conscious there is supreme fulfillment in store. Luxuriant gardens, vineyards, splendid companions well-matched, and a cup [of happiness] overflowing. (78:31-34)

Supreme fulfillment refers to all that a human being may ever desire, symbolized by "luxuriant gardens," etc. The term *kawib* means "glorious (or splendid) beings," without any definition of sex. In combination with the term *atrab*, it denotes, "splendid companions well-matched," alluding to the relationship of the blessed with one another and stressing the absolute mutual compatibility and equal dignity of all of them.

PURE COMPANIONS, BEAUTIFUL EYES

The God-conscious will find themselves in a secure state, amid gardens and springs, wearing [garments] of silk and brocade, facing one another [in love]. (44:51-53) And [with them will be their] companions pure, the most beautiful of eyes, like pearls that are still hidden in their shells **[as free of faults]**. *[And this will be] a reward for what they did [in life]. No empty talk will they hear, nor any call to sin, but only the tidings of inner soundness and peace. (56:22-26) And [with them will be their] spouses, raised high. We shall have brought them into being in a life renewed. Having resurrected them as virgins, full of love, well-matched with those who have attained righteousness a good many of olden times, and a good many of later times. (56:34-40)*

The term *zawj* denotes "a pair" or "a couple" or a spouse. It signifies either a husband or a wife. The noun *hur* rendered as "companions pure" is a plural of both *ahwar* (masculine) and *hawra* (feminine). Either of which describes "a person distinguished by "intense whiteness of the eyeballs and lustrous black of the iris." In a more general sense, it signifies simply "whiteness" or, as a moral qualification, "purity." Hence, the compound expression *hurin* refers to, "pure beings" or, "companions pure," "most beautiful of eyes." It is in the gender-neutral sense that the Quran uses the term *hur*. In the post-Quranic era or in the current form, the term *hur* has a feminine connotation, signifying the righteous women of humankind.

"As if they were hidden [ostrich] eggs" is an ancient Arabian figure of speech derived from the habit of the female ostrich, which buries its eggs in the sand for protection. Its application to women who attain Paradise becomes clear from 56:34, which states that all righteous women, irrespective of their age and condition at the time of death, will be resurrected as beautiful maidens. The Prophet stated on several occasions that all righteous women, however old and decayed they may have been on earth, will be resurrected as virginal maidens. They will, like their male counterparts, remain eternally young in paradise. The term "well-matched" denotes persons of similar age. However, this term is also used in the sense of persons equal in quality, that is, "well-matched," a significance which is eminently appropriate here, as it is meant to stress the equal excellence of all who have attained righteousness, whether they be men or women. In contrast with the foremost, who have always been closer to God, and of whom there are less and less. As time passes on, there will always be many of those who attain righteousness after initial stumbling and sinning.

SPOUSES WITH MODEST GAZE

Those who attain faith and do righteous deeds We shall bring into gardens through which running waters flow, therein to abide beyond the count of time. There they shall have spouses pure, and [thus] We shall bring them abounding happiness. (4:57) Let [all] this be a reminder [to those who believe in God]—for the most beauteous of all goals await the God-conscious. Gardens of perpetual bliss, with gates wide-open to them, where they will recline, [and] may [freely] call for many fruits and drinks, having beside them well-matched mates of modest gaze. This is what you are promised for the Day of Reckoning. This shall be Our provision [for you], with no end to it! (38:49-54)

The expression "modest gaze," or such as restraining their gaze and having eyes only for their mates, applies to the righteous of both sexes. These righteous persons in the life to come will be rejoined with those whom they loved and by whom they were loved in this world.

The primary meaning of *zill* is "shade." However, in ancient Arabic usage, the word *zill* also means "a state of ease, pleasure, and plenty," or simply "happiness." In the combination of *zill zalil*, "abundant happiness," seems to agree best with the allegorical implications of the term "paradise."

FAMILY REUNION

Everyone will be reunited with his or her family and spouses.

PRAYER OF ANGELS

"And O, our Sustainer, bring them into the garden of perpetual bliss, which Thou hast promised them, together with the righteous from among their forebears, and their spouses, and their offspring—for Thou alone art almighty, truly wise." (40:8)

REUNITING WITH OFFSPRING

And as for those who have attained faith and whose offspring will follow them in faith, We shall unite them with their offspring. We shall not let aught of their deeds go to waste: [but] every human being will be held in pledge for whatever he has earned. (52:21)

CONVERSATIONS OF THE BLESSED

No empty talk will be heard in that [paradise], nor any lies. [All this will be] a reward from thy Sustainer, a gift in accordance with [His Own] reckoning from the Sustainer of the heavens and the earth and all that is between them, the Most Gracious! (78:35-37)

The conversation of the blessed, which follows here, is allegorical and meant to stress the continuity of individual consciousness in the hereafter. The faithful are content, peaceful, and secure. Finally, human beings will conquer death, and they will remain young forever in everlasting life. All women, irrespective of their age and condition at the time of death, will be resurrected as beautiful maidens with eyes like guarded pearls.

REMINISCING ABOUT THE EARTHLY LIFE

They [dwellers of paradise] will all turn to one another, asking each other [about their past lives]. One of them [the blessed one] speaks thus: "Behold, I had [on earth] a close companion who used to ask [me]. 'Why—are you one of those who believe it to be true [that] after we have died and become mere dust and bones we shall, forsooth, be brought to judgment?'" [And] he [the blessed one] adds: "Would you like to look [and see him]?" And then he looks and sees that [companion of his] in the blazing fire and says: "By God! You have almost destroyed me [too, O my erstwhile companion]—for had it not been for my Sustainer's favor, I would surely be [now] among those who are given over [to suffering]! (37:50-57)

The "conversation" of the blessed is related to earthly life, where his close companion questioned the validity of the resurrection. Denial of the resurrection denies God's unlimited creation power and man's responsibility to God. The blessed one tried to look for his companion, who was in Blazing fire. This passage is meant to stress individual consciousness continuity in the hereafter.

NO EMPTY Talk

There will be no empty talk to be heard; nothing but [tidings of] inner soundness and peace. They will have their sustenance by day and by night. This is the paradise, which We grant as a heritage to Our servants. (19:62-63)

The term *rizq* (sustenance) applies to all that might benefit a living being, spiritually as well as physically. They hear no idle talk and face each other as brethren, all being equal in dignity. They enjoy fruits neither forbidden nor out of reach, meat, and cool drinks from shining streams of delicious wine, from which they suffer no hangover.

FREEDOM FROM UNWORTHY THOUGHTS AND FEELINGS

Those who attain faith and do righteous deeds, they are destined for paradise, therein to abide after We shall have removed whatever unworthy thoughts or feelings may have been [lingering] in their bosoms. (7:42-43) And [by then] We shall have removed whatever unworthy thoughts or feelings may have been [lingering] in their breasts, [and they shall rest] as brethren, facing one another [in love] upon thrones of happiness. No weariness shall ever touch them in this [state of bliss], and they will never have to forgo it. (15:47-48)

The soul will reach its fullest stage of spiritual development when all base instincts and desires are removed. There will be freedom from unworthy thoughts, sorrow, struggle, and weariness. None will suffer from bodily ailments or unpleasant bodily functions. The faithful are content, peaceful, and secure. Finally, human beings will conquer death, and they will remain young forever in everlasting life. All women, irrespective of their age and condition at death, will be resurrected as beautiful maidens with eyes like guarded pearls.

FREEDOM FROM SORROW, STRUGGLE, AND WEARINESS

They will say: "All praise is due to God, who has caused all sorrow to leave us. Our Sustainer is indeed much-forgiving, ever-responsive to gratitude. He who, out of His bounty, has made us alight in this abode of life enduring. This is where no struggle can assail us, and no weariness can touch us!" (35:34-35)

They will face each other as brethren and equals, and therefore be free from envy. The plural noun *surur*, which literally denotes "couches" or, occasionally, "thrones," also signifies seats or thrones of eminence or happiness. The sublime quality of these "thrones of happiness" is in some instances further symbolized by expressions like "gold-encrusted" (56:15) or "raised high" (88:13)

BRACELETS OF GOLD, SILK AND BROCADE GARMENTS

Upon those [blest] will be garments of green silk and brocade, and they will be adorned with silver bracelets. (76:21) [When you are promised splendors] as though [of] rubies and [of] pearls—which, then, of your Sustainer's power can you disavow? Could the reward of good be anything but good? (55:58-60) They will be adorned with bracelets of gold and pearls, and silk will be their raiment. They were [willing to be] guided towards the best of all tenets, and so they were guided onto the way that leads to the One unto whom all praise is due. (22:23-24) Those who attain faith and do righteous deeds, We do not fail to reward those who persevere in doing good. They will be adorned with gold bracelets and will wear green garments of silk and brocade, [and] upon couches they will recline. How excellent a reward, and how delightful a place to rest! (18:30-31)

The above reference to the "adornment" of the believers with gold, jewels, silk and their "reclining upon couches" is an allegory of splendor, the ever-fresh life (symbolized by "green garments"), and the restful fulfillment that awaits them. It is the result of the many acts of self-denial, their faith imposed on them during their earthly life. The active form of the above clause ("they will wear...") alludes to what the righteous will earn by virtue of their deeds. The passive form ("they will be adorned...") denotes all that will be bestowed on them by God above and beyond their deserts.

MANSIONS OF PARADISE

Those who have attained faith and wrought good works We shall most certainly assign mansions in that paradise through which running waters flow, therein to abide. How excellent a reward for those who labor, are patient in adversity and in their Sustainer place their trust! (29:58-59) They who of their Sustainer are conscious shall [in the life to come] have mansions raised upon mansions high, beneath which running waters flow. [This is] God's promises [and] never does God fail to fulfill His promise. (39:20)

PERFECT PEACE AND FULFILLMENT

Those who are destined for paradise shall today have joy in whatever they do. In happiness will they and their spouses recline on couches. [Only] delight will there be for them, and theirs shall be all that they could ask for: peace and fulfillment through the word of a Sustainer who dispenses all grace. (36:55-58)

In the Quranic descriptions of paradise, the term "shade" is often used as a metaphor for happiness. The "couches" on which the blessed are to recline are a symbol of inner fulfillment and peace of mind. Peace and fulfillment, a composite expression, is the nearest approach in English to the concept of Salam in the above context.

CONQUERING DEATH AND ACHIEVING EVERLASTING LIFE

[O my friends in paradise] is it [really] so that we are not to die [again] beyond our previous death, and that we shall never [again] suffer? (37:58-61) In that [paradise]they shall [rightfully] claim all the fruits [of their past deeds], resting in security; neither shall they taste death there, after passing through their erstwhile death, an act of thy Sustainer's favor and that will be the triumph supreme. (44:55-57)

HIGHER STAGE OF EVOLUTION FOR MAN

But as for those who [by virtue of their past deeds] will have been blessed with happiness, [they shall live] in paradise, therein to abide if the heavens and the earth endure. Unless thy Sustainer wills it otherwise—as a gift unceasing. (11:108) In that [paradise] they shall have whatever they may desire—but there is yet more with Us. (50:35)

God wills to bestow upon them yet a greater reward, or unless He opens to man a new, yet higher stage of evolution.

BIBLIOGRAPHY

Ali, Ameer. *A Short History of the Saracens.* Boston: Adamant Media Corporation, 2004.

Ali, Ameer. *The Spirit of Islam.* Whitefish, MT: Kessinger Publishing, 2003.

Allen, Jayne. *Jefferson's Declaration of Independence, Origins, Philosophy, and Theology.* Lexington, KY: University of Kentucky Press, 2000.

Armstrong, Karen. *A History of God.* New York: Ballantine Books, 1993.

Armstrong, Karen. *Islam: A Short History.* New York: Random House, 2002.

Buchanan, Patrick. *The Death of the West.* New York: St. Martin's Griffin, 2002.

Carlyle, Thomas. *The Hero As Prophet.* Seattle: CreateSpace Independent Publishing, 2011.

Encyclopedia Britannica. Moses, Christianity, Jesus Christ, Synoptic Gospels, Constantine, Original Sin, Salvation, Saint Paul, Biblical Literature, 2004.

Encyclopedia Britannica. Islam, Shariah, 2004.

Esposito, John L. *Islam: The Straight Path.* New York: Oxford University Press, 2010.

Haykal, Husein. *The Life of Muhammad.* Oak Brook IL: American Trust Publications, 2005.

Hitti, Philip K. *Islam: A Way of Life.* Minneapolis: University of Minnesota Press, 1970.

Holt, P.M., Lambton, Ann K.S., and Lewis, Bernard. *The Cambridge History of Islam.* New York: Cambridge University Press. 1970.

Lewis, Bernard: *What Went Wrong?* New York: Harper Perennial, 2003.

Parrinder, Geoffrey. *World's Religions.* New York: Facts on File Publications, 1971.

Radford, Mary F. *The Inheritance Rights of Women Under Jewish and Islamic Law.* Boston: Boston College International and Comparative Law Review, Volume 23, Issue 23, 2000.

Siljander, Mark D. *A Deadly Misunderstanding—: A Congressman's Quest to Bridge the Muslim-Christian Divide.* San Francisco: Harper One, 2008.

Smith, Huston. *The Religions of Man.* Chapter on Islam, pages 193–224. New York: Harper, 1964.

The Holy Bible, Authorized King James Version

The Readers' Digest Bible. Pleasantville, NY: Readers' Digest Association, 1982.

WHAT IS DIFFERENT ABOUT THIS BOOK SERIES

TRADITIONAL ARRANGEMENT

The Quran is a unique book, and unlike most other books, it does not have a beginning, middle, or end. Topics or subject matter are not divided into categories. The traditional Quran is arranged according to the inner requirements of its message and not in the chronological order in which the individual passages were revealed.

The seemingly abrupt transition from subject to subject is also in accordance with the Quranic principle of deliberately interweaving moral exhortation with practical legislation. This is in accordance with the teaching that man's life—spiritual, physical, individual, and social—is one integral whole. Therefore, it requires simultaneous consideration of all its aspects if the concept of a good life is to be realized. The Quran in its traditional form was meant for common people to read daily in small installments and ponder. The role of **Tafsir**, or exegesis of the Quran, is verse-by-verse and sometimes word-by-word explanation or interpretation of the text.

The Quran, in its original format, is difficult to understand. Discussion of varying subjects within the same chapter, which seems disconnected and may cause confusion and misunderstanding. This is particularly relevant to those unfamiliar with the Quran's uniqueness. Due to the randomness of the subject matter, the Quran is vulnerable to misinterpretation. The Quran's core message is very consistent, despite the randomness of the topics covered.

THE QURAN IN AN EASY-TO-UNDERSTAND FORMAT

The author of this seven-volume series has rearranged **The Message of the Qur'an** by Muhammad Asad according to specific topics and subject matter. This approach to organizing Quranic verses according to different topics is based on the central idea that conclusions should not be drawn from isolated verses. This is a first-ever attempt to present the Quran in an easy-to-understand format—a revolutionary paradigm in understanding the Quran. For example, divorce is discussed in the Quran in Chapters 2, 33, 58, 60, and 65. Compiling all divorce verses in one place gives the reader a quick reference and comprehensive understanding. For scholars, lawyers, and anyone who needs to study a particular issue, it would be handy to have it arranged by subject matter. I have added my comments to update some of the information, especially related to the scientific advances related to the Quranic verses.